ROAD BIKING™

Oregon

Lizann Dunegan

FALCON®

GUILFORD, CONNECTICUT
HELENA, MONTANA

AN IMPRINT OF THE GLOBE PEQUOT PRESS

Acknowledgments

Riding the backroads of Oregon has deepened my appreciation for the beauty and diversity of this beautiful state. Thanks to all of my riding partners who reviewed the manuscript and maps and waited for me while I took notes and photos. Thanks to Jeff Serena and everyone at Globe Pequot Press for giving me the opportunity to write the first road riding guidebook to the entire state of Oregon.

A FALCON GUIDE ®

Copyright © 2002 by The Globe Pequot Press

Road Biking is a trademark and Falcon and FalconGuide are registered trademarks of The Globe Pequot Press.

Text design by Lesley Weissman-Cook
Maps by Trailhead Graphics © The Globe Pequot Press

ISBN 0-7627-1193-0

Manufactured in the United States of America
First Edition/First Printing

Contents

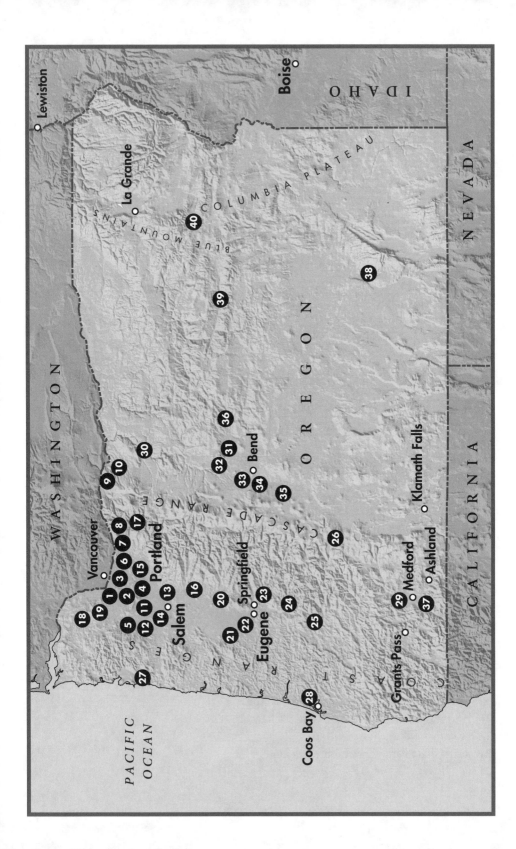

Resources

Introduction

Road Biking Oregon features forty tours that take you through the many beautiful landscapes of Oregon. You'll find a variety of tours in this book. You can wind down country lanes past historic covered bridges in the pastoral setting of the Willamette Valley, take grand city tours through historic neighborhoods and beautiful parks, pedal through the rugged terrain of the Cascade Mountains with its ancient volcanoes and high alpine lakes, or glide through the open spaces of the remote eastern Oregon desert. Each tour description provides you with essential information that will help you choose a tour that meets your interests and abilities.

GEOGRAPHY

Oregon has two distinct regions divided by the Cascade Mountain range. To the west are the rocky coastline and moist valleys, and to the east are high deserts and unique mountain ranges. On the western side of the Cascade Mountains, the Willamette Valley dominates the northern part of the state with its miles of fertile farmland and scenic rural roads. The Umpqua and Rogue River Valleys are south of the Willamette Valley and have been carved by large river systems that empty into the Pacific Ocean. The eastern side of the state includes the sage and juniper high desert of central Oregon and several distinct mountain ranges, including the Ochoco Mountains, Blue Mountains, Elkhorn Mountains, and Wallowa Mountains. The southeast section of the state is the least populated and is filled with dramatic open spaces. This part of the state is part of the Great Basin Desert and is characterized by fault block mountains, salt lakes, and vast sagebrush valleys.

WEATHER

The climate in the western valleys encourages biking all year. Moderated by the prevailing ocean breezes, the temperatures rarely go below freezing or exceed ninety degrees Fahrenheit. The late fall, winter, and spring bring the majority of this region's 40 inches of annual precipitation. The summer and early fall months are usually quite dry.

The temperatures along the coast are moderated to a greater extent with average summer temperatures in the sixties and winter temperatures in the upper forties. It is not uncommon to be sweltering in the valley summer heat while your friends on the coast ride in their winter gear. The average annual rainfall along the coast jumps to about 80 inches.

Heading into the Cascade Mountain range from the valley, you'll see lower temperatures and higher precipitation. During the winter, elevations above 3,000 feet are frequently snow packed. Though rare, snow squalls can occur during summer months.

Central and eastern Oregon have excellent biking weather during most of the year. The temperature ranges are more extreme, with summer highs into the nineties and winter lows sometimes below zero. Annual precipitation ranges between 8 and 20 inches for most areas. Summer thunderstorms and winter snowstorms are much more common than on the western side of the state.

ROAD AND TRAFFIC CONDITIONS

The tours in this guidebook are designed to meet the interests and abilities of all types of riders and to introduce you to the diverse landscapes of Oregon. On urban rides, of course, you'll have to contend with more road traffic and road obstacles than on rides in the country. Whenever possible, the urban tours in this book are designed to follow dedicated bike paths and routes in each city. However, there are some routes where you'll have to ride in high-traffic situations with no dedicated bike lane.

Tours in the country are designed to follow rural roads with less motor traffic. Although you'll have less traffic to contend with than urban rides, you'll find that the majority of the rural roads in Oregon do not have a shoulder. Remember to ride single file to avoid getting sideswiped by passing motorists, wear highly visible clothing, and make sure your bike is equipped with lights in case you have to ride at night.

TOUR PROFILES

Each tour profile in this book is categorized by difficulty level. There are four categories: rambles, cruises, challenges, and classics. **Rambles** are the easiest and shortest tours, are generally less than 35 miles long, and travel over flat or rolling terrain. **Cruises** are intermediate rides in terms of difficulty and distance, and are usually between 35 and 60 miles. An experienced and fit rider can easily complete cruises in one day. **Challenges** are generally between 50 and 90 miles long and often include steep climbing. Experienced cyclists will have to pedal hard to complete challenges in a day, and less experienced cyclists will want to complete challenges in two days. **Classics** are more than 100 miles and take two days to complete. Classics will usually have sustained climbing and often travel through remote and mountainous country.

Before you leave on a tour, always be sure to let someone know your itinerary. A cellular phone also can be helpful in emergencies, but keep in mind that this type of phone doesn't always work near steep terrain.

Bike Selection

Road bikes, touring bikes, recumbents, and mountain bikes all make fine touring steeds, each with their own benefits and trade-offs. Road bikes are built lightweight for climbing, have narrow high-pressure tires for speed, and are designed with a short wheelbase for quick maneuvering. For a more touring-capable road bike, select one with a triple front chain ring (for easier climbing) and 25mm or wider tires (for fewer flats and better shock absorption). If you are going to outfit your road bike with panniers, make sure the frame has brazons (threaded holes drilled into the bike frame) for mounting the racks. Also make sure there is enough clearance between your heels and the rear panniers.

Touring bikes are designed for long-distance, loaded excursions. They have a stretched geometry for riding comfort and gear accommodation, absorb a fair amount of shock with their wider tires, and are built stoutly to handle extra weight and rough roads.

Recumbents are incredibly comfortable, relieving stress in key areas—your derriere and wrists. They are fast on the downhill but tend to be a bit slower on the climbs.

Mountain bikes are also a fine choice for touring. They offer superior shock absorption and permit ventures off-pavement at your whim. Knobby tires, heavier frames, and active suspension components will decrease your cruising speed. To maximize your bike's efficiency, select narrower tires with smooth tread, and tighten down your suspension components. Full-suspension mountain bikes are not designed to mount panniers; however, an excellent alternative is a single-wheeled bike trailer. Whatever kind of bike you choose, have a knowledgeable bike shop fit you to the bike and select a quality seat.

Bike Gear

◆ *Tools.* A good set of tools and some basic repair skills contribute to your biking self-reliance. The dreaded flat tire is the most common repair. Bring along a pump for your type of valve (Presta or Schraeder), a patch kit, tire levers, and an extra tube. A warped wheel is also common, so pack your trusty spoke tool (note that this little tool can also cause great destruction, so brush up on your wheel truing skills). Other useful tools include pliers, a chain tool, Allen wrenches, a wrench set, a screwdriver, and chain lube. For extended voyages carry spare parts such as brake pads, brake and derailleur cables, extra spokes, extra chain, and an extra tire. You may want to wrap some duct tape around your down tube—the stuff invariably comes in handy. If you're not already bike-repair savvy, consider taking a class at a community college or bike shop.

◆ *Cyclometer.* A cyclometer is a bicycle computer that calculates wheel revolutions or pedal strokes. The options on these devices vary by brand, but most

Riding with a group is a great way to meet new cycling friends.

have a clock, odometer, stopwatch, and speedometer. A cyclometer is highly recommended so you can keep track of the detailed mileage directions in this guidebook.

♦ *Water Bottles and Holders.* Equip your bike with a minimum of two water bottle holders and two water bottles. Most bikes come with eyelets that allow you to attach water bottle holders on the seat tube and down tube of your bike. You can also purchase holders that attach to your seat post. Many riders also like to wear a backpack hydration system for really long rides or in hot weather.

♦ *Bike Rack/Panniers/Trailer.* A bike rack is a necessity if you plan on doing nonsupported touring. A rear rack allows you to attached bike panniers (bike backpacks) and also lets you strap on a tent, sleeping bag, and other camping gear. For extended tours you can also add a front rack to your bike to carry even more gear. Panniers come in many different styles and sizes. Panniers that are made of waterproof material work well in western Oregon's often wet climate. If you don't want to carry your gear on your bike, consider pulling a bike trailer with a waterproof duffel bag.

♦ *Lights/Reflectors.* As a minimum, equip your bike or helmet with a front white headlight that is visible for 500 feet in front of you and a rear flasher that is visible at least 600 feet in the rear in case you have to ride at night. Make sure you have spoke-mounted reflectors for side visibility. For low-riding recumbents, consider mounting a flag.

Rider Gear

♦ *Helmet.* Wear a helmet whenever you ride. Your head is a valuable commodity and should be well protected. Choose a helmet that meets ANSI (American National Standards Institute) and Snell safety standards. Look for a helmet that is lightweight and has good ventilation and a sun visor. If you plan on riding at night, try adding reflective tape to the helmet so you are more visible to motorists.

♦ *Eyewear.* Wear protective eyewear whenever you go road riding. Dust, rocks, glass, pollen, bugs, chemicals, exhaust, and other harmful agents can injure your eyes whenever you ride. In hot sunny conditions wear sunglasses with adequate UV protection. When riding in low light, rain, and cloudy conditions, wear clear glasses or ones tinted orange or yellow for better visibility.

♦ *Gloves.* Padded biking gloves provide cushion between your hands and the handlebars. Insulated gloves are essential for winter riding.

♦ *Cycle Shorts.* Padded cycle shorts provide cushioning between your body and the bicycle seat. Cycle shorts also wick moisture away from your body and prevent chafing. Form-fitting shorts are made from synthetic material and have smooth seams to avoid chafing. If you feel uncomfortable wearing form-fitting shorts, baggy-style padded shorts with pockets are available.

♦ *Other Clothing.* To prepare for Oregon's weather, it is best to dress in layers that can be added or removed as weather conditions change. In cold weather wear a wicking layer next to your skin made of a modern synthetic fiber. Avoid wearing cotton of any type. It dries slowly and does not wick moisture away from your skin, thus chilling you directly as it evaporates. The next layer should be a wool or synthetic insulating layer that helps keep you warm but also is breathable. A fleece jacket or vest works well as an insulating layer. The outer layer should be a jacket and pants or padded biking tights that are waterproof, windproof, and breathable. Your ears will also welcome a fleece headband when it's cold out. Look for cycling outerwear that also has reflective material and brighter colors so motorists can easily see you. Lime green and orange are highly visible colors during the day and night. See the Resources section for companies that sell bike gear.

EATING AND DRINKING

All of the tours in this book list recommended restaurants where you can stop and enjoy good local cuisine. However, some remote tours require that you take your own food and drink. Eating and staying well hydrated while you ride are top priorities. For longer tours stay hydrated with a sports drink instead of water. Sports drinks are designed to replace lost electrolytes, and they provide you with

Touring checklist

Use this checklist to aid you in preparing for an overnight tour.

Essentials

- [ ] cyclometer
- [ ] compass
- [ ] bungie cords
- [ ] panniers
- [ ] rear rack/front rack and/or bike trailer
- [ ] duct tape
- [ ] fenders
- [ ] multipurpose tool
- [ ] guidebook/maps
- [ ] water bottles
- [ ] water filter
- [ ] tool kit
- [ ] patch kit
- [ ] crescent wrench
- [ ] tire levers
- [ ] spoke wrench
- [ ] extra spokes
- [ ] chain rivet tool
- [ ] extra tubes
- [ ] tire pump

Clothing

- [ ] rain jacket/pants
- [ ] padded biking tights
- [ ] polar fleece jacket/vest
- [ ] helmet liner
- [ ] cycle shorts/jerseys
- [ ] cycling shoes
- [ ] swimsuit
- [ ] underwear
- [ ] bike gloves
- [ ] eyewear

First Aid Kit

- [ ] bandages (various sizes)
- [ ] gauze pads
- [ ] surgical tape
- [ ] antibiotic ointment
- [ ] hydrogen peroxide or iodine
- [ ] gauze roll
- [ ] Ace bandage
- [ ] aspirin
- [ ] antacid
- [ ] moleskin
- [ ] sunscreen
- [ ] skin lubricant to avoid chafing
- [ ] Benadryl
- [ ] insect repellent

Camping Items

- [ ] stove/fuel canister
- [ ] tent
- [ ] sleeping bag
- [ ] foam pad
- [ ] cooking and eating utensils
- [ ] can opener
- [ ] flashlight/batteries
- [ ] candle lantern
- [ ] zipper-seal plastic bags
- [ ] small duffels to organize gear

Miscellaneous Items

- [ ] camera/film/batteries
- [ ] notebook/pen
- [ ] paperback book
- [ ] toiletries

Knowing how to fix a flat tire is an essential skill.

an extra energy boost. You can carry fluids in water bottles or a backpack hydration system. For remote tours carry a lightweight water filter or iodine tablets to purify water obtained from a river or stream. To replace lost calories while you ride, bring sports bars and gels, dried fruit, bananas, bagels, chocolate bars, peanut butter and jelly sandwiches, apples, or gorp.

RULES OF THE ROAD

When you are road riding in Oregon, you can pedal on any public road except urban freeways. Always keep these tips in mind when you are riding:

♦ Follow the same driving rules as motorists. Be sure to obey all road signs and traffic lights.

♦ Wear a helmet and bright clothing so you are more visible to motorists. Bright colors, such as orange and lime green, are also highly visible at night.

♦ Oregon law requires that riders and passengers younger than age 16 wear a CPSC (Consumer Product Safety Commission)–approved helmet.

♦ Equip your bike with lights, and wear reflective clothing if you plan on riding at night. When riding at night the bicycle or rider must be equipped with a white light visible at least 500 feet to the front and a red light or reflector visible at least 600 feet to the rear.

♦ Pass motorists on the left, not on the right. Motorists are not expecting you to pass on the right, and they may not see you.

♦ Ride single file on busy roads so motorists can pass you safely.

♦ Stop off the roadway.

♦ Use hand signals to alert motorists of what you plan to do next.

♦ Ride with the traffic, not against it.

♦ Follow painted lane markings.

♦ Make eye contact with drivers. Assume they do not see you until you are sure they do.

♦ Ride in the middle of the lane at busy intersections and whenever you are moving at the same speed as traffic.

♦ Slow down and announce your presence when passing pedestrians, cyclists, and horses.

- Do not ride out to the curb between parked cars unless they are far apart. Motorists may not see you when you try to move back into traffic.
- Turn left by looking back, signaling, getting into the left lane, and turning. In urban situations, continue straight to the crosswalk, and walk your bike across the crosswalk when the pedestrian WALK sign is illuminated.
- Never ride while under the influence of alcohol or drugs. DUI laws apply when you are riding a bicycle.
- Avoid riding in extreme foggy, rainy, or windy conditions.
- Watch out for parallel-slat sewer grates, slippery manhole covers, oily pavement, gravel, wet leaves, and ice.
- Cross railroad tracks as perpendicularly as possible. Be especially careful when it's wet out. For better control as you move across bumps and other hazards, stand up on your pedals.
- Don't ride close to parked cars—a person opening the car door may hit you.
- Avoid riding on sidewalks. Instead, walk your bike. Pedestrians have the right of way on walkways. By law, you must give pedestrians audible warning when you pass. Use a bike bell or announce clearly, "On your left/right."
- Slow down at street crossings and driveways.

HOW TO USE THIS BOOK

This book contains forty scenic tours throughout Oregon. Each tour profile includes photos, a detailed map, and an elevation profile, and includes information that will help you choose a tour that matches your fitness level and interests.

Ride summary: Provides an at-a-glance paragraph of the tour highlights.

Start: Where the tour begins.

Length: The tour in miles, and indicates if the tour is a loop or an out-and-back route.

Season: Lists the time of year the ride is open.

Approximate riding time: A range of time in hours it will take the average cyclist to complete the route and to stop at points of interest.

Recommended start time: Recommended time of day you should start your tour to allow enough time to stop at points of interest and to complete the ride before it gets dark.

Terrain: Lists the type of roads (major highways, rural roads, forest service roads) and road surfaces (rough, potholes, gravel/dirt).

Traffic and hazards: Lists road hazards you should be aware of, including high traffic volume, presence or absence of road shoulders, presence of railroad or cattle guard crossings, and warnings for rough road surfaces.

Getting there: Detailed directions to the start of the tour.

Ride description: Detailed description of the tour, which may include information about attractions, history, geology, and wildlife.

Miles and directions: Lists the turn-for-turn mileage directions for the ride as well as additional options for exploring. It is highly recommended you ride with a cyclometer so you can use the mileage points for each profile.

Additional ride information: Lists park and recreational organizations that can provide you with additional information.

Local information: Lists local chamber of commerce offices, visitor centers, and other agencies that can provide you with information about the tour.

Local events/attractions: Lists fun events and attractions you may want to visit before, during, or after your tour.

Restaurants: Lists recommended restaurants at the start, middle, and end of the tour.

Accommodations: Lists recommended bed-and-breakfast inns, hotels, hostels, and campgrounds that are available on the tour.

Bike shops: Lists bike shops that are located in cities that are in close proximity to the tour.

Rest rooms: Lists the mileage points that have rest-room facilities.

Maps: Lists the U.S. Geological Survey (USGS) 7.5-minute quads for the route and the corresponding map number in DeLorme's *Oregon Atlas and Gazetteer.*

Sauvie Island Ramble

*L*ocated just minutes from Portland, the Sauvie Island Ramble takes you on a loop tour through a quiet, rural landscape filled with small farms, nurseries, and wild, open spaces. You'll have the chance to see hawks soaring above open fields, bald eagles nesting, and migratory waterfowl from the wildlife viewing areas that are present on this route. On a clear day you'll also have gorgeous views of prominent Cascade volcanoes, including Mount Rainier, Mount St. Helens, Mount Adams, and Mount Hood.

This 18-mile loop ride takes you through the quiet, rural landscape of 24,000-acre Sauvie Island, which is located at the confluence of two of Oregon's major rivers: the Willamette and the Columbia. Sauvie Island is the largest island in the Columbia River. At 4 miles wide and 15 miles long, it is made up of fertile farmland, shallow lakes, marshes, sloughs; and groves of cottonwood, willow, and ash. The island is home to more than 300 species of animals, including raccoon, beaver, mink, and black-tailed deer. It is located on the Pacific flyway, which attracts thousands of migrating birds each year.

The northern half of the island contains a 12,000-acre wildlife area that is managed by the Oregon Fish and Wildlife Service. This vast refuge contains designated viewing areas where you can see a variety of bird species. During the fall more than 150,000 ducks congregate in the wetlands on the island. You may see mallards, ruddy ducks, green-winged teals, buffleheads, pintails, and widgeons. Other additions to this cast of characters include sandhill cranes, blue herons, Canada geese, snow geese, and tundra swans. Bald eagles can also be seen roosting in trees on the island from December through March. This rich variety of bird life attracts not only bird-watchers but also hunters. The wildlife

Start: The parking area off NW Gillihan Loop Road on Sauvie Island. Sauvie Island is approximately 10 miles north of Portland off U.S. Highway 30.

Length: 18-mile loop.

Season: Year-round.

Approximate riding time: One to two hours.

Recommended start time: 11:00 A.M.

Terrain: Rural roads that are flat and fast with a variety of twists and turns.

Traffic and hazards: The shoulder on this ride varies from 1 to 2 feet at the start of the ride to no shoulder at all. The summer traffic can be thick on this route, and there are many blind curves where you will need to exercise caution. As a common courtesy, always be sure to ride single file. Also note that there are many places where you can pull off the road to let traffic by, which allows you more time to soak in the great views of the many picturesque farms and abundant bird life on the island.

Getting there: From I-405 in Portland, take the HIGHWAY 30 WEST/ST. HELENS exit, and follow the signs for St. Helens. Drive 9.3 miles north on Highway 30 until you see a sign indicating SAUVIE ISLAND WILDLIFE AREA. Exit to the right, and cross the bridge to the island. After crossing the bridge turn left onto NW Gillihan Loop Road, then take another immediate left into a large circular dirt parking area.

area is generally closed from October 1 through the middle of January for hunting season.

A group of Native Americans called the Flatheads were the first inhabitants of the island. They mainly subsisted on a diet of the tuberlike plant called wapato. This nutritious plant gained the attention of Lewis and Clark, who named the island Wappato when they passed through the area in 1805–1806. This name was later changed to Sauvie after a French-Canadian named Larent Sauve, who worked for the Hudson's Bay Company on a dairy farm in the early 1800s. In the mid-1850s much of the island was turned into large farms by settlers who were part of the great Oregon Trail migration. Today the farming tradition continues, and much of the southern half of the island is composed of nurseries, small farms, farmers' markets, and rural residences.

You'll begin this route by pedaling south on NW Gillihan Loop Road for a short distance. The road then swings north, taking you through a rolling landscape of open fields and pastures, nurseries, and large country homes. A variety of raptors can be seen soaring above the open landscape, including redtail hawks, Cooper's hawks, kestrels, and rough-legged hawks. Dotted along the route are many farm markets, which are fun to explore during the summer season. On a clear day you will have a magnificent view to the north and west of Mount Rainier, Mount St. Helens, Mount Adams, and Mount Hood.

After 6 miles, you'll turn right onto NW Reeder Road and continue your journey north. Along this section you'll pass by different wildlife area access points, and you can check out some of the island's great sandy beaches. Stop by the Reeder Beach RV Park and Store to get recommendations for beach access. After 8.9 miles you'll come to your turnaround point at a wildlife viewing platform that contains informative displays about the geology, history, and bird life of the island. When you are ready to continue on the route, you'll turn right (south) onto NW Reeder Road to the intersection with NW Sauvie Island Road. Turn left, and continue pedaling south, where you'll pass more open fields and farms. At 17 miles, be sure to explore the Bybee-Howell House in Howell Territorial Park. This two-story classical revival style house was built in the mid-1850s and is open to the public from 12:00 P.M. to 5:00 P.M. on the weekends (June through September).

If you plan on exploring the island more via car, be sure to pick up a $3.50 day-use parking permit at Sam's Cracker Barrel Store (you'll pass this store on your right at 17.8 miles), which is required at all wildlife viewing parking areas on the island.

LOCAL INFORMATION

♦ Oregon Department of Fish and Wildlife, Sauvie Island Wildlife Area, 18330 NW Sauvie Island Road, Portland, OR 97231, (503) 621–3488; www.dfw.state.or.us/ODFWhtml/InfoCntrWild/WildlifeAreas/Sauvie.html.
♦ Portland Visitors Information and Service Center, Two World Trade Center (Corner of SW Naito Parkway and SW Salmon Street), Portland, OR 97204, (877) 678–5263, www.pova.com/visitor/index.html.

Who says the dogs can't come along too?

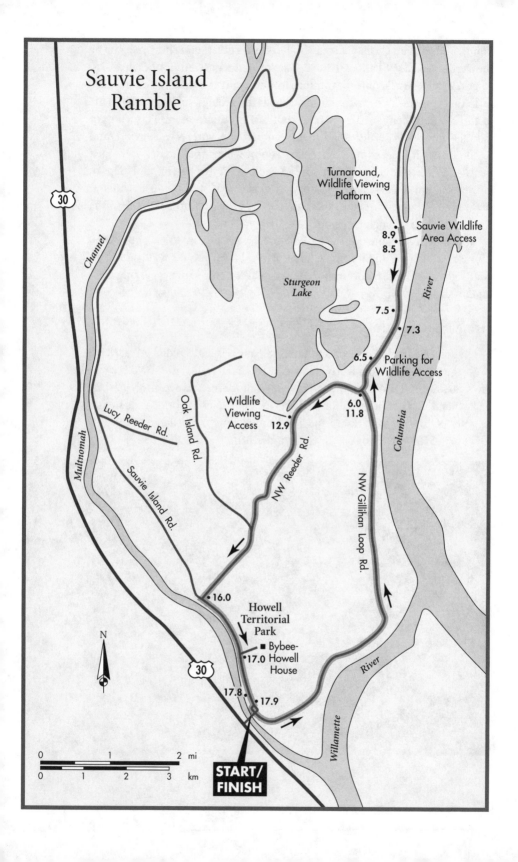

Sauvie Island Ramble

Turnaround,
Wildlife Viewing
Platform

Sauvie Wildlife
Area Access

8.9
8.5

Channel

30

Sturgeon
Lake

River

7.5
7.3

6.5
Parking for
Wildlife Access

Lucy Reeder Rd.

Oak Island Rd.

Wildlife
Viewing
Access
12.9

6.0
11.8

Multnomah

NW Reeder Rd.

Sauvie Island Rd.

NW Gillihan Loop Rd.

Columbia

16.0

Howell
Territorial
Park

Bybee-
Howell
House

17.0

N

30

River

17.8
17.9

Willamette

0   1   2 mi
0   1   2   3 km

START/
FINISH

Start by turning left (south) out of the parking area onto NW Gillihan Loop Road. Watch for traffic as you exit out of the parking area.

6.0 Turn right onto NW Reeder Road.

6.5 Pass a gravel parking area on your left, which is an access point to the Sauvie Island Wildlife Area. There is a portable rest room in this parking area.

7.3 Pass Reeder Beach RV Park and Store on your right. This is a good place to stop for snacks and drinks. There are portable rest rooms and a pay phone here.

7.5 Pass the Sauvie Island Bed & Breakfast on your right.

8.5 Pass another Sauvie Island Wildlife Area access point on your right.

8.9 Come to a wildlife viewing platform with interpretive signs and rest rooms. From this viewing platform you'll have the opportunity to view mallard, pintail, widgeon, and green-winged teal ducks; blue herons; tundra swans; and sandhill cranes. This is your turnaround point. To return to your starting point, turn right onto Reeder Road.

11.8 At the Y-junction, turn right (south), and continue riding on NW Reeder Road.

12.9 Pass another wildlife viewing area with rest rooms on the right.

16.0 At the T-intersection, turn left onto NW Sauvie Island Road.

17.0 Pass the historic Bybee-Howell House on your left.

17.8 Pass Sam's Cracker Barrel Store on your right. This is another good place to stock up on drinks and snacks. A pay phone is available.

17.9 Turn right onto NW Gillihan Loop Road.

18.0 Arrive back at your starting point on the left.

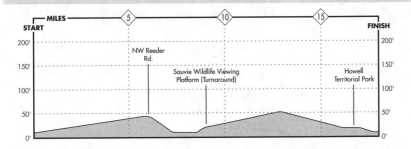

LOCAL EVENTS/ATTRACTIONS

♦ Portland Rose Festival, 5603 SW Hood Avenue, Portland, OR 97201, (503) 227–2681. Held June 1 through July 1.

♦ Providence Bridge Pedal, 1631 NE Klickitat Street, Portland, OR 97212, (503)281–9198; www.providence.org/oregon/services/cancer/bridge–pedal/default.htm. This annual event (held in mid-August) is a 27-mile bike ride crossing eight of Portland's historic bridges: Hawthorne, Ross Island, Marquam, Burnside, Steel, Fremont, St. Johns, and Broadway.

◆ The Bybee-Howell House, Howell Territorial Park, 13901 NW Howell Park Road on Sauvie Island, (503) 621–3344; www.metro-region.org/parks/ howellpage.html, was built in the mid-1850s and is open to the public from noon to 5:00 P.M. on weekends (June through September). A $2.00 donation is requested.

RESTAURANTS

◆ Portland Brewing Co. has great microbrews, German-style food, and moderate prices. 2730 NW 31st Avenue, Portland, OR 97210, (503) 226–7623, www.portlandbrew.com.

ACCOMMODATIONS

◆ Sauvie Island Bed & Breakfast, rooms $70–$85 per night, includes gourmet breakfast. 26504 NW Reeder Road, Portland, OR 97231, (503) 621–7821; www.moriah.com/sauvie.

BIKE SHOPS

Southwest Portland
◆ Bike Central Co-op, 732 SW 1st and Yamhill, Portland, OR 97201, (503) 227–4439; pdxnet.net/bikecentral.
◆ The Bike Gallery, 1001 SW Salmon Street, Portland, OR 97205, (503) 222–3821; bikegallery.com.
◆ En Selle the Road Bike Shop, 6200 SW Virginia Avenue, Portland, OR 97201, (503) 244–6754.
Northwest Portland
◆ Northwest Bicycles, 916 Northwest 21st Avenue, Portland, OR 97209, (503) 248–9142.

REST ROOMS

◆ Mile 6.5: Sauvie Island wildlife viewing parking area.
◆ Mile 7.3: Reeder Beach RV Park and Store.
◆ Mile 8.9: Wildlife viewing platform.

MAPS

◆ USGS 7.5-minute quads Sauvie Island and Linnton; *DeLorme Oregon Atlas and Gazetteer,* map 66.

Skyline Cruise

This route takes you on a tour of scenic Skyline Boulevard, which winds its way northwest along the ridge crest of the Tualatin Mountains and offers magnificent views of the Tualatin Valley. This hilly ride will challenge you as it takes you past expensive executive homes in Portland's West Hills; through the great expanse of Forest Park; and then through a rural landscape filled with mature forests, century-old farms, vineyards, and agricultural crops.

The ride starts by meandering through the green expanse of 332-acre Washington Park, which is crisscrossed with hiking trails that wind through a lush fern-filled forest. This park was established in 1871 and was originally just more than forty acres. Over the years adjacent lands were purchased until it reached its present size.

After almost a mile of uphill climbing, turn northwest onto Skyline Boulevard. This twisty road snakes its way along the crest of the Tualatin Mountains, which run in a northwest direction, separating Portland and the Willamette River to the east from the Tualatin Valley to the west. As you pedal on this winding road, you'll have many opportunities to stop and admire the views to the southwest of the Chehalem Mountains and the Tualatin Valley.

At the 2-mile mark, you'll pass Willamette Stone State Park, located on the west side of Skyline Boulevard. This 1.6-acre park has a small monument that commemorates an important surveying point where the Willamette meridian and the Willamette baseline meet. This site was the origin to sectioning all of the land in Oregon and Washington. As you continue riding on Skyline Boulevard, you'll pass the the great expanse of Forest Park to the east. At 5,000 acres Forest Park is one of the largest city parks in the world. This park contains more than 60 miles of hiking and biking trails that pass through a green

Start: The Vietnam Memorial parking lot in Washington Park. The Vietnam Memorial is located approximately 2.5 miles west of downtown Portland off U.S. Highway 26.

Length: 42.3-mile loop.

Season: Year-round. Some roads can be icy during the winter months.

Approximate riding time: Four to six hours.

Recommended start time: 10:00 A.M.

Terrain: Many twists and turns, and many steep ascents and descents on city and rural roads with no shoulder.

Traffic and hazards: Skyline Boulevard is a busy street with many blind curves and little or no shoulder. Some sections of Skyline Boulevard also have speed bumps. As you travel farther northwest on Skyline Boulevard, the route takes you into a more rural area, and there aren't as many cars. Watch for traffic when you cross NW Cornelius Pass Road at 12.1 miles. Rock Creek Road is bumpy and has some potholes. At 13.1 miles you'll have to stop for a railroad crossing. There are no railroad traffic lights, so you need to rely on your own judgment to look for trains before crossing the tracks. The rest of the roads on this ride have little or no shoulder with light to moderate traffic (depending on the time of day). This ride is best completed at midday or on a weekend. Avoid this ride during morning and evening rush hour.

Getting there: From downtown Portland, drive 1.8 miles west on U.S. Highway 26 toward Beaverton. Take exit 72 for the OREGON ZOO AND THE WORLD FORESTRY CENTER. At the end of the off-ramp, turn right on SW Knights Boulevard, and drive through the Oregon Zoo parking area. After 0.4 mile you'll pass the World Forestry Center on your left. At 0.6 mile turn right into a parking area directly across from the Vietnam Memorial at the intersection of SW Knights Boulevard and SW Kingston Boulevard.

landscape of big leaf maple, red alder, Douglas fir, sword fern, and Oregon grape. Originally Native Americans established routes over this vast ridge. As the area around Portland was settled, these routes were improved to allow settlers on the east side of Tualatin Mountain to bring their products for export into the growing city of Portland. Skyline Boulevard was a result of this expansion.

Continue pedaling northwest on Skyline Boulevard until you reach the 12.1-mile mark, where you'll cross busy NW Cornelius Pass Road. Along this section of Skyline Boulevard, you'll notice that you aren't the only one who is enjoying the view. Much of the western side of the ridge is being developed with expensive homes. As you continue heading northwest, the landscape opens up and becomes more rural. At 12.4 miles you'll turn onto Rock Creek Road. The road surface starts out a bit rough, and you'll have to dodge some potholes. This road takes you on a roller-coaster descent through a forested canyon and past several small farms where you may see horses, sheep, or cattle grazing. After the descent be ready for some steep climbing back to NW Skyline Boulevard at 17.7 miles.

The rest of this route has many steep ups and downs as it winds through rural Helvetia hill country. This countryside is filled with century-old farms, wineries, and elaborate homes. Just past 27 miles you'll pass Helvetia Tavern, a highly recommended local watering hole. This tavern serves delicious hamburgers and

Helvetia Community Church.

homemade fries. If you want to check out another local hangout, pedal a half mile farther and stop at Rock Creek Tavern. After you've had a chance to check out the local color, pedal your way back up to Skyline Boulevard, and return to your starting point.

LOCAL INFORMATION

♦ Portland Visitors Information and Service Center, Two World Trade Center (Corner of SW Naito Parkway and SW Salmon Street), Portland, OR 97204, (877) 678–5263, www.pova.com/visitor/index.html.
♦ Portland Wheelmen Touring Club, P.O. Box 2972, Portland, OR 97208-2972, 503-257-PWTC, www.pwtc.com.

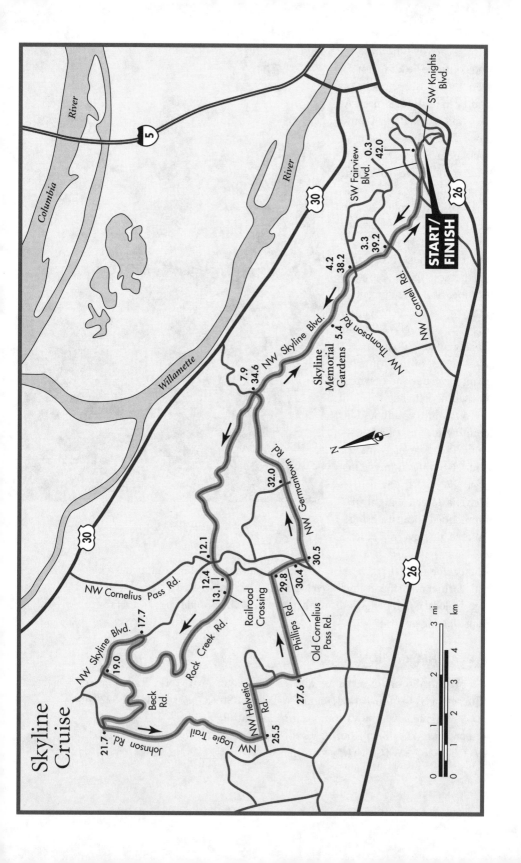

Skyline Cruise

Start by turning right out of the parking area onto SW Knights Boulevard. The route winds through Washington Park.

0.3 At the T-intersection turn left onto SW Fairview Boulevard.

0.9 Turn right onto SW Skyline Boulevard.

1.4 At the T-intersection turn left onto West Burnside.

1.6 At the Y-intersection stay to the right, following the signs for NW Skyline Boulevard.

2.0 Pass Willamette Stone State Park on your left. Watch for speed bumps over the next 0.5 mile.

3.3 At the four-way intersection and stop sign, continue straight (crossing NW Cornell Road), and continue riding on NW Skyline Boulevard. If you want to stop for some good burgers and shakes, Skyline Restaurant is located on your left at this intersection.

4.2 At the four-way intersection and stop sign, continue straight (crossing NW Thompson Road), and continue riding on NW Skyline Boulevard.

5.4 Pass Skyline Memorial Gardens on your left. This is a good place to stop and admire the view of the Tualatin Valley to the west.

7.7 Pass Skyline Tavern on your left. This is one of many good local watering holes you'll discover on this route.

7.9 At the four-way intersection and stop sign, continue straight (crossing NW Germantown Road) on NW Skyline Boulevard.

12.1 At the four-way intersection and stop sign, continue straight (crossing NW Cornelius Pass Road). Be cautious of the heavy traffic on this road. After crossing the highway you'll come to a stop sign. Turn left onto Old Cornelius Pass Road.

12.4 At the Y-intersection turn right onto Rock Creek Road. Note that this road is rough and has multiple potholes.

13.1 Stop for a railroad crossing.

17.7 At the T-intersection and stop sign, turn left onto NW Skyline Boulevard.

(continued)

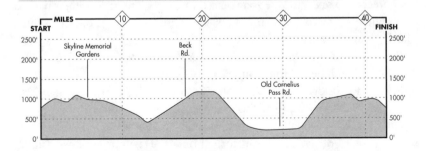

19.0 Turn left onto Beck Road.

21.7 At the T-intersection and stop sign, turn left onto Johnson Road. Note that Johnson Road eventually turns into NW Logie Trail.

25.5 At the T-intersection and stop sign, turn left onto NW Helvetia Road.

27.2 Pass Helvetia Tavern on your left. This tavern serves giant hamburgers and delicious homemade fries.

27.6 Turn left onto Phillips Road.

29.8 At the next T-intersection, turn right onto Old Cornelius Pass Road. Pass by Rock Creek Tavern at this intersection.

30.4 At the four-way intersection and stop sign, continue straight (crossing NW Cornelius Pass Road).

30.5 At the T-intersection and stop sign, turn left onto NW Germantown Road.

32.0 At the four-way intersection and stop sign, continue straight on NW Germantown Road (crossing NW Kaiser Road).

34.6 At the four-way intersection and stop light, turn right onto NW Skyline Boulevard.

38.2 At the four-way intersection and stop sign, continue straight on NW Skyline Boulevard (crossing NW Thompson Road).

39.2 At the four-way intersection and stop sign, continue straight on NW Skyline Boulevard (crossing NW Cornell Road).

40.9 At the Y-intersection and stop sign, turn left onto West Burnside Street.

41.1 Turn left onto SW Skyline Boulevard.

41.7 Turn left onto SW Fairview Boulevard.

42.0 Turn right onto SW Knights Boulevard.

42.3 Turn left into the parking lot and your starting point at the intersection of SW Knights Boulevard and SW Kingston Drive.

LOCAL EVENTS/ATTRACTIONS

♦ Oregon Zoo, 4001 SW Canyon Road, Portland, OR 97221, (503) 226–1561, www.oregonzoo.org. Visit the zoo and see a variety of animals in their natural environments. The zoo is open from 9:00 A.M. to 4:00 P.M. October 1 through March 31 and 9:00 A.M. to 6:00 P.M. the rest of the year.

♦ Portland Rose Festival, 5603 SW Hood Avenue, Portland, OR 97201, (503) 227–2681. Held June 1 through July 1.

♦ Providence Bridge Pedal, 1631 NE Klickitat Street, Portland, OR 97212 (503) 281–9198; www.providence.org/oregon/services/cancer/bridge_pedal/default.htm. This annual event (held in mid-August) is a 27-mile bike ride crossing eight of Portland's historic bridges: Hawthorne, Ross Island,

Marquam, Burnside, Steel, Fremont, St. Johns, and Broadway.
◆ World Forestry Center, 4033 SW Canyon Road, Portland, OR 97221, (503) 228–1367, www.worldforestry.org.

RESTAURANTS

◆ Helvetia Tavern, 10275 NW Helvetia Road, Hillsboro, OR 97124, (503) 647–5286.
◆ Rock Creek Tavern, 10000 NW Old Cornelius Pass Road, Portland, OR 97231, (503) 645–3822.
◆ Skyline Tavern, 8031 NW Skyline Boulevard, Portland, OR 97229, (503) 286–4788.

ACCOMMODATIONS

◆ Heron Haus, 2545 NW Westover Road, Portland, OR 97210, (503) 274–1846, home.europa.com/~hhaus.
◆ MacMaster House B&B, 1041 SW Vista, Portland, OR 97205, (800) 774–9523, www.macmaster.com.

BIKE SHOPS

Southwest Portland
◆ Bike Central Co-op, 732 SW 1st and Yamhill, Portland, OR 97201 (503) 227–4439, pdxnet.net/bikecentral.
◆ The Bike Gallery, 1001 SW Salmon Street, Portland, OR 97205, (503) 222–3821, bikegallery.com.
◆ En Selle the Road Bike Shop, 6200 SW Virginia Avenue, Portland, OR 97201, (503) 244–6754.
Northwest Portland
◆ Northwest Bicycles, 916 NW 21st Avenue, Portland, OR 97209, (503) 248–9142.

REST ROOMS

◆ Mile 7.7: Skyline Tavern.
◆ Mile 27.2: Helvetia Tavern.
◆ Mile 29.8: Rock Creek Tavern.

MAPS

◆ USGS 7.5-minute quads Linnton, Hillsboro, Dixie Mountain, and Portland; *DeLorme Oregon Atlas and Gazetteer,* map 66.

Portland Hilly Parks Cruise

This challenging city ride takes you to the top of three of Portland's most scenic parks: Mount Tabor, Joseph Wood Hill Park at Rocky Butte, and Council Crest Park. From the summits of these three parks you have spectacular views of the Portland metropolitan area. This route takes you past century-old homes in some of the Portland's historic neighborhoods. You'll also have the opportunity to ride across two of Portland's historic bridges—the Broadway and Hawthorne—which both offer scenic views of the Willamette River and downtown Portland. Additional highlights on this ride include a tour of downtown Portland and the urban greenery of Washington Park. Optional side trips include Waterfront Park, Oregon Zoo, World Forestry Center, Vietnam Memorial, Hoyt Arboretum, Portland Rose Gardens, and the Hawthorne District.

This ride begins in Mount Tabor Park, which is located about 4 miles east of downtown Portland. The 200-acre wooded park is a treasured urban sanctuary and has many hiking trails crisscrossing its steeply treed canopy. The park is a large butte that is the remnant of a 3-million-year-old volcano.

Begin this route by riding northeast from the park toward Rocky Butte. You'll ride on quiet backstreets through Portland's Northeast District, then climb to the 612-foot summit of Rocky Butte. After cranking the last steep incline, you'll arrive at an incredible stone monument that is part of Joseph Wood Hill Park. It is worth dismounting here to check out the far-reaching views of downtown Portland to the west, the Portland airport to the north, and

Start: North parking area at Mount Tabor Park. Mount Tabor Park is located approximately 4 miles east of downtown Portland.

Length: 33.3 miles.

Season: Year-round.

Approximate riding time: Four to six hours.

Recommended start time: 10:00 A.M.

Terrain: City streets and bike path.

Traffic and hazards: This ride follows city streets and has many busy intersections where you'll have to be cautious of traffic, including SE Stark Street, SE Washington Street, Burnside Street, NE Halsey Street, NE 82nd Avenue, NE Martin Luther King Boulevard, SW Broadway Street, SW Sixth, SW Terwilliger, SW Skyline Boulevard, and SE Hawthorne Boulevard. You'll also have two bridge crossings: the Broadway Bridge and the Hawthorne Bridge. Both bridges have a wide bike and pedestrian path. After you cross the Broadway Bridge, be very cautious of the traffic as the route takes you south through downtown Portland. Don't attempt this ride during peak morning and evening rush-hour traffic. It is recommended that you ride this route at midday or on a weekend.

Getting there: From downtown Portland, head 5.5 miles east on I-84 toward The Dalles. Exit the freeway at 82nd Avenue (exit 5). At the end of the off-ramp and stop sign, turn right, and drive 1 block to a stoplight and the intersection with NE 82nd Avenue. Turn left (south) onto NE 82nd Avenue, and drive 1.1 miles to the intersection with SE Yamhill Street. Turn right onto SE Yamhill Street and drive 0.3 mile west on Yamhill to the intersection with SE 76th Street. Turn right onto SE 76th Street, then take an immediate left onto SE Yamhill Street. Continue driving west for 0.3 mile to the intersection with SE 69th Street. Turn left onto SE 69th Street, drive 1 block, and turn right onto an unmarked paved road at the base of Mount Tabor Park. Drive 0.2 mile to a parking area on the right side of the road.

the magnificent Columbia River Gorge to the east. This park is popular with local climbers, who like to boulder on the knobby stone walls that surround the park. After you soak in the views from this prominent butte, get ready for a fun downhill sail from the summit. From the base of Rocky Butte, you'll head west and ride through quiet city streets in some of Portland's original neighborhoods, including Alameda and Irvington, which feature wide tree-lined avenues and historic homes.

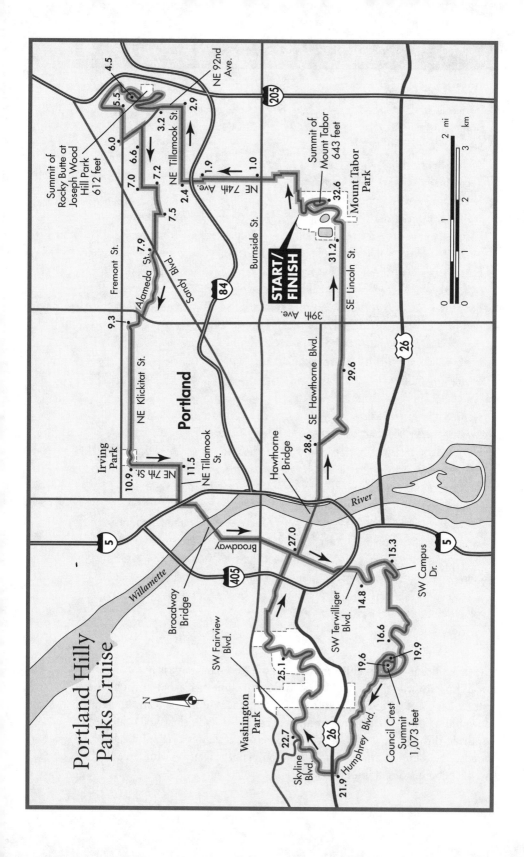

Start by turning left out of the parking area onto the paved park road.

0.2 Turn left onto SE 69th Street. Ride 50 yards, then turn right onto SE Yamhill Street.

0.3 Cross SE 71st Street, and continue pedaling a fast downhill on SE Yamhill Street.

0.5 At the stop sign turn left onto SE 76th Avenue.

0.7 Cross SE Washington Street, and continue pedaling straight on SE 76th Street. Ride about 50 yards. At the next stoplight turn left onto SE Stark Street.

0.8 Turn right onto SE 75th Street, pedal a short distance, then turn left onto SE Pine Street.

0.9 At the stop sign turn right onto SE 74th Street.

1.0 Cross Burnside Street, and continue straight on NE 74th Street.

1.9 At a stoplight, turn left onto NE Halsey Street, then take an immediate right onto NE 74th Street.

2.1 At the T-intersection and stop sign, turn right onto NE Tillamook Street.

2.4 Cross NE 82nd Avenue.

2.9 At the T-intersection and stop sign, turn left onto NE 92nd Avenue.

3.2 At the Y-intersection turn right onto NE Rocky Butte Road, and begin a steep ascent to the top of Rocky Butte. Note that there is no shoulder on NE Rocky Butte Road.

3.5 Ride through a tunnel—be sure to watch for cars.

4.5 At the T-intersection turn right. Be sure to explore Joseph Wood Hill Park on your left by following the trail up to a viewpoint. From the 612-foot summit of Rocky Butte, you can see downtown Portland, the Portland Airport, and the Columbia River Gorge. At the next unmarked Y-intersection (located across from the trail to the park), veer right and ride a fun downhill on NE Rocky Butte Road. This road turns into NE 91st Avenue near the bottom of the hill.

5.5 At the stop sign turn right onto NE Fremont Street.

6.0 Turn left onto NE Fremont Drive.

6.3 Turn right onto NE Siskiyou Street. *(continued)*

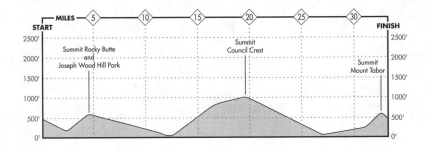

6.5 At the stoplight cross NE 82nd.

6.6 Pass Glenhaven Park on your left, which has rest rooms and water.

7.0 At the stop sign turn left onto NE 72nd Street.

7.2 Turn right onto NE Sacramento Street.

7.5 Turn right onto NE 66th Street. Ride 1 block, then turn left onto NE Alameda Street.

7.9 At the stoplight cross NE Sandy Boulevard, and continue riding on NE Alameda Street.

9.3 Turn left onto NE Klickitat Street.

9.5 Cross NE 35th Avenue, and continue riding straight on NE Klickitat Street, where a sign indicates DO NOT ENTER. This sign applies to cars only.

9.6 Cross NE 33rd Avenue.

10.5 Cross NE 14th Avenue, and start riding on a bike-only path. The path crosses NE 13th Avenue, NE 12th Avenue, and NE 11th Avenue. Stay on the bike path, and continue riding west through Irvington Park.

10.8 Pass by rest rooms.

10.9 Turn left onto NE 7th Avenue.

11.5 Turn right onto NE Tillamook Street.

11.7 Cross Martin Luther King Boulevard, and continue riding on NE Tillamook Street.

11.9 Cross North Vancouver.

12.0 Turn left onto North Flint.

12.2 Turn right onto North Broadway.

12.4 Cross the Broadway Bridge over the Willamette River, and continue riding south on SW Broadway as it takes you through downtown Portland.

13.2 Cross Burnside Street, and continue riding south on SW Broadway.

13.5 Ride past Pioneer Courthouse Square and Pioneer Place on your left.

14.3 At the stoplight at the intersection with SW Broadway Drive, stay to the left (this turns into SW 6th Avenue). Follow signs to SW Barbur Boulevard and the Ross Island Bridge.

14.4 Continue riding on SW 6th Avenue, and stay to the right where a sign indicates 6TH AVE. TO TERWILLIGER BLVD/OREGON HEALTH SCIENCES UNIVERSITY/VA HOSPITAL.

14.5 At the stoplight continue straight on SW 6th Street.

14.8 At the stoplight turn left onto SW Terwilliger Boulevard.

15.3 Turn right onto SW Campus Drive, and begin a steep uphill climb.

15.7 At the T-intersection turn left onto SW Sam Jackson Park Road.

15.9 At the Y-intersection veer right onto SW Gibbs Street (SW Gibbs Street eventually turns into SW Marquam Hill Road).

(continued)

16.6 Turn left onto SW Fairmount Boulevard.

18.9 At the four-way stop, turn right onto SW Talbot Terrace.

19.1 Turn right onto SW Greenway Avenue.

19.3 At the Y-intersection stay to the right, and continue riding on SW Greenway Avenue. Begin riding the summit loop at Council Crest Park.

19.6 Arrive at the 1,073-foot summit of Council Crest. There is a drinking fountain at this location. Finish riding the summit circle.

19.9 At the stop sign, turn left onto SW Greenway Avenue.

20.2 Turn left onto SW Talbot Terrace.

20.3 At the four-way stop, continue riding straight on SW Talbot Road.

20.5 At the four-way stop, continue riding straight on SW Humphrey Boulevard (crossing SW Patton Road). There is a Chevron station on your left that has a rest room and phone.

21.9 Turn right onto the bike-only path. Ride 15 feet, and turn right onto SW Skyline Boulevard. Continue straight on SW Skyline Boulevard. Ride through a busy intersection and stoplight.

22.7 Turn right onto SW Fairview Boulevard.

23.3 Turn right onto SW Knights Boulevard. You have the option here of taking a side trip to the Vietnam Memorial, World Forestry Center, Hoyt Arboretum, or Oregon Zoo.

23.6 Turn left onto SW Kingston Drive.

25.1 At the four-way stop, turn right on SW Sherwood. There are rest rooms, water, a phone, and bike racks at this location. You can also explore the Portland Rose Gardens.

25.8 At the stop sign turn right onto Lewis and Clark Circle.

25.9 Turn right onto SW Park Place.

26.2 Take a short jog to the right on SW King Avenue, then turn left onto SW Salmon Street.

26.8 Pass by the Bike Gallery on your right (a good place to stock up on any biking supplies).

26.9 Turn right onto SW Broadway.

27.0 Turn left onto SW Madison Street.

27.3 Cross the Hawthorne Bridge. Continue riding straight on SE Hawthorne Boulevard.

28.6 After crossing SE 12th veer right onto SE Ladd Avenue.

28.8 Turn right onto SE Ladd Avenue Circle.

28.9 Turn right onto SE Harrison Street.

(continued)

29.0 Turn right onto SE Locust. Ride 1 block, then turn left onto SE Harrison Street. At this intersection you'll pass Palio Coffee and Dessert House on the right. Continue riding east on SE Harrison Street.

29.6 Cross SE 30th Avenue, and continue riding east on SE Lincoln Street (SE Harrison Street ends at this intersection).

30.2 At the stoplight cross SE 39th Avenue, and continue riding east on SE Lincoln Street.

31.2 Cross 60th Avenue, and continue straight on SE Lincoln Street.

31.4 SE Lincoln Street ends. Turn left into Mount Tabor Park at the entrance sign, and begin pedaling to the summit.

31.7 At the Y-intersection stay to the left.

32.1 At the Y-intersection stay to the left.

32.3 Take a very sharp left turn, and pedal around a closed gate. No cars are allowed on the summit of Mount Tabor.

32.6 Stay to the right, and ride counterclockwise around the 643-foot Mount Tabor Park summit loop.

32.9 End the summit loop, and begin descending.

33.0 Go around the closed metal gate, then turn left and keep pedaling downhill.

33.3 At the T-intersection and stop sign, turn left, then take an immediate right into the parking area and to your vehicle.

After pedaling 12.4 miles you'll cross the Broadway Bridge and swing south through downtown Portland. The Broadway Bridge was built during 1911 and 1912 and is a double-leaf bascule span. Amazingly, this bridge is the largest of only four bridges in the country of this type. In the downtown area, you may want to stop and explore the red-brick Pioneer Courthouse Square and the many shops located in the Pioneer Place mall. You can ride 6 blocks east from the square and tour Waterfront Park, which parallels the Willamette River and offers outstanding views of Portland's historic bridges. From downtown you'll continue south and begin a difficult climb through the Oregon Health Sciences University medical campus and quiet West Hills neighborhoods to the 1,073-foot summit of Council Crest. From this spectacular summit you'll have expansive views of Portland and Mount Hood to the west and Tualatin Valley to the east. From Council Crest Park you'll wind through more West Hills neighborhoods and descend into Washington Park. This park is another one of Portland's beautiful urban green spaces and contains many popular Portland attractions, including the Vietnam Memorial, World Forestry Center, Oregon Zoo, Hoyt Aboretum, and Portland Rose Gardens. After you've explored this scenic spot, check your brakes and quick releases, then zoom down through the city center.

Enjoying the view from the 1,043-foot summit of Council Crest.

From downtown you'll head east across the spectacular Hawthorne Bridge. Built in 1910, this bridge is the most used bicycle and pedestrian bridge in Oregon. You'll continue east on busy SE Hawthorne Boulevard. If you're feeling thirsty, you might want to check out the Lucky Labrador Brew Pub located at 915 SE Hawthorne Boulevard. This friendly local pub immortalizes the Labrador retriever and all other hounds and has named many of its brews with a canine twist. If you stop here try the Lucky Lab IPA, Black Lab Stout, or the Hawthorne Bitter. Be aware that on the back patio you may be sipping suds in the company of dogs. You should also know that if you continue a couple more miles east on Hawthorne Boulevard, you'll arrive in the center of the popular Hawthorne District. This Portland district is filled with unique shops, pubs, bookstores, and the Bagdad Theater (3702 SE Hawthorne Boulevard), where you can watch movies, eat pizza, and drink beer all at the same time. If you decide to check out the Hawthorne District, ride east on one of the side streets that parallel SE Hawthorne Boulevard because this high-traffic thoroughfare does not have a bike lane. This area is prone to bike theft, so be sure to lock up your bike if you decide to go exploring.

You'll soon abandon this busy boulevard for the tranquil Ladd's Edition neighborhood, which is characterized by large trees, rose gardens, and historic homes. If you have the urge for something sweet, stop by Palio Coffee and Dessert House (1996 SE Ladd Street), which serves up scrumptious desserts. Before you know it you'll be soaring up to the 643-foot summit of Mount Tabor, where you'll have superb views of Portland's east side and downtown areas. Looking west, you may also spot Mount Hood peaking through the trees. From the summit cruise downhill to your starting point.

LOCAL INFORMATION

♦ Portland Visitors Information and Service Center, Two World Trade Center (Corner of SW Naito Parkway and SW Salmon Street), Portland, OR 97204, (877) 678–5263, www.pova.com/visitor/index.html.
♦ Portland Wheelmen Touring Club, P.O. Box 2972, Portland, OR 97208-2972, (503) 257-PWTC, www.pwtc.com.

LOCAL EVENTS/ATTRACTIONS

♦ Oregon Zoo, 4001 SW Canyon Road, Portland, OR 97221, (503) 226–1561, www.oregonzoo.org. See a variety of animals in their natural environments. The zoo is open from 9:00 A.M. to 4:00 P.M. October 1 through March 31 and 9:00 A.M. to 6:00 P.M. the rest of the year.
♦ Portland Rose Festival, 5603 SW Hood Avenue, Portland, OR 97201. Held June 1 through July 1, (503) 227–2681.
♦ Providence Bridge Pedal, 1631 NE Klickitat Street, Portland, OR 97212 (503) 281–9198, www.providence.org/oregon/services/cancer/bridge_pedal/default.htm. This annual event (held in mid-August) is a 27-mile bike ride crossing eight of Portland's historic bridges: Hawthorne, Ross Island, Marquam, Burnside, Steel, Fremont, St. Johns, and Broadway.
♦ World Forestry Center, 4033 SW Canyon Road, Portland, OR 97221, (503) 228–1367, www.worldforestry.org.

RESTAURANTS

♦ McMenamin's Bagdad Theater and Pub, 3702 SE Hawthorne Boulevard, Portland, OR 97215, (503) 225–5555, www.mcmenamins.com.
♦ Lucky Labrador Brewing Company, 915 SE Hawthorne Boulevard, Portland, OR 97214, (503) 236–3555, www.luckylab.com.
♦ Palio Coffee and Dessert House, 1996 SE Ladd Street, Portland, OR 97214, (503) 232–9412.
♦ Una Mas!, 3832 SE Hawthorne Boulevard, Portland, OR 97215, (503) 236–5000.
♦ Ya Hala Lebanese Cuisine, 8005 SE Stark Street, Portland, OR 97215, (503) 256–4484.

ACCOMMODATIONS

♦ Portland International Youth Hostel, 3031 SE Hawthorne Boulevard, Portland, OR 97214, (503) 236–3380, www.teleport.com/~hip.
♦ Portland's White House, 1914 NE 22nd Avenue, Portland, OR 97212, (800) 272–7131, www.portlandswhitehouse.com.

BIKE SHOPS

Southwest Portland

♦ Bike Central Co-op, 732 SW 1st and Yamhill, Portland, OR 97201 (503) 227–4439, pdxnet.net/bikecentral.

♦ The Bike Gallery, 1001 SW Salmon Street, Portland, OR 97205, (503) 222–3821, bikegallery.com.

♦ En Selle the Road Bike Shop, 6200 SW Virginia Avenue, Portland, OR 97201, (503) 244–6754.

Northwest Portland

♦ Northwest Bicycles, 916 NW 21st Avenue, Portland, OR 97209, (503) 248–9142.

Southeast Portland

♦ Bike N Hike, 1734 SE Martin Luther King Boulevard, Portland, OR 97214, (503) 736–1074.

♦ Bob's Bicycle Center, 10950 SE Division Street, Portland, OR 97266, (503) 254–2663.

♦ City Bikes, 1914 SE Ankeny Street, Portland, OR 97214, (503) 239–0553.

♦ River City Bicycles, 706 SE Martin Luther King Boulevard, Portland, OR 97214, (503) 233–5973.

♦ Sellwood Cycle Repair, 7639 SE Milwaukie Avenue, Portland, OR 97202, (503) 233–9392, www.sellwoodcycle.com.

Northeast Portland

♦ Gateway Bicycles, 11905 NE Halsey Street, Portland, OR 97220, (503) 254–0800, www.gatewaybicycles.com.

REST ROOMS

♦ Mile 0.0: Mount Tabor.

♦ Mile 6.6: Glenhaven Park.

♦ Mile 10.8: Irvington Park.

♦ Mile 13.5: Pioneer Place.

♦ Mile 20.5: Chevron station.

♦ Mile 25.1: Portland Rose Garden.

MAPS

♦ USGS 7.5-minute quads Portland, Mount Tabor, and Lake Oswego; *DeLorme Oregon Atlas and Gazetteer,* map 66.

Portland Bridges–Tryon Creek State Park Ramble

T *his out-and-back scenic city ride begins on the east side of the Willamette River on the East Bank Esplanade. This magnificent multiuse path features many interpretive plaques, art sculptures, and a floating boardwalk. You'll cross the Steel Bridge and pedal through popular Waterfront Park. After a short but intense passage through downtown Portland, you'll head up shady Terwilliger Boulevard. The route stays fun until you cross Barbur Boulevard and contest with a bit of automotive congestion. After about a mile of this, you'll turn onto a tranquil multiuse path that meanders through Tryon Creek State Park to its nature center.*

This loop route begins in southeast Portland and heads north along the banks of the Willamette River on the East Bank Esplanade—an exceptional multiuse path. Along the way you can stop and read interpretive signs that give you an inside look at Willamette River history and development. The Willamette River begins in the Cascade Mountains, then flows north past Eugene, Corvallis, Albany, and Salem. It continues its northward journey and travels past Oregon City and Portland, where it joins the Columbia River at the southern tip of Sauvie Island (about 10 miles north of Portland off U.S. Highway 30). Lewis and Clark first canoed past the entrance to the Willamette in the fall of 1805 and the spring of 1806. At that time the Willamette was a

Start: SE Caruthers Street in Southeast Portland.

Length: 18.1-mile loop.

Season: Year-round.

Approximate riding time: Two to three hours.

Recommended start time: 10:00 A.M.

Terrain: City streets and bike paths.

Traffic and hazards: Take care when traveling among pedestrians on the multiuse paths along the East Bank Esplanade and Waterfront Park. Use caution when riding on city streets in downtown Portland, including SW Taylor, SW Broadway, SW 6th Avenue, and SW Madison. Use crosswalks when crossing the busy intersections at SW Terwilliger and SW Boones Ferry Road.

Getting there: From I-5 south in Portland, take exit 300B and get into the left lane. Follow the brown OMSI (Oregon Museum of Science and Industry) signs that take you to SE Belmont Avenue, where you'll head east. Turn right (south) onto 7th Avenue, and drive to the intersection with SW Clay Street. Turn right (west) onto Clay Street, and drive to the intersection with SE Water Avenue. Turn left (south) onto Water Avenue, and proceed to OMSI. Once you reach OMSI, continue driving south on Water Avenue for another 0.3 mile to the intersection with SE Caruthers Street. Turn right onto SE Caruthers, and park where SE Caruthers dead-ends at a cul-de-sac.

From I-5 north in Portland, take exit 300 toward I-84/THE DALLES/PORTLAND AIRPORT. Get into the right lane and exit at a sign that indicates OMSI/CENTRAL EASTSIDE INDUSTRIAL DISTRICT. Turn right (south) onto SE Water Street. Proceed 0.7 mile (you'll pass OMSI after 0.4 mile) to the intersection with SE Caruthers Street. Turn right onto SE Caruthers Street, and park where SE Caruthers dead-ends at a cul-de-sac.

pristine watershed teeming with salmon and bordered by green meadowlands, marshes, and thick stands of fir and cedar.

Portland was incorporated in 1851, and the government decreed that settlers were entitled to 1 square mile of free land. It wasn't long before timber was cut, houses were built, and warehouses sprang up to store and receive cargo from ships traveling up the Columbia River from Astoria. By 1859 most of the Native Americans who once enjoyed the bounty of this rich river valley were displaced by white settlers. As the city grew the marshes and ponds were filled

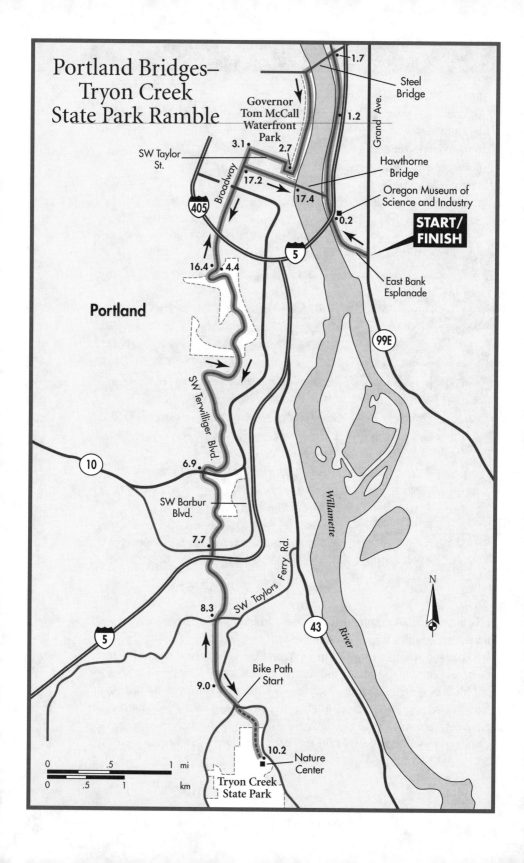

Portland Bridges–
Tryon Creek
State Park Ramble

Steel
Bridge

1.7

Governor
Tom McCall
Waterfront
Park

1.2

Grand Ave.

3.1

2.7

SW Taylor
St.

17.2

Hawthorne
Bridge

Oregon Museum of
Science and Industry

17.4

405

Broadway

0.2

START/
FINISH

5

East Bank
Esplanade

16.4   4.4

Portland

99E

SW Terwilliger Blvd.

10

6.9

SW Barbur
Blvd.

Willamette

7.7

SW Taylors Ferry Rd.

N

8.3

43

River

5

9.0

Bike Path
Start

10.2   Nature
Center

0   .5   1 mi

0   .5   1 km

Tryon Creek
State Park

Start riding west on SE Caruthers Street until it dead-ends at the start of the multiuse East Bank Esplanade. Turn right (north) onto the East Bank Esplanade, which parallels the Willamette River.

0.2 Pass the oregon Museum of Science and Industry (OMSI) on the right.

1.2 Turn left at the ASH STREET sign, then ride down a ramp and follow the path as it continues north. You are now riding on a floating ramp.

1.7 Cross the Steel Bridge.

1.9 After crossing the Steel Bridge, turn left (south), and follow the paved path as it takes you through Waterfront Park.

2.7 Pass the Salmon Street Fountain on your right. Turn right here, then take another right when you reach Front Avenue. Walk your bike 1 block along Front Avenue.

2.8 Use the crosswalk to cross Front Avenue. After crossing continue riding west on SW Taylor Street.

3.1 Turn left onto SW Broadway.

3.9 At the stoplight head left toward BARBUR BLVD/ROSS ISLAND BRIDGE/HOSPITALS.

4.0 At the stoplight turn right where a sign indicates 6TH AVE./TERWILLIGER BLVD./ OHSU/VA HOSPITALS.

4.1 Cross SW Sherman, and continue to the right on 6th Avenue (SW Broadway turns into SW 6th Avenue).

4.4 At the stoplight turn left onto SW Terwilliger Boulevard.

6.9 At the stoplight cross Capitol Highway, and continue riding straight on SW Terwilliger Boulevard.

7.7 At the stoplight cross SW Barbur Boulevard, and continue riding straight on SW Terwilliger Boulevard.

8.3 At the stoplight cross SW Taylors Ferry Road, and continue riding straight on SW Terwilliger Boulevard.

9.0 The road forks here, with Terwilliger heading left and Boones Ferry going right. Stay to the right on Boones Ferry, and immediately catch a series of crosswalks

(continued)

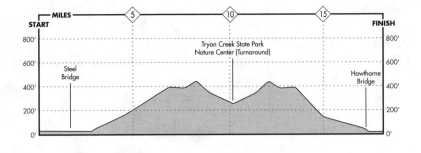

to the other side of Boones Ferry. Begin riding on a paved bike path that heads into the forest.

10.0 Arrive at a junction. Head right, and continue riding on the bike path.

10.1 Arrive at a junction with the entrance road to Tryon Creek State Park. Check for traffic, cross the entrance road, and veer right toward the nature center.

10.2 Arrive at the nature center. Lock up your bike and explore the center and the trails in the park. Rest rooms and water are available here. When you are finished exploring, head north on the bike path back toward downtown Portland.

10.3 Arrive at a junction. Turn left (north). Cross the entrance road to Tryon Creek State Park, and continue riding north on the bike path.

11.4 The bike path ends. Cross two crosswalks, and continue riding north on SW Terwilliger Boulevard.

16.2 At the stoplight turn right, and continue riding on SW Terwilliger Boulevard.

16.4 Cross SW Sheridan, and continue riding straight on SW 6th Avenue (SW Terwilliger Boulevard turns into SW 6th Avenue).

17.2 Turn right onto SW Madison.

17.4 Cross the Hawthorne Bridge over the Willamette River.

17.9 Turn right onto the bike ramp that heads south along the Willamette River.

18.1 Arrive at SE Caruthers Street on your left.

to build rail lines and rail yards. In addition a 25-foot channel was dredged in the Willamette River from Portland to where it meets the Columbia River to allow ships to pass more easily into the Portland Harbor. By the 1920s the river became so polluted it was not suitable for fishing, swimming, or boating. The once bountiful salmon runs plummeted. Beginning in the 1970s new laws were adopted to clean up the Willamette River, and in the mid-1980s the city began working on solving the problem of frequent sewer overflows when excess storm water and untreated waste flowed into the river. Despite these efforts, in December 2000 the Portland Harbor was designated as a Superfund site because of its extreme pollution, including contaminants such as lead, arsenic, benzene, mercury, and pesticides that enter the river from agricultural runoff and industrial wastes. So on a hot day, don't be tempted to take a dip! Nonprofit groups such as the Willamette RiverKeeper and OSPIRG (Oregon Student Public Interest Research Group) are working with local communities and government agencies to help clean up the Willamette with the goal of restoring wildlife habitat, fish runs, and water quality.

As you ride north you'll have an unobstructed view of Portland's skyline and its many historical bridges. After 0.2 mile you'll pass the Oregon Museum of Science and Industry. Established in 1944, this world-class science museum is a popular Portland attraction. It teaches visitors about the wonder of science through hands-on demonstrations, interactive exhibits, and science labs. It also features the OMNIMAX Theater—a five-story domed screen with viewers seated in the middle of the movie action. You'll cross the Steel Bridge on a special walkway for pedestrians and cyclists built on the south side of the bridge next to the bottom deck.

After crossing, you'll swing south and cruise through Tom McCall Waterfront Park. When you are on this section of the route, you may want to stop at Saturday Market (open on week-

Stunning artwork in Waterfront Park.

ends only), located under the Burnside Bridge, to check out handcrafted items and to try some delicious ethnic foods. After riding through Waterfront Park for about a mile, you'll reach the Salmon Street Fountain. In the summer months adults and kids enjoy cooling off in this circular fountain.

The route continues south through downtown Portland, then hooks up with SW Terwilliger Boulevard after 4.4 miles. This winding road boasts an excellent bike lane that travels through the Portland West Hills and Burlingame District until it reaches Tryon Creek State Park. It is worth taking a break from the saddle here to check out the nature center and to hike on some of the

Enjoying Willamette River views on the East Bank Esplanade.

forested trails that surround the park. The nature center hours are 9:00 A.M. to 5:00 P.M. Monday through Friday, and 9:00 A.M. to 4:00 P.M. on weekends. From the park you'll backtrack to downtown Portland, then head east across the Hawthorne Bridge on expansive bike lanes. After crossing the bridge you'll turn south onto the bike and pedestrian path that leads you back to your starting point.

LOCAL INFORMATION

♦ Oregon State Parks and Recreation, 1115 Commercial Street NE, Suite 1, Salem, OR 97301-1002, (800) 551–6949, www.oregonstateparks.org.
♦ Portland Parks and Recreation, 1120 SW Fifth Avenue, Suite 1302, Portland, OR 97204, (503) 823–PLAY, www.parks.ci.portland.or.us.
♦ Portland Visitors Information and Service Center, Two World Trade Center (Corner of SW Naito Parkway and SW Salmon Street), Portland, OR 97204, (877) 678–5263, www.pova.com/visitor/index.html.

◆ Portland Wheelmen Touring Club, P.O. Box 2972, Portland, OR 97208-2972, (503) 257-PWTC, www.pwtc.com.

LOCAL EVENTS/ATTRACTIONS

◆ Oregon Museum of Science and Industry (OMSI). 1945 SE Water Avenue, Portland, OR 97214-3354, (800) 955–6674, www.omsi.edu. Visit a world-class science museum that teaches kids about science with interactive exhibits and hands-on demonstrations. Call for current admission rates and hours.
◆ Portland Rose Festival, 5603 SW Hood Avenue, Portland, OR 97201, (503) 227–2681. Held June 1 through July 1.
◆ Providence Bridge Pedal, 1631 NE Klickitat Street, Portland, OR 97212 (503) 281–9198, www.providence.org/oregon/services/cancer/bridge_pedal/default.htm. This annual event (held in mid-August) is a 27-mile bike ride crossing eight of Portland's historic bridges: Hawthorne, Ross Island, Marquam, Burnside, Steel, Fremont, St. Johns, and Broadway.
◆ Saturday Market, 108 West Burnside, Portland, OR 97209, (503) 222–6072. The marketplace is located under the Burnside Bridge and features arts and crafts from local artists and fabulous ethnic food from a wide assortment of vendors. Saturday Market is open March 1 through Christmas Eve, Saturdays 10:00 A.M. to 5:00 P.M. and Sundays 11:00 A.M. to 4:30 P.M.

RESTAURANTS

◆ Bijou Café, 132 SW 3rd Avenue, Portland, OR 97204, (503) 222–3187. This restaurant serves delicious omelets and vegetarian dishes.
◆ Typhoon!, 400 SW Broadway, Portland, OR 97204, (503) 224–8285. This restaurant serves delicious Thai food.

ACCOMMODATIONS

◆ Terwilliger Vista B&B, 515 SW Westwood Drive, Portland, OR 97201, (888) 244–0602, www.terwilligervista.com.

BIKE SHOPS

Southwest Portland
◆ Bike Central Co-op, 732 SW 1st and Yamhill, Portland, OR 97201, (503) 227–4439, pdxnet.net/bikecentral/.
◆ The Bike Gallery, 1001 SW Salmon Street, Portland, OR 97205, (503) 222–3821, bikegallery.com.
◆ En Selle the Road Bike Shop, 6200 SW Virginia Avenue, Portland, OR 97201, (503) 244–6754.

Southeast Portland

♦ Bike N Hike, 1734 SE Martin Luther King Boulevard, Portland, OR 97214, (503) 736–1074.

♦ Bob's Bicycle Center, 10950 SE Division Street, Portland, OR 97266, (503) 254–2663.

♦ City Bikes, 1914 SE Ankeny Street, Portland, OR 97214, (503) 239–0553.

♦ River City Bicycles, 706 SE Martin Luther King Boulevard, Portland, OR 97214, (503) 233–5973.

♦ Sellwood Cycle Repair, 7639 SE Milwaukie Avenue, Portland, OR 97202, (503) 233–9392, www.sellwoodcycle.com.

REST ROOMS

♦ Mile 10.2: Nature Center at Tryon Creek State Park.

MAPS

♦ USGS 7.5-minute quads Portland and Lake Oswego; *DeLorme Oregon Atlas and Gazetteer,* maps 60 and 66.

Hagg Lake Ramble

This ride begins at the historic McMenamin's Grand Lodge in Forest Grove and takes you through the rural farm country of Washington County. On this route you'll have the opportunity to stop and taste fine wines at the Montinore Winery and cruise around scenic Hagg Lake, where you can stop and hike, have a picnic, or take a refreshing swim.

This ride begins at the historic McMenamin's Grand Lodge. Located on thirteen acres of gardens, this Greek Revival–style lodge was originally built in 1922 as a Masonic lodge. The McMenamin brothers purchased the lodge in 1999 when the Masonic and Eastern Star Home moved to a new location. The magnificent red-brick accommodations feature seventy-seven European-style rooms that have a shared bathroom in the hall. A homemade breakfast is included and served in the pub. The lodge features a movie theater, restaurant and pub, soaking pool, day spa, specialty bars, classic artwork, and live music. For those on a budget, you can stay in a hostel-style room for $40 per night (breakfast is not included with hostel-style rooms). Even if you don't plan on staying here, it is highly recommended that you tour the building and check out the unique artwork and the grand architectural details.

You'll start this route by riding south on Highway 47, which has a wide shoulder and can have moderate to heavy traffic during peak morning and evening rush hour. You may want to take an optional side trip to the Momokawa Saké Brewery, located on the east side of Highway 47. This brewery was the first to produce saké in the Northwest and is open from noon to 5:00 P.M. daily. (The turnoff to this brewery is on your left at the 1.4-mile mark.) You'll ride on Highway 47 for only a few miles before you turn off the

Start: The parking lot at McMenamin's Grand Lodge at the intersection of U.S. Highway 47 and Pacific Avenue in Forest Grove.

Length: 28.7-mile loop.

Season: Year-round.

Approximate riding time: Two to four hours.

Recommended start time: 11:30 A.M.

Terrain: Major highway with wide shoulder and rural country roads with no shoulder.

Traffic and hazards: Be cautious of heavy traffic when you cross Pacific Avenue at 0.1 mile. This is the most congested intersection you will find on this route. U.S. Highway 47 has a wide shoulder, but you still need to watch for heavy traffic during peak morning and afternoon rush hour. Be cautious of logging trucks transporting logs to Stimson Mill, located off Scoggins Valley Road. Stringtown Road, SW Dilley Road., SW Dudney Road, and Old Highway 47 do not have shoulders, but the traffic is usually light. Scoggins Valley Road has a 2-foot shoulder, and traffic on this road can be moderate to heavy during the peak summer season. There is also a 2-foot shoulder on the route circling the lake, and the traffic can be moderate to heavy on busy summer weekends.

Getting there: From Portland, head 21 miles west on U.S. Highway 26 to a Y-intersection with Highway 6. Turn left onto Highway 6 (toward Banks, Forest Grove, and Tillamook), and drive 2.5 miles to the intersection with Highway 47. Turn onto Highway 47, and drive 7 miles south to McMenamin's Grand Lodge parking lot, located on the right side of the highway at the intersection with Pacific Avenue in Forest Grove.

highway and begin pedaling on rural roads that wind past fields of grapes, grass-seed crops, dairies, and nurseries. Just shy of 4 miles, you'll pass the entrance to Montinore Vineyards on your right. This European-style winery is the fifth-largest winery in Oregon and is located on 711 acres. It is well known for its handcrafted pinot noir, pinot gris, chardonnay, Müller-Thurgau, gewürztraminer, and Riesling. At the turn of the century, the original owner named the estate Montinore, which is short for "Montana in Oregon." The winery is open every day from noon to 5:00 P.M. (April through December), and from noon to 5:00 P.M. on weekends the rest of the year.

As you continue on your route, you'll pass through picturesque farm country and arrive at the small town of Dilley. This historic community was established in 1873 and was named after Milton E. Dilley, who was one of the original settlers in this area. If you are working up an appetite or need to stock up on drinks, be sure to stop at the Lake Stop Store, which you'll pass after 6.8 miles. This store features deli fried chicken and other food and drink. Continue another 2.6 miles to Hagg Lake and the intersection with West Shore Drive. From here, you'll begin your 10.5-mile ride around the scenic 1,113-acre lake. This much-loved lake was developed in the mid-1970s and provides irrigation water for the Tualatin Valley and supplemental drinking

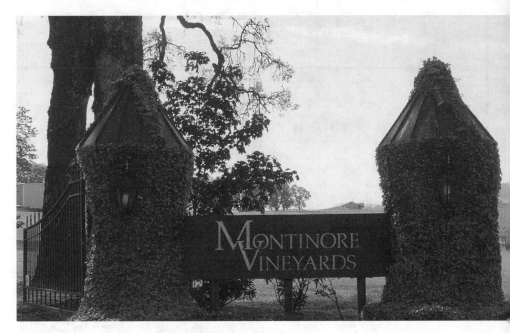

Pick up a bottle of wine for a picnic at Hagg Lake.

water to surrounding communities. The route around the lake features rolling hills, travels past thick woods and open grassy meadows, and offers plenty of opportunities for exploring. The lake is surrounded by Scoggins Valley Park, which features a 15-mile hiking and mountain-biking trail that circles the lakeshore. This scenic, winding trail can be accessed from any of the lake's picnic areas or from other roadside access points. Wildlife you may see includes deer, coyotes, bobcats, osprey, hawks, bald eagles, songbirds, and a variety of waterfowl. If it's a hot summer day, you should take a refreshing plunge into the lake. Juicy blackberries can be found near the lake's edge in mid-August.

Cyclists and hikers aren't the only people enjoying this popular park. Boaters, water skiers, and anglers also use the lake. The east end is used by motor boaters and water skiers—the no-wake speed limit is not enforced. The west end is reserved for canoeing, sailing, and kayaking. Triathlons are held at the lake, with the Hagg Lake Triathlon (held the second weekend in July) being the most well known. Because of its close proximity to a large metropolitan area, this park can be very crowded during the summer months, and the car traffic on the lakeside road can be moderate to heavy. To avoid the crowds, ride this route in the early spring and late fall. If you visit during the summer months, try to arrange your ride on a weekday. Note that the road around Hagg Lake is open year-round, but the park facilities are only open from mid-April through the end of October. The park is open from sunrise to sunset and does not allow camping.

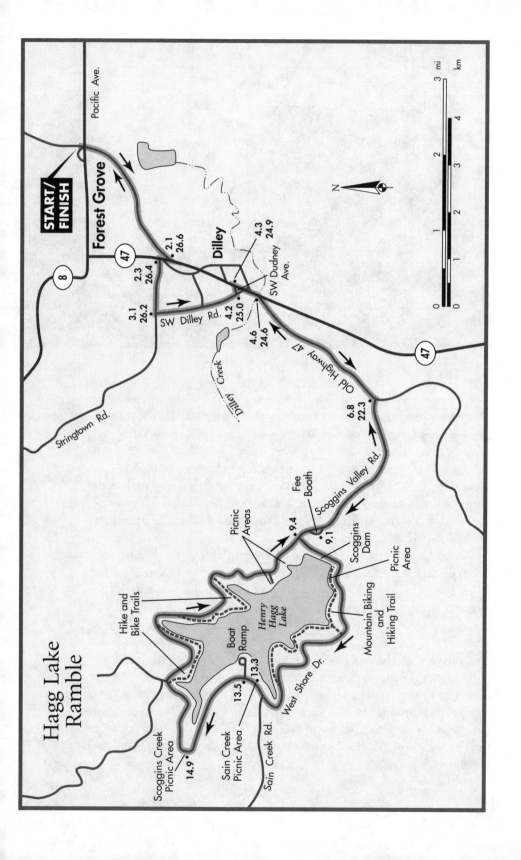

Hagg Lake Ramble

START/FINISH

8
47

Pacific Ave.

Forest Grove

2.1
26.6

Dilley

2.3
26.4

3.1
26.2

SW Dilley Rd.

4.2
25.0

4.3
24.9

SW Dudney Ave.

4.6
24.6

Old Highway 47

47

6.8
22.3

Scoggins Valley Rd.

Stringtown Rd.

Dilley Creek

Fee Booth

9.4

Scoggins Dam

9.1

Picnic Areas

Picnic Area

Mountain Biking and Hiking Trail

Henry Hagg Lake

Hike and Bike Trails

Boat Ramp

13.3

13.5

Sain Creek Rd.

West Shore Dr.

Sain Creek Picnic Area

Scoggins Creek Picnic Area

14.9

N

0   1   2   3 mi
0 1 2 3 4 km

Start by turning right (south) onto Highway 47 from the McMenamin's Grand Lodge parking lot.

0.1 Cross Pacific Avenue, and continue riding straight on Highway 47. Use caution at this intersection—it has heavy car traffic. Highway 47 has a wide shoulder, and some sections along the highway have a separate bike path.

1.4 Pass the turnoff to the Momokawa Saké Brewery on your left.

2.1 At a flashing yellow light, turn right onto an unmarked road.

2.3 Turn left onto Stringtown Road.

3.1 Turn left onto SW Dilley Road.

3.9 You'll pass the entrance to Montinore Vineyards on your right. The winery is open every day from noon to 5:00 P.M. (April through December), and from noon to 5:00 P.M. on weekends the rest of the year.

4.2 Turn left onto SW Dudney Avenue (SW Dilley dead-ends.)

4.3 Turn right onto Highway 47. Be cautious of traffic on this section of the route.

4.6 Turn right onto Old Highway 47. Be cautious of traffic; there is no shoulder on this section of the route.

6.8 Pass the Lake Stop Store on the right. You may want to stock up on drinks and snacks here. This store also serves great fried chicken. Just past the store you'll come to a stop sign; turn right onto SW Scoggins Valley Road. Be cautious of logging trucks heading for Stimson Mill zipping by you.

9.1 Pass the fee booth on your left. Ride past the booth, and continue pedaling up a short hill. You won't have to pay a fee when riding a bike.

9.4 Turn left onto West Shore Drive, and ride across Scoggins Dam. From this point, begin circling the lake in a clockwise direction on a series of fun rolling hills for about 10.5 miles.

10.3 Pass rest rooms and a large gravel parking area on the right.

13.3 Pass Sain Creek Picnic Area on your right. This is a good place to stop for lunch. There are rest rooms and picnic tables at this location. You can also access a hiking and mountain-biking trail that circles the lake from here.

(continued)

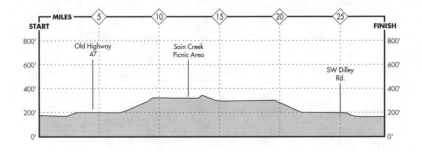

13.5 Pass Boat Ramp C on your right. There are rest rooms at this location.

14.9 Pass Scoggins Creek Picnic Area on your right. There are rest rooms here, too.

22.3 Turn left onto Old Highway 47. Be cautious of traffic.

24.9 Turn left onto SW Dudney Avenue.

25.0 Turn right onto SW Dilley Road.

26.2 Turn right onto SW Stringtown Road.

26.4 At the road intersection turn right, and ride 0.2 mile to the intersection with Highway 47.

26.6 Turn left onto Highway 47, and ride north toward Forest Grove.

28.7 Arrive at McMenamin's Grand Lodge parking lot and your vehicle on your left.

If you are still feeling spunky after completing the lake loop, you may want to go for another round. For a different perspective, reverse your direction. When you're done with your lake riding, head back on the same route to your starting point.

LOCAL INFORMATION

♦ Forest Grove Chamber of Commerce, 2417 Pacific Avenue, Forest Grove, OR 97116, (503) 357–3006, www.fgchamber.com.

♦ Portland Wheelmen Touring Club, P.O. Box 2972, Portland, OR 97208-2972, 503-257-PWTC, www.pwtc.com.

♦ Washington County Parks, Facilities Management Division, Support Services Department, 111 SE Washington Street, Hillsboro, OR 97123, (503) 846–3692, www.co.washington.or.us/deptmts/sup_serv/fac_mgt/parks/hagglake.htm.

LOCAL EVENTS/ATTRACTIONS

♦ Hagg Lake Triathlon, AA SPORTS, LTD., 4840 SW Western Avenue, Suite 400, Beaverton, OR 97005, (503) 644–6822, www.racecenter.com/hagglake/index.htm. This triathlon is held annually the second weekend in July.

♦ Momokawa Saké Brewery, 820 Elm Street, Forest Grove, OR 97116, (800) 550–7253, www.momokawa.com. Open noon to 5:00 P.M. daily.

♦ Montinore Vineyards, 3663 SW Dilley Road, Forest Grove, OR 97116, (503) 359–5012, www.montinore.com. Well known for their handcrafted pinot noir, pinot gris, chardonnay, Müller-Thurgau, gewürztraminer, and Riesling. Open daily from noon to 5:00 P.M. April through December, and from noon to 5:00 P.M. on weekends the rest of the year. Closed major holidays.

RESTAURANTS

♦ Lake Stop Grocery, 8015 SW Old Highway 47, Gaston, OR 97119, (503) 357–4270. Good fried chicken and other deli items.

♦ The Yardhouse Pub at the Grand Lodge, 3505 Pacific Avenue, Forest Grove, OR 97116, (503) 992–3442. Serves delicious McMenamin's handcrafted micro-brews, wines, and hearty food and features live music and outdoor seating during the summer months.

ACCOMMODATIONS

♦ McMenamin's Grand Lodge, 3505 Pacific Avenue, Forest Grove, OR 97116, (503) 992–9533, www.mcmenamins.com/grandlodge/index.html. Rates at this historic lodge are $40–$200 per night, depending on the season and time of the week. This lodge has a theater, restaurant and pub, soaking pool, day spa, specialty bars, and live music.

BIKE SHOPS

♦ Boomer Bikes, 2019 Pacific Avenue, Forest Grove, OR 97116, (503) 359–1280.

♦ Schlegel's Cycling and Fitness Centers, 1913 19th, Forest Grove, OR 97116, (503) 357–9807.

REST ROOMS

♦ Mile 0.0: McMenamin's Grand Lodge.
♦ Mile 10.3: Hagg Lake parking area.
♦ Mile 13.3: Sain Creek Picnic Area.
♦ Mile 13.5: Boat Ramp C.
♦ Mile 14.9: Scoggins Creek Picnic Area.

MAPS

♦ USGS 7.5-minute quads Gaston, Gales Creek, Laurelwood, and Forest Grove; *DeLorme Oregon Atlas and Gazetteer,* maps 59 and 65.

Columbia River–Springwater Corridor Ramble

T his route is a great introduction to some prime multiuse bike paths on the east side of Portland. These include the I–205 bike corridor, the Columbia River Trail, and the Springwater Corridor Trail. The expansive views along the Columbia and the wild isolation of the Springwater make this an enjoyable loop.

Portland has worked hard to develop a series of bike paths throughout the metropolitan area. This loop route takes you on three well-known bike and pedestrian paths: the I–205 bike corridor, the Columbia River Trail, and the Springwater Corridor Trail. These three multiuse paths are part of the 40-mile-loop trail system in Portland that links metropolitan parks and green spaces throughout the city. This link system provides both recreation opportunities and a haven for wildlife in the densely populated Portland metropolitan area.

The 40-Mile Loop Land Trust oversees the current

Cruising on the Columbia River Trail.

trail system and recommends new trail development for the future. Curiously this trail system totals more than 40 miles, so the name is misleading. John and Frederick Olmsted made the original proposal for the 40-mile loop in 1903. These two ambitious landscape architects were asked by the Municipal Park Commission of Portland to complete a park planning study. The report recommended a 40-mile trail system around the city of Portland that connected a series of parks. Today this loop system totals almost 150 miles and links more than thirty parks around Portland.

This ride begins at the Gateway Park and Ride in northeast Portland. Light rail trains from the far reaches of eastern and western Portland as well as the airport converge here. During non–rush-hour periods you can bring your bicycle aboard. From this parking area you'll head north on the I–205 bike and pedestrian path, which parallels the I–205 freeway. As you ride north you'll have to contend with some freeway noise, but you will only have to deal with car traffic at major intersections with Columbia Boulevard and Sandy Boulevard. After 3.8 miles you'll leave the freeway noise behind and turn east on Marine Boulevard. This main thoroughfare parallels the mighty Columbia River, which is the dividing line between Oregon and Washington. At 5.4 miles you'll cross Marine Drive and ride on the Columbia River Trail, a dedicated bike and pedestrian path that parallels the Columbia River. This scenic

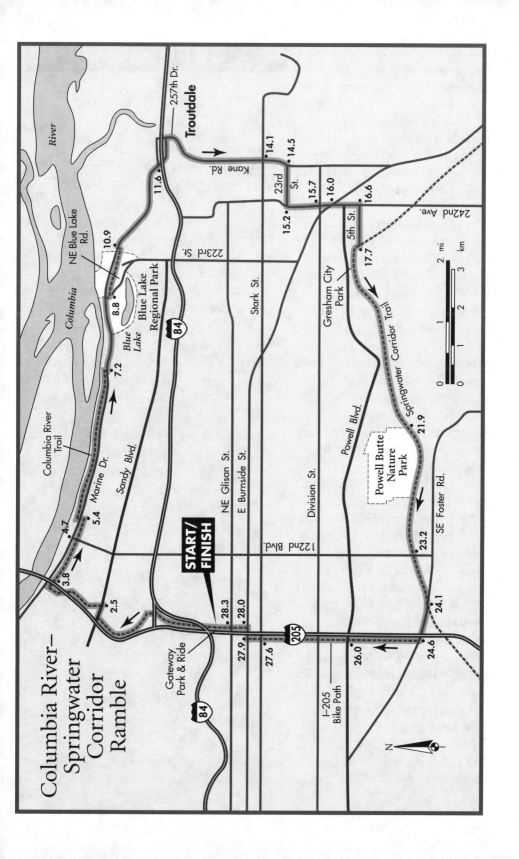

Start the route by heading west from the parking lot, crossing the train tracks, and heading north on the I–205 bike path.

2.0 Arrive at a Y-junction. Continue to the left, and ride north, paralleling I–205.

2.1 At the Y-junction go right where a sign indicates COLUMBIA BLVD .3 MILE.

2.4 The bike path intersects with Columbia Boulevard. Follow the bike sign to the right.

2.5 At the stoplight cross Sandy Boulevard. At the next intersection cross Columbia Boulevard, using the crosswalk, and then continue riding on the bike path.

3.6 Arrive at a junction. Continue straight. (If you go left here, you would be heading toward Vancouver, Washington.)

3.8 Turn right onto Marine Drive, and ride east in the bike lane toward Troutdale and Gresham.

4.7 Cross NE 122nd Boulevard, and continue riding on the bike path.

5.4 Cross Marine Drive, and continue riding east on the Columbia River Trail, which parallels the river.

7.2 The Columbia River Trail ends. Cross Marine Drive, and ride east on the bike lane on Marine Drive.

8.8 Arrive at a junction with NE Blue Lake Road. Turn right, follow the bike lane 200 yards, cross NE Blue Lake Road, and continue riding east on the bike lane. *Note:* This bike lane has some very rough sections. Instead of riding on the bike path, you may want to ride on the shoulder of Marine Drive, which has a smoother riding surface. You also have the option here of exploring Blue Lake Regional Park. To enter the park, continue riding on NE Blue Lake Road to the entrance road on your right. Blue Lake Regional Park has rest rooms, water, and picnic tables.

9.4 Cross an exit road for FAIRVIEW/GRESHAM, and continue riding on the bike path.

10.3 Use caution as you cross a set of railroad tracks. You'll enter the community of Troutdale.

10.9 The bike path ends and you'll need to continue riding on the shoulder on Marine Drive.

(continued)

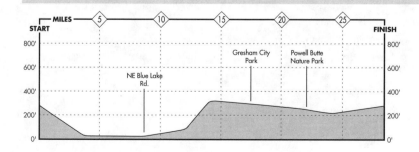

11.6 Ride under the I–84 freeway, and turn left onto a paved frontage road. You'll pass by numerous fast-food restaurants on your right, including McDonalds, Arbys, and Subway.

12.1 At the stoplight turn right onto 257th Drive, and begin a long climb.

12.2 At the stoplight you have the option of turning left onto 257th Way and exploring the Columbia Outlet Stores.

12.4 At the stoplight you'll cross the Old Columbia River Highway. You have the option of turning left and exploring the shops in downtown Troutdale. Continue straight on 257th Drive.

14.1 Cross Stark Street, and continue riding straight.

14.5 Turn right onto 23rd Street.

15.2 At the stoplight turn left onto 242nd Avenue.

15.7 Cross Division Street, and continue riding straight on 242nd Avenue.

16.0 Continue on 242nd Avenue across Burnside Street.

16.3 Cross Powell Boulevard, and continue riding straight on 242nd Avenue.

16.6 Turn right onto 5th Street.

17.2 Turn right onto Roberts Avenue.

17.3 Turn left onto the bike lane (the entrance to the bike lane is right across from 4th Street). You'll enter Gresham City Park.

17.4 Arrive at a junction. Turn left, and cross over a bridge.

17.6 Ignore the side path and bridge on the right, and continue riding straight on the bike path.

17.7 Ride across a strip of grass, then turn right (west) onto the Springwater Corridor.

18.5 Cross Eastman Parkway.

19.5 Cross Pleasant View Drive.

21.9 Pass the entrance trail to Powell Butte Nature Park on your right.

22.5 Pass the Country Market on your left. You may want to stock up on snacks and drinks at this store. Cross SE 136th Street.

22.9 Cross SE 128th Street.

23.2 Cross SE 122nd Avenue.

24.1 Turn right onto SE Foster Road.

24.6 Go under the I–205 Freeway. Cross SE 94th, then turn right (north) onto the I–205 bike path.

25.4 Cross SE Holgate Boulevard.

26.0 Cross SE Powell Boulevard. Be sure to use the crosswalk at this busy intersection.

(continued)

27.5 Cross SE Washington Street. Be sure to use the crosswalk at this busy intersection.

27.6 Cross SE Stark Street. Be sure to use the crosswalk at this busy intersection.

27.9 Arrive at East Burnside Street. Turn right onto the sidewalk to ride over the I–205 freeway.

28.0 After crossing the bridge over the freeway, use the crosswalk to cross East Burnside Street. Use caution at this intersection! Once you cross East Burnside Street, continue riding north on the I–205 bike path.

28.3 Cross NE Glisan Street using the crosswalk. Continue riding north on the I–205 bike path.

28.5 Arrive at the Gateway Park and Ride on your right.

pathway offers tremendous views of the Columbia River and the Columbia River Gorge.

After 8.8 miles you have the option of exploring Blue Lake Regional Park. This park has expansive lawns, picnic areas, and a swimming area at the lake. At the west end of the lake you can explore a small wetland area that is made up of two ponds that support rushes, willows, and cattails and are home to red-winged blackbirds, common yellowthroats, swallows, sparrows, and muskrats. The ponds are shaded by alder, cottonwood, and willows and have brushy undergrowth of Oregon grape, thimbleberry, and flowering currant.

After about 10 miles you'll enter the community of Troutdale and begin heading south. The Columbia Outlet Stores and the shops in historic downtown Troutdale may be of interest. Not far past Troutdale you'll enter the large community of Gresham. The car traffic can be congested as you travel through this area, but soon you will escape and ride through quiet Gresham City Park, which hooks into the Springwater Corridor Trail, a nonmotorized multiuse path, at 17.7 miles. The Springwater Corridor Trail follows an old rail line that has linked Portland and Boring since 1903. The trail is 16.8 miles long. It starts in Boring and heads west toward Southeast McLoughlin Boulevard in Portland. More than 600,000 people annually use this trail for commuting and recreation.

You'll pedal west on the Springwater Corridor Trail for the next 6.5 miles. Along the way you'll ride past farms, quiet residential areas, and huge thickets of blackberries that begin to ripen at the beginning of August. Bring extra containers so you can enjoy some of these delicious berries after your ride (empty water bottles also work well). On this section of the route you'll pass by the entrance to Powell Butte Nature Park at mile 21.9. This 570-acre nature park is a maze of woodlands and open meadows and has more than 9 miles of trails to explore.

You'll finish your loop by hooking up with Foster Road, then swinging north on the I–205 bike path.

ADDITIONAL RIDE INFORMATION

♦ Portland Parks and Recreation, 1120 SW Fifth Avenue, Suite 1302, Portland, OR 97204, (503) 823–PLAY, www.parks.ci.portland.or.us.

LOCAL INFORMATION

♦ Portland Visitors Information and Service Center, Two World Trade Center (Corner of SW Naito Parkway and SW Salmon Street), Portland, OR 97204, (877) 678–5263, www.pova.com/visitor/index.html.
♦ Troutdale Chamber of Commerce, 338 East Columbia River Highway, Troutdale, OR 97060, (503) 669–7473, www.troutdalechamber.org.

LOCAL EVENTS/ATTRACTIONS

♦ Harlow House Museum, 726 East Historic Columbia River Highway, Troutdale, OR 97060, (503) 661–2164.
♦ Portland Rose Festival, held June 1 through July 1, Portland. Call (503) 227–2681 for an event schedule.
♦ Providence Bridge Pedal, Portland, (503) 281–9198, www.providence.org/oregon/services/cancer/bridge_pedal/default.htm. This annual event (held in mid-August) is a 27-mile bike ride crossing eight of Portland's historic bridges: Hawthorne, Ross Island, Marquam, Burnside, Steel, Fremont, St. Johns, and Broadway.
♦ Depot Rail Museum, 473 East Historic Columbia River Highway, Troutdale, OR 97060, (503) 661–2164.

RESTAURANTS

♦ Black Rabbit Restaurant at McMenamin's Edgefield, 2126 SW Halsey Street, Troutdale, OR 97060, (503) 492–3086.

ACCOMMODATIONS

♦ McMenamin's Edgefield, 2126 SW Halsey Street, Troutdale, OR 97060, (503) 669–8610. This 103-room European-style hotel features comfy rooms, a winery, brewery, movie theater, and restaurant. Room rates here are $85–$120 or you can opt for a hostel room, which is only $20 per person. Room prices include breakfast (except if you are staying in the men's or women's hostel dormitory).

BIKE SHOPS

♦ Gateway Bicycles, 11905 NE Halsey Street, Portland, OR 97220, (503) 254–0800, www.gatewaybicycles.com.
♦ Gresham Bicycle and Fitness Center, 567 NE 8th Street, Gresham, OR 97030, (503) 661–2453.

REST ROOMS

♦ Mile 8.8: Blue Lake Regional Park.

MAPS

♦ USGS 7.5-minute quads Damascus, Camas, Gladstone, and Mount Tabor; *DeLorme Oregon Atlas and Gazetteer,* maps 60, 61, 66, and 67.

Larch Mountain Cruise

T his challenging ride takes you to the summit of 4,055-foot Larch Mountain, located in the Columbia River Gorge. On your way to the summit, you'll stop at two magnificent viewpoints—Portland Women's Forum State Park and Crown Point—that offer breathtaking views of the Columbia River Gorge. At Crown Point you'll also have the opportunity to look inside of the historic Vista House, which was built in 1917. After exploring the Vista House you'll pedal for 14 miles and gain 3,270 feet in elevation to the summit of Larch Mountain. At the summit you can take a quarter-mile hike to 4,055-foot Sherrard Point, where you can enjoy the views of Mount St. Helens, Mount Rainier, Mount Hood, and Mount Jefferson.

This challenging tour to the summit of 4,055-foot Larch Mountain starts out innocently enough by following a gentle grade on the historic Columbia River Highway parallel to the shores of the Sandy River. Lewis and Clark gave the river this name in November 1805 because of its soft, quicksand bottom.

You'll arrive in the town of Springdale just shy of a mile. This small rural town was established in the 1880s by Danish immigrants. The town was named Springdale after the numerous natural springs that can be found in the area. The original commerce in Springdale was a mercantile and creamery. By the 1920s the town had expanded, with the newly built Columbia River Highway paving the way for more new commerce. While you are pedaling through Springdale, be sure to stop at Mom's Bakery and Café to fuel up before the long climb to the summit of Larch Mountain.

Start: Dabney State Park, 4 miles east of Troutdale, off the Historic Columbia River Highway.

Length: 39.8-mile loop.

Season: June through October.

Approximate riding time: Four to six hours.

Recommended start time: 9:00 A.M.

Terrain: Rolling hills and one long, difficult 14-mile climb to the summit of Larch Mountain with 3,270 feet of elevation gain. The reward for all of your work is a very fast, very cool descent from the summit. (Be sure to bring extra clothing layers!) Note that because of snow, Larch Mountain Road is not often open until the first part of May.

Traffic and hazards: This route follows the Historic Columbia River Highway, which has a 2-foot shoulder for almost 6 miles. You'll be riding on this highway with moderate car traffic. After 5.8 miles, the highway has no shoulder, and it has blind curves when you descend to Crown Point State Park and the Vista House. The 14-mile climb to the summit of Larch Mountain is difficult, and there is no shoulder on Larch Mountain Road. Wear bright clothing and bring extra layers for the fast, brisk descent from the summit. Larch Mountain Road can also have moderate traffic on summer weekends. The return loop follows rural roads with mostly no shoulder and light to moderate traffic.

Getting there: From the intersection of I-205 and I-84 in Portland, drive 9 miles east on I-84 to exit 18 for LEWIS & CLARK STATE PARK. At the end of the off-ramp, turn left onto the Columbia River Highway. Continue 0.5 mile, and you'll arrive at a stop sign and intersection. Turn left where a sign indicates HISTORIC HIGHWAY, CORBETT, DABNEY STATE PARK. Proceed 2.7 miles on the Columbia River Highway to the entrance to Dabney State Park on the right. Note the sign for the park is small and difficult to see. There is a $3.00 day-use fee for this state park. You can obtain a day-use pass at the self-pay station in the parking area. There are rest rooms and water here.

After you ride through Springdale, you'll continue pedaling through scenic countryside filled with small farms and dotted with crops of blueberries and fruit trees. You'll arrive in Corbett after 3.5 miles. This community was named after Henry Winslow Corbett, a U.S. senator and Portland businessman who settled in this area in the early 1900s. In the early part of this century, Corbett was a thriving timber and agricultural center.

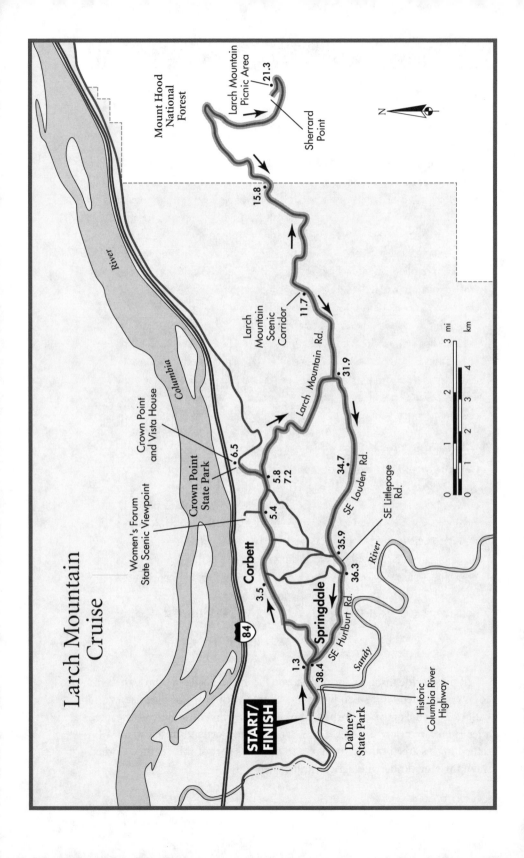

Start by turning right out of the Dabney State Park entrance onto Historic Columbia River Highway. There is a 1- to 2-foot shoulder on this section of the road. Rest rooms and water are available here.

0.8 Enter the small community of Springdale.

1.2 Pass Mom's Garden Bakery and Café on the right. You might want to stock up on bakery goodies for the long, difficult climb to the summit of Larch Mountain.

1.3 At the Y-intersection, go right where a sign indicates HISTORIC HIGHWAY, CORBETT, MULT-NOMAH FALLS, and continue riding on the Historic Columbia River Highway. At the next road junction, stay left.

3.5 Arrive in the small town of Corbett.

4.1 Pass Corbett Country Market on your left. You may want to stop and stock up on snacks and make sure you have enough to drink; there is no water at the summit of Larch Mountain. There is a phone at this store.

5.4 Pass Portland Women's Forum State Scenic Viewpoint and Chanticleer Point. Be sure to stop and check out the gorgeous view of the Columbia River Gorge and Crown Point, and to read the interpretive signs that describe the geology of the Gorge.

5.8 Turn left where a sign indicates HISTORIC HIGHWAY, CROWN POINT, MULTNOMAH FALLS, and begin descending on a narrow, curvy road with no shoulder to Crown Point State Park and the Vista House.

6.5 Turn right, and enter the parking area to Crown Point State Park and the Vista House. Be sure to take the time to view the historic 1917 Vista House (open April through October). Once you are finished exploring and soaking in the view, turn left out of the parking area and head back uphill. Note that this is your last chance to fill your water bottles before the long, difficult climb to the summit of Larch Mountain.

7.2 At the intersection and stop sign, take a very sharp left onto Larch Mountain Road. From this point you will begin a very steep, difficult climb to the Larch Mountain summit parking and picnic area.

(continued)

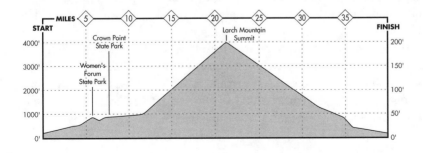

11.7 Enter the Larch Mountain Scenic Corridor.

15.8 Enter the Mount Hood National Forest.

21.3 Arrive at the Larch Mountain summit parking area. There are rest rooms and picnic tables but no water. Be sure to hike the quarter-mile trail to the viewpoint at the top of Sherrard Point. After you've enjoyed the view, head back down Larch Mountain Road. Wear extra layers—the descent can be very chilly!

31.9 Turn left onto SE Louden Road. This road takes on a mostly downhill cruise through picturesque foothills filled with farms and livestock.

34.7 Begin a steep, curvy downhill descent. Be cautious—there is no shoulder on this section of the route.

35.9 At the T-intersection and stop sign, turn left onto SE Littlepage Road.

36.1 At the stop sign turn right onto SE Hurlburt Road.

36.3 At the four-way intersection and stop sign, continue riding straight on SE Hurlburt Road.

38.4 At the stop sign turn left onto the Columbia River Highway, heading west toward Troutdale.

39.8 Turn left into Dabney State Park and your starting point. The sign for this state park is difficult to see, and this turnoff is easy to miss!

After 5.4 miles you'll arrive at Portland Women's Forum State Scenic Viewpoint and Chanticleer Point. This scenic viewpoint has a grand view of the Vista House and Crown Point looking east, and more spectacular views of the cliff-lined gorge looking west toward Portland. Chanticleer Point was named after the Chanticleer Inn, which was built in 1912 by Mr. and Mrs. A. R. Morgan. When the Columbia River Highway opened in 1915, many flocked to the inn for its delicious food and gorgeous view. Unfortunately the inn burned down in the 1930s, and now only old photos depict its former grandeur.

After 6.5 miles you'll arrive at Crown Point State Park and the historic Vista House, built in 1917. This classic, domed structure perches on a 733-foot cliff overlooking Columbia River Gorge. It was the vision of Samuel Lancaster, the chief engineer of the original Columbia River Highway project. He wanted "an observatory from which the view both up and down the Columbia could be viewed in silent communion with the infinite." Inside the Vista House you'll find old photos documenting the construction of the highway, as well as a museum, gift shop, interpretive displays, rest room, and small snack bar that serves espresso, soft drinks, and ice cream. (The Vista House is open from April through October.) Also note that this is your last watering hole for the remainder of this ride. (The Larch Mountain summit picnic area does not have water.)

As the westernmost high point in the Columbia River Gorge, Larch Mountain is a spectacular natural area. Douglas fir, silver fir, and noble fir grace its slopes, along with a thick understory of sword fern, licorice fern, and maidenhair fern. Ironically, no Larch trees grow on Larch Mountain—these trees typically grow only on the eastern side of the Cascades. Loggers often mistakenly called the noble fir a Larch, which leads to the misleading name. When you arrive at the Larch Mountain summit picnic area, stash your bike behind some trees (or better yet, lock it up), and be sure to hike the quarter-mile trail to the summit of 4,055-foot Sherrard Point. The rocky promontory of Sherrard Point rises sharply above a deep, extinct volcano. From the viewing area at the top, you can see (on a clear day) four prominent Cascade volcanoes: 8,363-foot Mount St. Helens; 14,410-foot Mount Rainier; 11,235-foot Mount Hood; and 10,497-foot Mount Jefferson. After you've spent some time enjoying the view, get ready for a fast, exhilarating downhill that is the great reward for all of your elevation gain. Be sure to throw on some extra layers for the very cool descent. Also, be cautious of traffic on this curvy, shoulderless road. After you've traveled 10.6 miles, swing a left onto SE Louden Road. The rest of your return trip will be a fun romp on rural roads through the Sandy River foothills to your starting point at Dabney State Park.

Admiring the view of Crown Point from Portland Women's Forum State Park.

The historic Vista House was built in 1917.

ADDITIONAL RIDE INFORMATION

♦ Columbia River Gorge National Scenic Area, 902 Wasco Avenue, Suite 200, Hood River, OR 97031, (541) 386–2333, www.fs.fed.us/r6/columbia/.

♦ Oregon State Parks and Recreation, 1115 Commercial Street NE, Suite 1, Salem, OR 97301-1002, (800) 551–6949, www.oregonstateparks.org.

LOCAL INFORMATION

♦ Corbett Country Market, 36801 East Historic Columbia River Highway, Corbett, OR 97019, (503) 695–2234.

♦ Troutdale Chamber of Commerce, 338 East Columbia River Highway, Troutdale, OR 97060, (503) 669–7473, www.troutdalechamber.org.

LOCAL EVENTS/ATTRACTIONS

♦ Crown Point and Vista House, located 11 miles east of Troutdale on the Historic Columbia River Highway. Contact Oregon State Parks at 1115 Commercial Street NE, Suite 1, Salem, OR 97301-1002, (800) 551–6949, www.oregonstateparks.org/park_150.php or www.vistahouse.com.

♦ Dabney State Park, located 4 miles east of Troutdale on the Historic Columbia River Highway. Contact Oregon State Parks at 1115 Commercial Street NE, Suite 1, Salem, OR 97301-1002, (800) 551–6949, www.oregonstateparks.org/park_150.php.

♦ Harlow House Museum, 726 East Historic Columbia River Highway, Troutdale, OR 97060, (503) 661–2164.

♦ Portland Women's Forum State Park, located 9 miles east of Troutdale on the Historic Columbia River Highway. Contact Oregon State Parks at 1115 Commercial Street NE, Suite 1, Salem, OR 97301-1002, (800) 551–6949, www.oregonstateparks.org/park_164.php.

♦ Depot Rail Museum, 473 East Historic Columbia River Highway, Troutdale, OR 97060, (503) 661–2164.

RESTAURANTS

♦ Black Rabbit Restaurant at McMenamin's Edgefield, 2126 SW Halsey Street, Troutdale, OR 97060, (503) 492–3086.

♦ Mom's Garden Bakery and Café, 32030 East Historic Columbia River Highway, Springdale, OR 97060, (503) 695–3285.

♦ Tad's Chicken'n Dumplins, 1325 East Columbia River Highway, Troutdale, OR 97060, (503) 666–5337.

ACCOMMODATIONS

♦ Chamberlain House Bed & Breakfast, 36817 Historic Columbia River Highway, Corbett, OR 97019, (503) 695–2200.

♦ McMenamin's Edgefield, 2126 SW Halsey Street, Troutdale, OR 97060, (503) 669–8610. This 103-room European-style hotel features comfy rooms, a winery, brewery, movie theater, and restaurant. Room rates here are $85–$120, or you can opt for a hostel room for only $20 per person. Room prices include breakfast (except if you are staying in the men's or women's hostel dormitory).

BIKE SHOPS

♦ Bike Gallery, 2332 East Powell Boulevard, Gresham, OR 97080, (503) 669–5190.

♦ Gateway Bicycles, 11905 NE Halsey Street, Portland, OR 97220, (503) 254–0800, www.gatewaybicycles.com.

♦ Gresham Bicycle and Fitness Center, 567 NE 8th Street, Gresham, OR 97030, (503) 661–2453.

REST ROOMS

♦ Mile 0.0: Dabney State Park.
♦ Mile 6.5: Crown Point State Park and the Vista House.
♦ Mile 21.3: Larch Mountain summit picnic area.

MAPS

♦ USGS 7.5-minute quads Washougal, Bridal Veil, and Multnomah Falls; *DeLorme Oregon Atlas and Gazetteer,* map 67.

Columbia River Gorge Waterfall Cruise

This tour travels on a restored section of the Historic Columbia River Highway, where you'll ride through one of the highest concentrations of waterfalls in North America. Other trip highlights include spectacular views of the Columbia River Gorge from Chanticleer Point, the opportunity to tour the historic Vista House, and chances to stop and hike at many of the state parks on this route.

This ride starts at Lewis and Clark State Park and takes you east on a restored section of the Historic Columbia River Highway, where you'll visit multiple cascading waterfalls and numerous scenic state parks. The construction of the Historic Columbia River Highway was thought to be one of the greatest engineering projects of its time. One of the original visionaries for the highway was Samuel C. Hill, also known as the father of the Columbia River Highway. Hill was a strong supporter of the "good roads" movement that was spawned from the development of the first commercially produced Model T Ford automobile. In 1900 Hill invited Samuel Lancaster, a well-respected road-building engineer, to the Northwest to discuss his vision for the Columbia River Highway. By 1913 Lancaster and his crew built a series of impressive roads on Hill's 7,000-acre Maryhill Estate in Washington. To help gain support for his vision for the Columbia River Highway, Hill invited members of the Oregon legislature to his estate to view the magnificent roadwork. Legislative members were so inspired by what they saw that they created the Oregon State Highway Commission to help oversee the development of the Columbia River Highway. Samuel Lancaster was appointed supervising engineer for the project, and before survey work began in 1913, Lancaster commented, "Our first order of business was to find the beauty spots, or those points where the most beautiful things along the line might be seen in the best advantage, and if possible to locate the road in such a way as to reach them." Work began in 1913 to build the highway that would stretch from Astoria to The Dalles. In June 1922 the highway was finally completed and consisted of eighteen bridges, three tunnels, seven viaducts, two footbridges, and 73.8 miles of roadway.

This tour starts by following the shores of the Sandy River and taking you past Dabney State Park at mile 3.1. This state park is a good place to go for a swim on a hot summer's day. Over the next 5 miles, the highway takes you past berry farms and orchards, and through the historic communities of Springdale and Corbett. If you are cycling in July and August, be on the lookout for U-PICK signs along this section of the highway. At mile 8.4 you'll arrive at Portland Women's Forum State Park and Chanticleer Point. Here you have a gorgeous view of the dramatic cliffs and forested ridges of Columbia River Gorge. This magnificent gorge was sculpted by castastrophic floods that occurred near the end of the ice age (19,000–12,000 years ago). These floods were created when the climate began to warm up, causing 2,000-foot ice dams that held 3,000-square-mile Lake Missoula in Montana to break. These floods poured through east-

THE BASICS

Start: From Lewis and Clark State Park, located approximately 16 miles east of Portland, off the Historic Columbia River Highway.

Length: 41.8 miles out and back.

Season: Year-round.

Approximate riding time: Five to seven hours.

Recommended start time: 9:00 A.M.

Terrain: This route follows the Historic Columbia River Highway east for 20.9 miles, starting at Lewis and Clark State Park and ending at Ainsworth State Park in the Columbia River Gorge. From Ainsworth State Park you'll retrace your route back to Lewis and Clark State Park for a total mileage of 41.8.

Traffic and hazards: This route follows the Historic Columbia River Highway, which has a 2-foot shoulder for almost 6 miles. After 8.8 miles, the highway has no shoulder, and it has blind curves when you descend to Crown Point State Park and the Vista House. You'll continue on a twisty, shoulderless descent for approximately 2 more miles. The route then continues east for another 10 miles to your turnaround point at Ainsworth State Park. You can expect moderate to heavy car traffic on this highway on the weekends and light to moderate traffic on weekdays. It is recommended that you attempt this tour on a weekday.

Getting there: From the intersection of I–205 and I–84 in Portland, drive 9 miles east on I–84 to exit 18 for Lewis and Clark State Park. At the end of the off-ramp, turn left onto the Columbia River Highway. Continue 0.2 mile on the Columbia River Highway, and turn left into the Lewis and Clark State Park parking area.

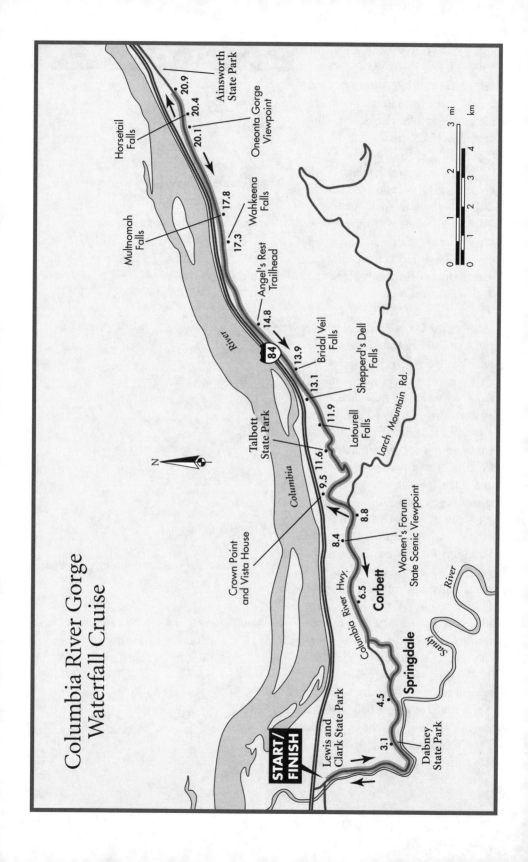

Columbia River Gorge
Waterfall Cruise

Start by turning left out of the Lewis and Clark State Park parking area onto the Historic Columbia River Highway. Water and rest rooms are available here.

0.2 At the stop sign turn left where a sign indicates HISTORIC HIGHWAY, CORBETT, DABNEY STATE PARK.

0.6 Pass Tad's Chicken'n Dumplins restaurant on your right.

3.0 Pass Dabney State Park on your right. Water and rest rooms are available here.

3.9 Enter the small community of Springdale.

4.2 Pass Mom's Garden Bakery and Café on your right.

4.5 At the Y-intersection go right where a sign indicates HISTORIC HIGHWAY, CORBETT, MULTNOMAH FALLS, and continue riding on the Columbia River Highway.

6.5 Arrive in the small town of Corbett.

7.1 Pass Corbett Country Market on your left.

8.4 Arrive at Portland Women's Forum State Scenic Viewpoint and Chanticleer Point. Be sure to stop and check out the gorgeous view of the Columbia River Gorge and Crown Point, and to read the interpretive signs that describe the geology of the Gorge.

8.8 Turn left where a sign indicates HISTORIC HIGHWAY, CORBETT, MULTNOMAH FALLS, and begin descending on a narrow, curvy, shoulderless road to Crown Point State Park and the Vista House.

9.5 Turn right, and enter the parking area to Crown Point State Park and the Vista House. Be sure to take the time to view the historic 1917 Vista House. The Vista House is open April through October and has interpretive displays, a gift shop, rest rooms, water, and a small espresso and snack stand.

11.6 Pass the turnoff to Talbot State Park on your left. Rest rooms and water are available here.

11.9 Latourell Falls. At this stop you can hike a 2.3-mile loop to view the lower and upper falls.

13.1 Shepperd's Dell State Park. Hike to the east end of the bridge to view Shepperd's Dell Falls.

(continued)

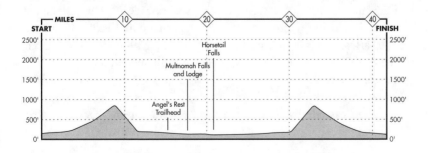

13.9 Bridal Veil State Park is your next stop on the left. At this state park you can take a short 0.6-mile round-trip hike to view Bridal Veil Falls. Picnic tables, rest rooms, and water are available here.

14.8 Angel's Rest Trailhead is on your right. You have the option here of hiking 4.4 miles out and back to a spectacular viewpoint at the top of Angel's Rest.

17.3 Arrive at Wahkeena Falls on your right.

17.8 Arrive at Multnomah Falls and Multnomah Falls Lodge. Watch for vehicle and pedestrian traffic. A restaurant, gift shop, visitor center, rest rooms, and water are located here.

20.1 Arrive at a viewpoint for Oneonta Gorge on your right.

20.4 Pass Horsetail Falls on your right. You have the option of hiking a 2.7-mile loop that takes you past Horsetail Falls, Ponytail Falls, and Oneonta Falls.

20.9 Arrive at Ainsworth State Park. Picnic tables, rest rooms, and water are available here. This is your turnaround point.

41.8 Arrive at Lewis and Clark State Park.

ern Washington, turned southwest across the Columbia Plateau, and finally escaped through the Columbia River drainage, widening the valley floor and carving the cliffs you see today. As a result of these floods, the lower courses of many of the valley's tributary streams were cut off, creating an area with spectacular waterfalls.

From Portland Women's State Park, pedal less than a mile downhill to Crown Point State Park and the historic Vista House (built in 1917). Be sure to enjoy the view and to explore the Vista House, which has interpretive displays, a gift shop, rest room, and small snack bar that serves espresso, soft drinks, and ice cream. (The Vista House is open from October through March.) From Crown Point sail downhill on a series of winding curves to Talbot State Park at 11.6 miles. This scenic picnic spot was donated to the state by Guy W. Talbot in 1929. Port Orford cedars, Douglas firs, alders, and big leaf maples provide welcoming shade if you want to break from the saddle. Latourell Falls, located in Talbot State Park, is your next stop at 11.9 miles. From the parking area you can walk a 2.3-mile loop trail to view the shooting cascade of 249-foot Lower Latourell Falls and the twisting cascade of Upper Latourell Falls. Shepperd's Dell State Park and falls is your next destination. This 519-acre park was given to the state of Oregon as by George G. Shepperd in remembrance of his wife. From the east end of the bridge, a short trail leads to a viewing area by the falls.

Next you'll arrive at Bridal Veil State Park and Bridal Veil Falls. You can view this two-tiered cascade by walking on the 0.6-mile out-and-back trail that begins behind the rest rooms. You'll travel down a rocky dirt path into the creek

Bridal Veil Falls.

canyon to a viewing area below the falls. Wild roses, lupine, and penstemons line the trail with their vivid colors. On a hot summer's day, you can cool off in the shallow pool at the base of the waterfall.

Wahkeena Falls is your next waterfall destination. This spectacular 542-foot, two-tiered cascade can be viewed from a paved trail accessed from the highway. Travel another 0.5 mile east, and stop to view the spectacular 642-foot cascade of Multnomah Falls. At this location you can also view Multnomah Falls Lodge, which was built in 1925. Inside the lodge is a restaurant, gift shop, visitors center, and public rest rooms. If you don't mind braving the crowds, you can hike a steep mile to the top of the falls on a paved trail. The clifftop viewpoint is well worth the effort spent.

At 20.1 miles you'll pass a viewpoint of Oneonta Gorge on your right. Hidden a half mile up this dramatic chasm is a 100-foot waterfall. On a hot summer's day, you can wade up the canyon to view the falls. Continue east to 176-foot Horsetail Falls. This trail swishes and swirls, mimicking the movement of a horse's tail. If you want to view two more wonderful falls, hike up the paved trail 0.2 mile, take a right, and arrive at Ponytail Falls at 0.4 mile. The trail takes you behind the falls in an open circular cave. After 1.4 miles you'll arrive at a wooden bridge that affords outstanding views of 60-foot Oneonta Falls. The turnaround point for this tour is 20.9 miles at Ainsworth State Park, which has a shady picnic area, rest rooms, and water. If you want to spend more time exploring this area, you can camp at Ainsworth State Park campground, located another 0.5 mile east.

ADDITIONAL RIDE INFORMATION

♦ Columbia River Gorge National Scenic Area, 902 Wasco Avenue, Suite 200, Hood River, OR 97031, (541) 386–2333, www.fs.fed.us/r6/columbia.
♦ Oregon State Parks and Recreation, 1115 Commercial Street NE, Suite 1, Salem, OR 97301-1002, (800) 551–6949, www.oregonstateparks.org.

LOCAL INFORMATION

♦ Corbett Country Market, 36801 East Historic Columbia River Highway, Corbett, OR 97019, (503) 695–2234.
♦ Troutdale Chamber of Commerce, 338 East Columbia River Highway, Troutdale, OR 97060, (503) 669–7473, www.troutdalechamber.org.

LOCAL EVENTS/ATTRACTIONS

♦ Harlow House Museum, 726 East Historic Columbia River Highway, Troutdale, OR 97060, (503) 661–2164.
♦ Depot Rail Museum, 473 East Historic Columbia River Highway, Troutdale, OR 97060, (503) 661–2164.

RESTAURANTS

♦ Black Rabbit Restaurant at McMenamin's Edgefield, 2126 SW Halsey Street, Troutdale, OR 97060, (503) 492–3086.
♦ Multnomah Falls Lodge Restaurant, 50000 Historic Columbia River Highway, Bridal Veil, OR 97010, (503) 695–2376, www.multnomahfallslodge.com.
♦ Tad's Chicken'n Dumplins, 1325 East Columbia River Highway, Troutdale, OR 97060, (503) 666–5337.

ACCOMMODATIONS

♦ Bridal Veil Lodge Bed and Breakfast, PO Box 87, Bridal Veil, OR 97010-0087, (503) 695–2333.
♦ Chamberlain House Bed & Breakfast, 36817 Historic Columbia River Highway, Corbett, OR 97019, (503) 695–2200.
♦ McMenamin's Edgefield, 2126 SW Halsey Street, Troutdale, OR 97060, (503) 669–8610. This 103-room European-style hotel features comfy rooms, a winery, brewery, movie theater, and restaurant. Room rates here are $85–$120, or you can opt for a hostel room for only $20 per person. Room prices include breakfast (except if you are staying in the men's or women's hostel dormitory).

BIKE SHOPS

♦ Gateway Bicycles, 11905 NE Halsey Street, Portland, OR 97220, (503) 254–0800, www.gatewaybicycles.com.
♦ Gresham Bicycle & Fitness Center, 567 NE 8th Street, Gresham, OR 97030, (503) 661–2453.

REST ROOMS

♦ Mile 0.0: Lewis and Clark State Park.
♦ Mile 3.1: Dabney State Park.
♦ Mile 9.5: Crown Point State Park and the Vista House.
♦ Mile 11.6: Talbot State Park.
♦ Mile 13.9: Bridal Veil State Park.
♦ Mile 17.8: Multnomah Falls and Lodge.
♦ Mile 20.9: Ainsworth State Park.

MAPS

♦ USGS 7.5-minute quads Washougal, Bridal Veil, and Multnomah Falls; *DeLorme Oregon Atlas and Gazetteer,* map 67.

Hood River Valley Ramble

T his loop route takes you through the orchards and farms of the scenic Hood River Valley. Majestic Mount Hood, Mount Adams, and Mount St. Helens provide a stunning backdrop as you ride uphill from Tucker Park in Hood River to the community of Parkdale. In Parkdale you can explore the Hutson Museum, have lunch at the Elliot Glacier Public House, and admire artwork at the Mount Hood Artisans Market.

Located in the Columbia River Gorge, Hood River is a fantastic place to cycle. This dynamic town has many rural roads that begin at the outer limits of town and wind through the broad expanse of the Hood River Valley. The rich volcanic soils and moist climate in the valley produce the perfect microclimate for many agricultural crops, including a variety of flowers, herbs, berries, apples, cherries, pears, and seasonal vegetables. Amazingly this valley is one of the premier pear-growing districts in the world and produces 11 percent of the nation's supply of Bartlett pears and 30 percent of the country's Anjous, Bosc, and Comice pears. In addition to agricultural crops, the valley has many farms that raise cattle, llamas, alpacas, and horses.

This loop tour starts at the outskirts of Hood River in Tucker Park. From this quiet roadside stop, you'll pedal uphill on a fairly mild grade through pine-scented forest and pear and apple orchards for 12.4 miles until you reach the Hutson Museum. It is worth taking the the time to explore this small Parkdale museum. The museum houses a special rock collection, arrows, spear points, mortars, and grinding tools, as well as historical artifacts from Parkdale's history. This location is also the ending point for the Mount Hood Railroad. The railroad originally began running in 1906 and carried lumber and agricultural crops from the Hood River Valley to Hood River. The train reopened in the early 1980s as a tourist train. You can take a four-hour scenic train ride from Hood River to Parkdale and back, as well as have dinner or brunch aboard the train. The train runs from April through December and is another fun way to enjoy the spectacular beauty of the Hood River Valley.

Continue your tour by heading south from Parkdale on Clear Creek Road. On this section of the route, you'll continue uphill past more orchards and farms. Keep a sharp eye out for fruit markets that are open during the summer months. (Note that strawberries are ripe in June, cherries in July, apricots in late July, blueberries and peaches in August, pears in mid-August through September, and apples in mid-August through October.) After 15.6 miles you'll hook up with Cooper Spur Road and begin a fast downhill with gorgeous views of the Columbia River Gorge and the glistening peaks of Mount Adams and Mount St. Helens to the north. Just shy of 19 miles, you'll arrive at the Elliot

Glacier Public House and Brew Pub in Parkdale. It is highly recommended that you stop at this superb local watering hole to try a handcrafted microbrew and to refuel on a homemade sandwich or one of the other delicious daily specials. After lunch take the time to check out the Mount Hood Artisans Market next door to the brew pub. This market features handcrafted pottery, paintings, dolls, candles, soap, and other crafts made by local artists. After exploring Parkdale you'll finish your loop by heading downhill through the communities of Mount Hood and Odell to your starting point at Tucker Park. If you are looking for some after-ride nourishment, turn left onto Tucker Road from

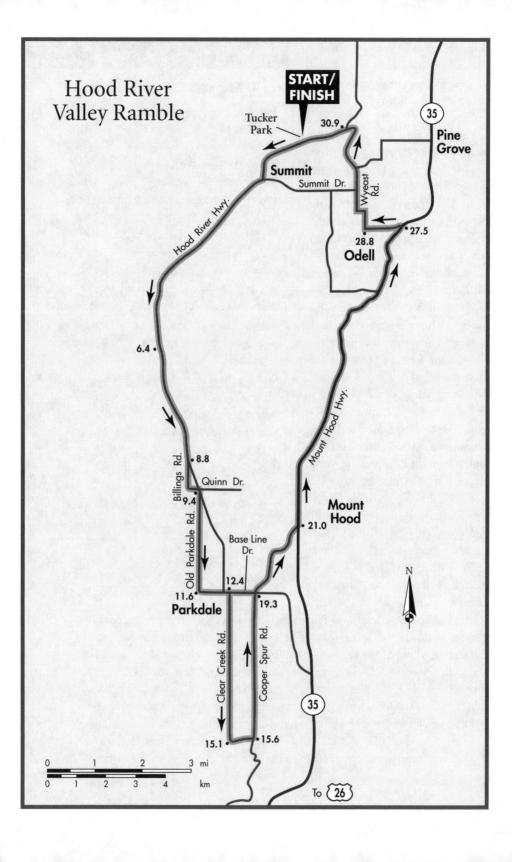

Hood River Valley Ramble

START/FINISH

Tucker Park

30.9

35

Pine Grove

Summit

Summit Dr.

Wyeast Rd.

27.5

Hood River Hwy.

28.8

Odell

6.4

Mount Hood Hwy.

Billings Rd.

8.8

Quinn Dr.

9.4

Old Parkdale Rd.

Base Line Dr.

21.0

Mount Hood

12.4

11.6

Parkdale

19.3

N

Clear Creek Rd.

Cooper Spur Rd.

35

15.1

15.6

To 26

0   1   2   3 mi

0   1   2   3   4 km

Start by turning right onto the Hood River Highway.

6.4 Arrive at a Y-intersection. Stay left where a sign indicates PARKDALE 5 MILES.

7.5 Cross the railroad tracks.

8.8 Turn right onto Alexander Drive. You'll have spectacular views looking south at Mount Hood.

8.9 At the stop sign turn left onto Billings Road. After 0.3 mile, Billings Road turns into Quinn Drive.

9.4 At the stop sign turn right (south) onto the Hood River Highway. Ride 200 yards, then turn right onto Old Parkdale Road.

11.6 Turn left onto Base Line Drive.

12.3 At the stop sign continue straight, and enter the small town of Parkdale.

12.4 Turn right onto Clear Creek Road. After you make this turn, pass the Hutson Museum on your left (rest rooms and water are available here) and the Mount Hood Railroad.

15.1 Arrive at a Y-intersection. Turn left. (Clear Creek Road turns into Evans Creek Drive.)

15.6 At stop sign and T-intersection, turn left onto Cooper Spur Road. Begin a fun downhill ride. You'll have great views of Mount Adams and Mount St. Helens to the north.

18.4 At the stop sign and four-way intersection, turn left onto Base Line Drive toward Parkdale. From here you'll head into Parkdale for lunch and some exploring.

18.9 Pass the Elliot Glacier Public House & Brew Pub on your left. You can eat lunch and try a microbrew at this friendly local restaurant. Once you are done be sure to check out local artwork at the Mount Hood Artisans Market right next door to the brew pub. From the brew pub turn right (east) onto Base Line Drive.

19.3 At a four-way intersection, turn left on Cooper Spur Road toward ODELL AND HOOD RIVER. You'll start a fun downhill after this intersection.

21.0 Enter the small town of Mount Hood. At the stop sign turn left onto Highway 35 toward ODELL AND HOOD RIVER. Begin a long gradual downhill north toward Hood River.

(continued)

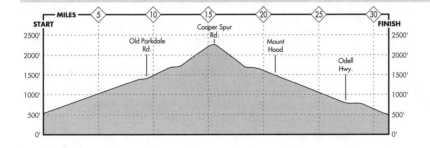

27.5 Turn left onto the Odell Highway, where a sign indicates ODELL 1 MILE/HOOD RIVER
BEND FARM & COUNTRY STORE 3½ MILES.

28.4 Odell.

28.8 Turn right onto unsigned Wyeast Road.

30.9 At the stop sign turn left onto unsigned Tucker Road.

31.3 Arrive at Tucker Park on the right.

Tucker Park and head 0.5 mile to the River Bend Farm & Country Store (located at 2363 Tucker Road). This friendly establishment serves mouth-watering slices of apple and berry pie and huckleberry milkshakes. They also offer a wide assortment of jams and jellies and other handmade gifts.

LOCAL INFORMATION

♦ Hood River Chamber of Commerce, 405 Portway Avenue, Hood River, OR 97031, (800) 366–3530, www.hoodriver.org.

LOCAL EVENTS/ATTRACTIONS

♦ Gorge Games, mid-July, 550 Riverside Drive, Suite 3, Hood River, OR 97031, (541) 386–7774, www.gorgegames.com.

♦ Hood River Blossom Festival, held the third week in April, 405 Portway Avenue, Hood River, OR 97031, (541) 354–2865.

♦ Hood River Harvest Festival, held the third week in October at the Hood River Expo on the Waterfront, 405 Portway Avenue, Hood River, OR 97031, (800) 366–3530.

♦ Hood River Vineyards, 4693 Westwood Drive, Hood River, OR 97031, (541) 386–3772.

♦ Hutson Museum, PO Box 501, Parkdale, OR 97041, (541) 352–6808. $1.00 admission fee.

♦ Mount Hood Artisans Market, 4933 Base Line Drive, Parkdale, OR 97041, (541) 352–3582.

♦ Mount Hood Scenic Railroad, 110 Railroad Avenue, Hood River, OR 97031, (800) 872–4661, www.mthoodrr.com.

♦ River Bend Farm & Country Store, 2363 Tucker Road, Hood River, OR 97031, (541) 386–8766, www.riverbendstore.com. This store features home-made apple and berry pies, huckleberry milkshakes, flowers and gifts, and jams and jellies.

♦ Wine and Arts Festival, held the third week in May, Sixth Street Bistro, Sixth and Cascade Street, Hood River, OR 97031,(541) 386–5737.

RESTAURANTS

♦ Elliot Glacier Public House & Brew Pub, 4945 Base Line Drive, Parkdale, OR 97041, (541) 352–1022.
♦ Full Sail Tasting Room & Pub, 506 Columbia Street, Hood River, OR 97031, (541) 386–2247, www.fullsailbrewing.com.
♦ Hood River Bagel Company, 13 Oak Street, Hood River, OR 97031, (541) 386–2123.
♦ Mike's Ice Cream, 504 Oak Street, Hood River, OR 97031, (541) 386–6260.

ACCOMMODATIONS

♦ Columbia Gorge Hotel, 4000 Westcliff Drive, Hood River, OR 97031, (800) 345–1921, www.columbiagorgehotel.com.
♦ Old Parkdale Inn, 4932 Base Line Drive, Parkdale, OR 97041, (541) 352–5551, www.hoodriverlodging.com. Enjoy a cozy room at this inn located in quaint downtown Parkdale. Room rates are $125–$145 per night and include a homemade breakfast.
♦ Panorama Lodge Bed and Breakfast, 2290 Old Dalles Drive, Hood River, OR 97031, (888) 403–2687, www.panoramalodge.com. Rates for this fun bed-and-breakfast are $65–$90 per night.

Mount Hood is a well-known Hood River Valley landmark.

BIKE SHOPS

♦ Discover Bicycles, 205 Oak Street, Hood River, OR 97031, (541) 386–4820, www.discoverbicycles.com.
♦ Mountain View Cycle & Fitness, 411 Oak Street, Hood River, OR 97031, (541) 386–2453.

REST ROOMS

♦ Mile 0.0: Tucker Park.
♦ Mile 12.4: Hutson Museum.
♦ Mile 18.8: Elliot Glacier Public House & Brew Pub.

MAPS

♦ USGS 7.5-minute quads Parkdale, Dog River, and Hood River; *DeLorme Oregon Atlas and Gazetteer,* maps 62 and 68.

Columbia River Highway East Cruise

T his ride takes you on a scenic journey on the Historic Columbia River Highway through the magnificent Columbia River Gorge. It begins in historic Hood River and heads east toward Gorge Discovery Center in The Dalles. The first 4.6 miles are open to bikers and pedestrians only and offer many viewpoints of the cliff-lined gorge, Mount St. Helens, and Mount Adams, as well as the opportunity to explore the restored Mosier Twin Tunnels. As you continue east, you'll pass through the small town of Mosier. The route then travels uphill through cherry orchards to the Memaloose Overlook and Rowena Crest Viewpoint. From the Rowena Crest Viewpoint, you'll have a sweeping descent down hairpin curves to a straightaway that takes you past Mayer State Park and through the small community of Rowena to your turnaround point at Columbia Gorge Discovery Center and Wasco County Historical Museum in The Dalles. Be sure to start this route early in the day so you can have time to explore the informative displays at this one-of-a-kind interpretive center.

On this classic route you'll explore the east end of the Columbia River Gorge, which is well known for its wide open plateaus, wildflower meadows, agricultural valleys, cloud-capped cliffs, and endless opportunities for outdoor fun. This ride takes you on a tour of a restored section of the Historic Columbia River Highway, which was originally completed in 1922 and ran east from Portland and ended in The Dalles. This first major paved roadway in Oregon

THE BASICS

Start: The Hood River West Trailhead, located 54 miles east of Portland off I-84 in the Columbia River Gorge.

Length: 37.8 miles out and back.

Season: Year-round. The roads on this route can be icy during the winter months.

Approximate riding time: Three to five hours.

Recommended start time: 9:00 A.M.

Terrain: A 9.2-mile section of this route is on a nonmotorized bicycle and pedestrian path. The remaining 28.6 miles of the route you'll share with motorists, and there are many twists, turns, steep ascents and descents, and no shoulder.

Traffic and hazards: The first 4.6 miles (and last 4.6 miles) of this route you'll share only with pedestrians. You'll ride on a wide, smooth paved path. The remaining part of the route continues east on the Historic Columbia River Highway, and you'll have to share the roadway with motorists. Note that the Historic Columbia River Highway is a very narrow, twisty road, and you'll have to be constantly on the lookout for cars. Be especially cautious when you are riding downhill from the Rowena Crest Viewpoint on the hairpin curves that have many blind corners.

Getting there: From the intersection of I-205 and I-84 in Portland, drive 54 miles east on I-84 toward Hood River and The Dalles. Turn off the highway at exit 64, where a sign indicates HOOD RIVER HIGHWAY 35/ WHITE SALMON/GOVERNMENT CAMP. At the end of the off-ramp, turn right (south) toward Hood River. Drive 0.3 mile to a stop sign and a four-way intersection. Turn left (east) onto the Historic Columbia River Highway. You'll also see a sign indicating HISTORIC STATE PARK TRAIL. Drive 1.3 miles on the Historic Columbia River Highway until you reach a parking area and visitor center and the trailhead located on the left side of the road. There is a $3.00 day-use permit that is required to park at the visitors center. You can obtain the permit from the self-pay station in the parking lot or inside the visitors center. The visitors center also sells a $25 annual pass that is good for all Oregon state parks.

was the accomplishment of lawyer and visionary Samuel C. Hill and the talented engineer Samuel Lancaster. This duo and a dedicated team of skilled tradesmen defied the odds of nature and built a highway that complemented the landscape and offered motorists a unique look at the magnificent Columbia River Gorge. Samuel Hill once said about the highway, "We will cash in, year

Historic wagon at the Living History Park at the Gorge Discovery Center.

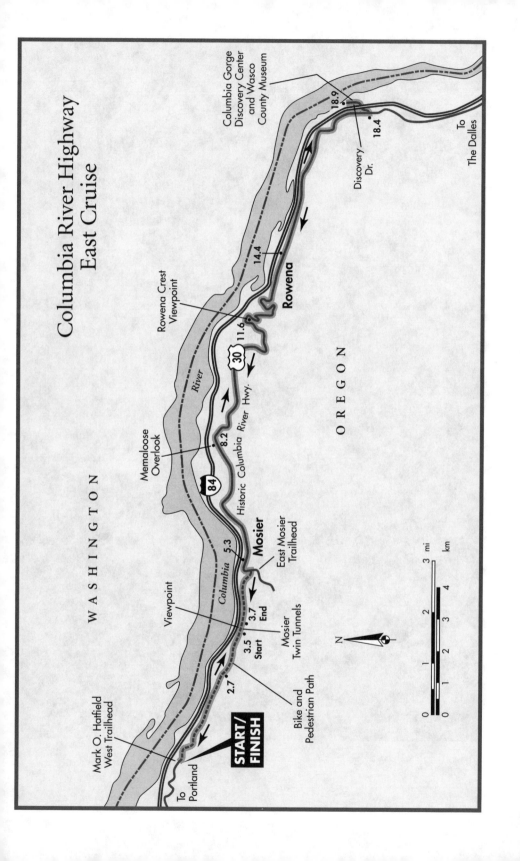

Columbia River Highway
East Cruise

WASHINGTON

OREGON

Columbia River

Mark O. Hatfield
West Trailhead

To
Portland

START/
FINISH

2.7

Viewpoint

3.5
Start

3.7
End

Bike and
Pedestrian Path

Mosier
Twin Tunnels

Mosier

East Mosier
Trailhead

5.3

Historic Columbia River Hwy.

Memaloose
Overlook

8.2

84

30

11.6

Rowena Crest
Viewpoint

14.4

Rowena

Columbia Gorge
Discovery Center
and Wasco
County Museum

18.9

18.4

Discovery
Dr.

To
The Dalles

N

0   1   2   3 mi

0   1   2   3   4 km

Start by riding east on the paved trail adjacent to the visitors center where a sign indicates MARK. O. HATFIELD WEST TRAILHEAD. The visitors center has rest rooms, water, and a phone.

2.7 Pass a viewpoint on your left.

3.5 Enter the Mosier Twin Tunnels.

3.7 Exit the Mosier Twin Tunnels.

4.4 At the T-intersection and stop sign, turn left onto Rock Creek Road. You have the option here of turning right and riding 0.2 mile uphill to the East Mosier trailhead, which has water, rest rooms, and a phone.

5.3 You'll arrive at a T-intersection. Turn left (east) onto the Historic Columbia River Highway, and continue pedaling through the small town of Mosier. As you ride through Mosier, be on the lookout for the Route 30 Ice Cream Store (on the right side of the highway in the center of town), where you can eat delicious ice cream and view vintage Porsche cars.

6.6 Ride through a long section filled with cherry orchards. The cherries are ripe in July, and there are many U-PICK stops along this route.

8.2 Pass the Memaloose Overlook on your left.

11.6 Arrive at the Rowena Crest Viewpoint on your right, where you can soak in fantastic views of the gorge. You'll also pass by Governor Tom McCall Preserve (on the left), which offers many hiking opportunities.

14.2 Pass the turnoff to Mayer State Park on your left. There are rest rooms at this state park.

14.4 Ride through the small town of Rowena.

18.4 Turn left onto Discovery Drive at the COLUMBIA GORGE DISCOVERY CENTER/WASCO COUNTY HISTORICAL MUSEUM sign.

18.9 Arrive at the Columbia Gorge Discovery Center and the Wasco County Historical Museum. Be sure to check out the displays and interpretive trails before you turn around and head back to your vehicle on the same route.

37.8 Arrive back at the Hood River Trailhead and your vehicle.

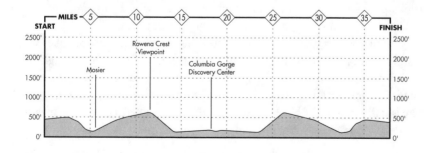

after year, on our crop of scenic beauty, without depleting it in any way."

When I–84 was built in the 1950s, many sections of the historic highway were abandoned. However, when the original Columbia River Highway highway was recognized as a National Historic Landmark in May 2000, there was a resurgence of interest in restoring unused sections of the highway for everyone to enjoy. In July 2000, a 4.6-mile section of the highway was opened as a hiker/biker-only trail between Hood River and Mosier. This impressive $5.6 million restoration project included paving the original highway route, building landslide protective retaining walls, and reopening the Mosier Twin Tunnels, which were filled with rock in the mid-1950s. These impressive tunnels were originally designed by Conde B. McCullough, a famous Oregon bridge engineer, and you'll have the opportunity to ride through them and gaze at the cliff-lined gorge through arched viewing portals. These tunnels act as a gateway between two different ecosystems—the wetter, western side of the gorge and the dryer, eastern side of the Columbia River Plateau.

After the hiker/biker trail ends at the Mosier Trailhead, you'll cruise down Rock Creek Road into downtown Mosier. From this point forward you'll be sharing the road with motorists. As you continue east you'll start ascending and riding through hillsides covered with cherry orchards, whose cherries ripen in July. Watch for U-PICK signs.

After cruising on this scenic stretch of road for just more than 8 miles, you'll arrive at the Memaloose Overlook, where you can view Memaloose Island—the location of a traditional Native American burial site. As you continue riding east, you'll continue climbing to a spectacular roadside viewpoint at Rowena Crest. From this cliff-top vantage point, you'll see the wheat-covered hills of the Columbia Basin Plateau to the east, catch views of Mount St. Helens and Mount Adams to the north, and be able to soak in more wondrous views of the Columbia River Gorge. The Rowena Crest Viewpoint sits on the Rowena Plateau, which is literally bursting with a profusion of wildflowers during the spring months (peak blooming season is April and May). If you want to take a break from riding, be sure to hike through the Tom McCall Preserve, which has some of the highest concentrations of wildflowers in this area. Varieties you may spot are the bright yellow balsamroot, the bluish-purple blooms of broadleaf lupine, white yarrow, wild parsley, penstemons, and wild lilies. If you decide to hike here, be sure to keep your eye out for poison oak! You can access a hiking trail to these bountiful wildflower meadowlands just opposite the entrance road to the Rowena Crest Viewpoint parking area.

Continuing east, the highway corkscrews down the cliff face and takes you past Mayer State Park (which has rest room facilities) and then through the small town of Rowena. The change in landscape is quite dramatic from the wetter, heavier vegetation in the western part of the gorge. Nature's architecture here is characterized by black basalt cliffs, dramatic bluffs and grassy plateaus, and deeply carved canyons. Just short of 19 miles, you'll arrive at your turnaround point at the Columbia Gorge Discovery Center and Wasco County Historical Museum. Be sure to take the time to explore this interpretive center and museum, which describes the geological formation of the gorge and the fascinating history of the people who lived here. This complex also has a living history park where you can see reenactments of life on the Oregon Trail, the experiences of Lewis and Clark, and much more.

LOCAL INFORMATION

♦ Oregon State Parks and Recreation, 1115 Commercial Street NE, Suite 1, Salem, OR 97301-1002, (800) 551–6949, www.oregonstateparks.org.

LOCAL EVENTS/ATTRACTIONS

♦ Columbia Gorge Discovery Center and the Wasco County Historical Museum, 5000 Discovery Drive, The Dalles, OR 97058, (541) 296–8600, www. gorgediscovery.org. Summer hours are 10:00 A.M. to 6:00 P.M. April through October, and 10:00 A.M. to 4:00 P.M. the rest of the year. General admission is $6.50 for adults, $5.50 for seniors (sixty-two and older), $3.50 for children ages six to sixteen, and free for children younger than age five.
♦ Hood River Blossom Festival, held the third week in April, 405 Portway Avenue, Hood River, OR 97031, (541) 354–2865.
♦ Gorge Games, mid-July, 550 Riverside Drive, Suite 3, Hood River, OR 97031, (541) 386–7774, www.gorgegames.com.
♦ Mount Hood Scenic Railroad, 110 Railroad Avenue, Hood River, OR 97031, (800) 872–4661, www.mthoodrr.com.
♦ Wine and Arts Festival, held the third week in May, Sixth Street Bistro, Sixth and Cascade Street, Hood River, OR 97031, (541) 386–5737.

RESTAURANTS

♦ Full Sail Tasting Room & Pub, 506 Columbia Street, Hood River, OR 97031, (541) 386–2247, www.fullsailbrewing.com.
♦ Hood River Bagel Company, 13 Oak Street, Hood River, OR 97031, (541) 386–2123.
♦ Mike's Ice Cream, 504 Oak Street, Hood River, OR 97031, (541) 386–6260.

ACCOMMODATIONS

♦ Columbia Gorge Hotel, 4000 Westcliff Drive, Hood River, OR 97031, (800) 345–1921, www.columbiagorgehotel.com.
♦ Mosier House B&B, 704 3rd Avenue, Mosier, OR 97040, (541) 478–3640, www.mosierhouse.com.
♦ Memaloose State Park, located 11 miles west of The Dalles (I–84 westbound exit only), Oregon State Parks, 1115 Commercial Street NE, Suite 1, Salem, OR

97301-1002, (800) 551–6949, www.oregonstateparks.org/park_163.php. This
state park campground has tent sites and RV sites.

BIKE SHOPS

♦ Discover Bicycles, 205 Oak Street, Hood River, OR 97031, (541) 386–4820,
www.discoverbicycles.com.
♦ Mountain View Cycle & Fitness, 411 Oak Street, Hood River, OR 97031,
(541) 386–2453.

REST ROOMS

♦ Mile 0.0: Hood River Trailhead.
♦ Mile 4.6: Mosier Trailhead.
♦ Mile 14.2: Mayer State Park.
♦ Mile 18.9: Gorge Discovery Center.

MAPS

♦ USGS 7.5-minute quads White Salmon, Lyle, and The Dalles; *DeLorme
Oregon Atlas and Gazetteer,* map pages 68 and 69.

Champoeg State Park Ramble

Τhis tour begins in Champoeg State Park and travels on rural roads through the farming country of French Prairie. Highlights of this tour include fascinating history and geology exhibits at the Champoeg State Park Visitors Center, the Robert Newell House Museum, a stop along the scenic Willamette River, and a tour through the historic community of St. Paul.

Established in 1901, Champoeg State Park is your starting point for this leisurely ride through the scenic Willamette Valley farming country known as French Prairie. Located on the banks of the Willamette River, this state park features white oak woodlands and open grassy meadows, a large campground, hiking and biking trails, historic buildings, and a large visitors center.

Native peoples lived here 6,000 years before white settlers arrived. They burned the area in order to maintain the open white oak savannah, which allowed the growth of native plants and made it easier to hunt game. One of the largest tribes of Native Americans to live in the valley was the Calapooya. They hunted small game, fished in the Willamette River, and harvested camas roots. This onionlike plant grows in open sunny meadows and has a 2-foot long stem that has ten to thirty bluish-purple blooms. When prepared, the bulbs of this native plant taste like sweet potatoes.

In 1811 hunters and fur traders of the Hudson's Bay Company arrived on the scene. With their arrival a warehouse, mill, and town were built, and Champoeg became an important site for trading beaver pelts and wheat. The word *Champoeg* is thought to be derived from the French word *champ* ("field") and the Native American word *pooich* ("root"). While the white settlers prospered, the Native American population was dessimated by the diseases that were introduced. Before the white settlers' arrival, the Native American popu-

Start: Champoeg State Park Visitors Center parking lot, located approximately 30 miles southwest of Portland and northwest of Salem off I-5.

Length: 24.5-mile loop.

Season: Year-round.

Approximate riding time: One and one-half to two and one-half hours.

Recommended start time: 11:00 A.M.

Terrain: This route follows rural country roads that lead you through the farming area of French Prairie and the small community of St. Paul.

Traffic and hazards: Highway 219 has a wide shoulder and moderate traffic. Use caution when riding on and crossing this highway. The rest of the route travels on rural roads with no shoulder and light traffic.

Getting there: This route starts in Champoeg State Park, which is about a 30-mile drive southwest of Portland and northwest of Salem. From I-5, take exit 278 for DONALD/AURORA/ CHAMPOEG STATE PARK. Turn west, and drive 3.5 miles on Ehlen Road/Yergen Road. Turn right onto Case Road. Continue for 1.3 miles on Case Road, and turn left onto Champoeg Road. Proceed 0.8 mile on Champoeg Road to the entrance to Champoeg State Park. Turn right onto the park entrance road, and take the first right into the visitors center parking lot. There is a $3.00 day-use permit that is required to park here. You can obtain the permit inside the visitors center.

lation was more than 13,000; by the mid-1800s their numbers plummeted to around 2,000.

In May 1843 a provisional government was established—this was the first American government on the Pacific Coast—and the Champoeg settlement continued to grow. Although this new government moved to Oregon City in 1844, by 1850 Champoeg's population had swelled to more than 200, and the settlement contained more than thirty buildings. In 1861 the mood of the Willamette River turned foul, and a disastrous flood almost destroyed the entire community. By 1892 another record-breaking flood turned the area into a ghost town.

The route begins right in the heart of this historical landscape at Champoeg State Park. Before you start your ride, be sure to check out the exhibits in the visitors center, which feature Native American history, stories of the Oregon Trail, geology of the Willamette Valley, and information on flora and fauna. You'll start by pedaling northwest on quiet country roads. At 0.1 mile you can explore the Robert Newell House Museum. The museum's namesake was born in 1807 in Butler County, Ohio. His many titles included saddlemaker, civic leader, mountain man, and entrepreneur. He brought the first wagon train over the Blue Mountains into the Willamette Valley and settled in Champoeg in 1843. He built a house at this location and lived here for more than nineteen years. The museum is a 1959 reconstruction of the original house and features six rooms decorated in 1860s style, West Coast Native American baskets, nineteenth-century quilts and coverlets, and inaugural gowns worn by the wives of Oregon governors.

A unique historic home.

Continue on the tour as it travels over small rolling hills past open grassy meadows; fields of hops, sugar beets, and grass seed; and a large dairy farm. At 11.7 miles hop off your bike to check out the Willamette River views at a small boat landing at the end of Horseshoe Lake Road. From here the route travels south through a rural landscape dotted with majestic white oak trees and century-old farms.

St. Paul is your next stop at 15.2 miles. This historic community was named after the Apostle Paul by Archbishop Francis Norbert Blanchet, who started the St. Paul Mission in 1839. The St. Paul Catholic Church is one of many historical buildings in this small town. It was built in 1846 and is made of 300,000 bricks that were fired on the building site. The church features a dramatic spire, stained glass windows, and 2-foot-thick walls. From St. Paul the route swings north and takes you through more pastoral landscape to your ending point at the visitors center and your vehicle at 24.5 miles.

LOCAL INFORMATION

♦ Champoeg State Heritage Area, 7679 Champoeg Road NE, St. Paul, OR 97137, (503) 678–1251.

♦ Oregon State Parks and Recreation, 1115 Commercial Street NE, Suite 1, Salem, OR 97301-1002, (800) 551–6949, www.oregonstateparks.org/park_113.php.

♦ Portland Wheelmen Touring Club, P.O. Box 2972, Portland, OR 97208-2972, 503-257-PWTC, www.pwtc.com.

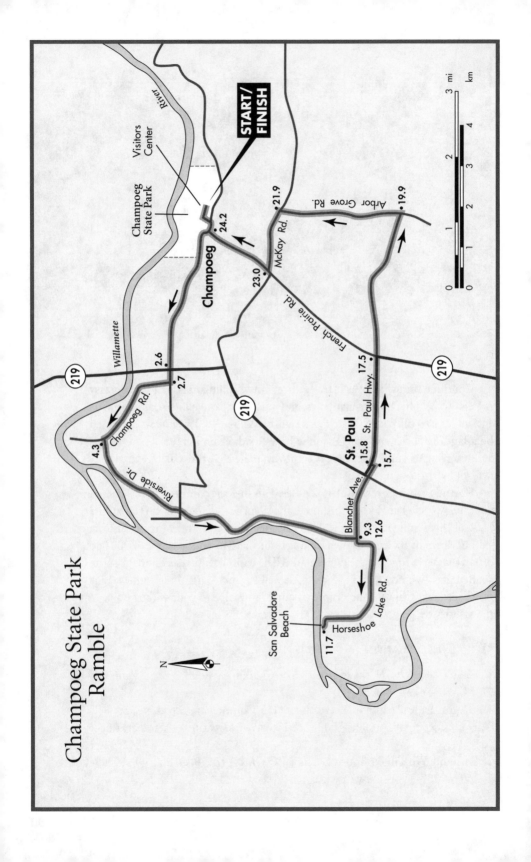

Start by turning left out of the visitors center parking area on the park's entrance road. The visitors center has a phone, rest room, water, gift shop, and interpretive displays.

0.1 Turn right onto Champoeg Road. You'll pass the Robert Newell House Museum on your right. This museum has displays that explore the pioneering history of the area.

0.2 At the T-intersection and stop sign, turn right onto French Prairie Road.

2.6 At the stop sign cross Highway 219, and continue riding on French Prairie Road.

2.7 At the Y-intersection turn right onto Champoeg Road.

4.3 Turn left onto Riverside Drive.

9.3 At the T-intersection turn right onto Horseshoe Lake Road.

11.7 Arrive at the end of Horseshoe Lake Road at a boat ramp to the Willamette River and San Salvadore Beach. This is a good spot to check out the river and take a break from pedaling. Turn around and retrace your route on Horseshoe Lake Road.

12.6 Arrive at a road intersection. Continue straight on Blanchet Avenue.

15.2 Enter the small town of St. Paul.

15.6 Cross Main Street in downtown St. Paul, and continue riding on Blanchet Avenue.

15.7 Turn left onto 4th Street.

15.8 Turn right onto the St. Paul Highway 219.

17.5 At a road intersection turn left and continue straight. You'll cross French Prairie Road at this intersection.

19.9 Turn left onto Arbor Grove Road.

21.9 At the T-intersection and stop sign, turn left onto McKay Road.

23.0 Turn right onto French Prairie Road.

24.2 Turn right onto Champoeg Road.

24.4 Turn left onto the entrance road to Champoeg State Park.

24.5 Turn right into the visitors center parking lot.

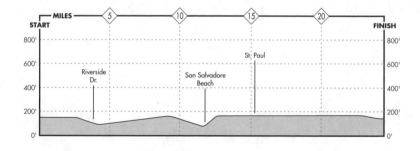

LOCAL EVENTS/ATTRACTIONS

♦ American Revolution Mothers Memorial Cabin, 8035 Champoeg Road NE, St. Paul, OR 97137, (503) 633–2237.

♦ Champoeg Wine Cellars, 10375 Champoeg Road NE, Aurora, OR, 97002, (503) 678–2144, www.champoegwine.com. This winery is open 11:00 A.M. to 6:00 P.M. May through October and noon to 5:00 P.M. on weekends November through April.

♦ Robert Newell House, Champoeg State Park, 8089 Champoeg Road NE, St. Paul, OR 97137, (503) 678–5537. Hours are 1:00 to 5:00 P.M. Friday, Saturday, and Sunday from March 1 through November 1. Admission is $1.00 for children ages four to eleven and $2.00 for adults.

♦ St. Paul Rodeo, St. Paul Rodeo Association, PO Box 175, St. Paul, OR 97137, (800) 237–5920. This famous rodeo is held June 30 through July 4 and has a variety of events, including concerts, a carnival, specialty acts, rodeo clowns, food vendors, a parade, dancing, and spectacular fireworks.

RESTAURANTS

♦ Margaret's Place, 4113 Church Street NE, St. Paul, OR 97137, (503) 633–4100.

ACCOMMODATIONS

♦ Best Western Willamette Inn, 30800 SW Parkway, Wilsonville, OR 97070, (888) 682–0101.

♦ Champoeg State Park Campground, Oregon State Parks and Recreation, 1115 Commercial Street NE, Suite 1, Salem, OR 97301-1002, (800) 551–6949, www.oregonstateparks.org/park_113.php. This state park has tent sites, RV sites, and yurts you can reserve. Call ahead for current rates.

BIKE SHOPS

♦ Bike N Hike Centers, 887 Commercial Street SE, Salem, OR 97302, (503) 581–2707.

♦ Bike Peddler, 174 Commercial Street NE, Salem, OR 97301, (503) 399–7741.

♦ R.E.I., 7410 SW Bridgeport Road (exit 290 off I–5), Tigard, OR 97224, (503) 624–8600, www.rei.com.

♦ Santiam Bicycle Way of Life, 388 Commercial Street NE, Salem, OR 97301, (503) 363–6602.

♦ Scotts Cycle, 147 Commercial Street SE, Salem, OR 97301, (503) 363–4516.

REST ROOMS

♦ Mile 0.0: Champoeg State Park Visitors Center.

MAPS

♦ USGS 7.5-minute quads Newberg, St. Paul, and The Dalles; *DeLorme Oregon Atlas and Gazetteer,* maps 59 and 60.

12

Yamhill County Winery Ramble

T his loop route takes you through the scenic oak-forested foothills of Yamhill County and past three unique wineries.

The tour begins in downtown Yamhill. This small community was established in 1901 and is thought to be named after the Yamhelas Indian tribe. The town of Yamhill resides in Yamhill County, which was established in July 1843 and covers about 714 square miles. At that time the county was much larger. Its boundaries were the Willamette River to the east and the Pacific Coast to the west. Its northern boundary was the Columbia River, and its southern boundary was the California border.

You'll begin this tour by traveling west from Yamhill on Highway 240, which takes you through one of Oregon's finest wine-growing regions. The northern latitude, long summer days, cool autumn, and marine air from the Coast Mountains provide a perfect environment for growing

Taking a break from the saddle.

Start: Yamhill-Carlton High School in downtown Yamhill.

Length: 25.9-mile loop.

Season: Year-round.

Approximate riding time: Two to three hours.

Recommended start time: 11:30 A.M.

Terrain: Major highways combined with rural roads.

Traffic and hazards: Be cautious of the moderate car traffic when riding on Highway 47 and Highway 240.

Getting there: From Portland drive 21 miles west on U.S. Highway 26 to a Y-intersection with Highway 6. Turn left onto Highway 6 (toward Banks, Forest Grove, and Tillamook) and drive 2.5 miles to the intersection with Highway 47. Turn south onto Highway 47, and drive 22.3 miles to Yamhill-Carlton High School on the left side of the road in downtown Yamhill.

wine grapes. Oregon is host to more than 170 wineries; 40 of them are located in Yamhill County. Varietal wine grapes that thrive in this unique growing environment include pinot noir, pinot gris, chardonnay, Riesling, cabernet sauvignon, merlot, gewurztraminer, zinfandel, and sauvignon blanc. It is thought that the first wine grapes planted in Oregon were by the Jesuits in St. Paul; vines were also brought to Oregon by early settlers to the area. You'll have your first opportunity to taste some of Oregon's unique wines at the WillaKenzie Winery, just shy of the 2-mile mark. This winery covers 420 acres in the scenic Chalem Hills and features a bistro-style tasting room. Featured wines include pinot noir, pinot meunier, pinot blanc, pinot gris, chardonnay, and gamay noir.

After 5.6 miles you'll turn south onto Kuehne Road and pedal through a wide valley in a pastoral setting of open hay fields, century-old farms, and rural residences. After about 6 miles you'll arrive at Laurel Ridge Winery. This winery specializes in sparkling and dessert wines, and other well-known wines found in Oregon. After another mile you'll arrive in historic Lafayette, which was incorporated in 1878. Lafayette was the first county seat and was originally called Yamhill Falls. The town was located on the overland trail, and many immigrants settled here in the early 1840s. Over the next twenty years, most of the land in the county was taken by settlers, and as you ride through this rolling hill country, you'll see some of the original homesteads. While you are in Layfayette, you have the option of exploring the Yamhill County Historical Museum, located at 605 North Market Street. This museum features pioneer art, implements, and antique farming equipment.

From Lafayette the route heads north on Mineral Springs Road. Chateau Benoit Winery is your next stop. Perched high on a hill overlooking a wide valley, this winery features a French country-style tasting room. A vast patio filled with picnic tables is a great place to taste Chateau Benoit's award-winning wines and enjoy the panoramic view of the surrounding Yamhill County countryside. Chateau Benoit specializes in producing chardonnay, sauvignon blanc, pinot gris, white Riesling, gewürztraminer, pinot noir, and delicious dessert wines. The tour ends in Yamhill, and if you have an appetite, be sure to stop at the Yamhill Café downtown.

LOCAL INFORMATION

♦ Forest Grove Chamber of Commerce, 2417 Pacific Avenue, Forest Grove, OR 97116, (503) 357–3006, www.fgchamber.com.
♦ Portland Wheelmen Touring Club, P.O. Box 2972, Portland, OR 97208-2972, 503-257-PWTC, www.pwtc.com.
♦ Yamhill County Wineries Association, PO Box 25162, Portland, OR 97298, (503) 646–2985, www.yamhillwine.com.

LOCAL EVENTS/ATTRACTIONS

♦ Chateau Benoit, 6580 NE Mineral Springs Road, Carlton, OR 97111, (503) 864–2991 or (800) 248–4835, www.chateaubenoit.com. This winery features chardonnay, pinot gris, pinot noir, white Riesling, and dessert wines. It is open 10:00 A.M. to 5:00 P.M. daily.
♦ Laurel Ridge Winery, PO Box 456, Yamhill, OR 97116, (503) 359–5436. This winery produces a variety of white and red wines as well as dessert wines. The winery is open noon to 5:00 P.M. daily February through December.
♦ WillaKenzie Estate Winery, 19143 NE Laughlin Road, Yamhill, OR 97148, (503) 662–3280 or (888) 953–9463, www.willakenzie.com. The winery is open noon to 5:00 P.M. Memorial Day through Labor Day.
♦ Yamhill County Historical Museum, 605 North Market Street, Lafayette, OR 97127, (503) 472–6070. Admission is free. The museum is open 1:00 to 4:00 P.M. weekends (September through May), and 1:00 to 4:00 P.M. Friday and Sunday, and 10:00 A.M. to 4:00 P.M. on Saturday (June through August).

RESTAURANTS

♦ Yamhill Café, 240 South Maple, Yamhill, OR 97148, (503) 662–3504.
♦ The Yardhouse Pub at the Grand Lodge, 3505 Pacific Avenue, Forest Grove, OR 97116, (503) 992–3442. Serves delicious McMenamin's handcrafted micro-brews and wines and hearty food; features live music and outdoor seating during the summer months.

ACCOMMODATIONS

♦ Flying M Ranch, 23029 Northwest Flying M Road, Yamhill, OR 97148, (503) 662–3222, www.flying-m-ranch.com. This resort features cabin rentals and also offers regular rooms.

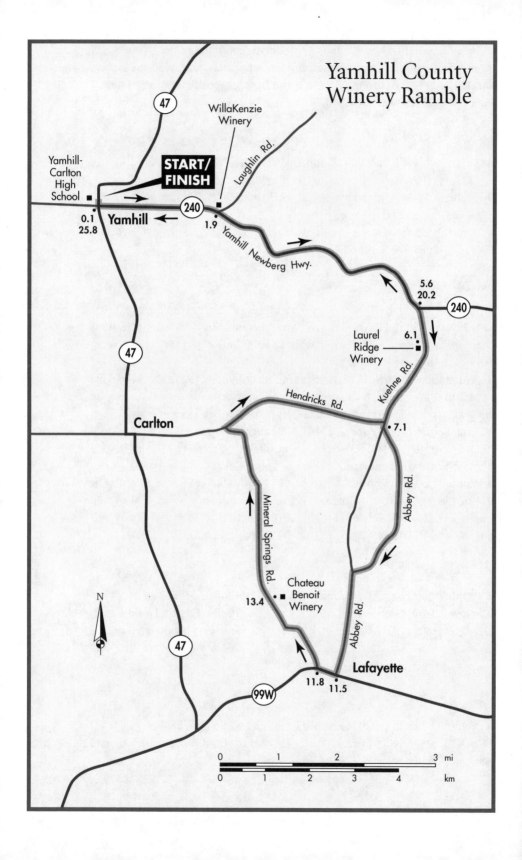

Yamhill County Winery Ramble

START/FINISH

WillaKenzie Winery

Laughlin Rd.

47

Yamhill-Carlton High School

Yamhill

0.1
25.8

240

1.9

Yamhill Newberg Hwy.

5.6
20.2

240

Laurel Ridge Winery

6.1

Kuehne Rd.

47

Hendricks Rd.

Carlton

7.1

Abbey Rd.

Mineral Springs Rd.

Chateau Benoit Winery

13.4

N

Abbey Rd.

Lafayette

11.8

11.5

99W

| 0 | 1 | 2 | 3 mi |

| 0 | 1 | 2 | 3 | 4 km |

MILES AND DIRECTIONS

Start by turning left from the Yamhill-Carlton High School parking lot onto Highway 47.

0.1 Turn left onto East Main Street (Highway 240) toward Chahalem Valley/Newberg.

1.9 Pass the turnoff to WillaKenzie Winery on the left.

5.6 Turn right (south) onto Kuehne Road.

6.1 Pass the turnoff to Laurel Ridge Winery on the right.

7.1 Turn left onto Abbey Road toward Lafayette.

11.2 Enter the town of Lafayette. You can explore the Yamhill County Historical Museum at 605 North Market Street.

11.5 Turn right onto 3rd Street (Highway 99W).

11.8 Turn right onto Mineral Springs Road.

13.4 Pass the turnoff to Chateau Benoit Winery on your right.

15.9 Turn right onto Hendricks Road.

18.3 Hendricks Road turns into Kuehne Road.

20.2 Turn left onto Highway 240 toward Yamhill.

25.8 Turn right onto Highway 47.

25.9 Arrive back at the Yamhill-Carlton High School parking area on your right.

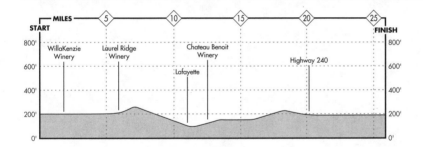

♦ Kelty Estate B&B, 675 Third Street, Lafayette, OR 97127, (800) 867–3740, www.moriah.com/kelty/. Historic house located in downtown Lafayette. Rates are $90–$95 per night, which includes a homemade breakfast.

♦ McMenamin's Grand Lodge, 3505 Pacific Avenue, Forest Grove, OR 97116, (503) 992–9533 or www.mcmenamins.com/grandlodge/index.html. Rates at this historic lodge are $40–$200 per night, depending on the season and time of the week. This lodge has a theater, restaurant and pub, soaking pool, day spa, specialty bars, and live music.

BIKE SHOPS

Forest Grove

♦ Boomer Bikes, 2019 Pacific Avenue, Forest Grove, OR 97116, (503) 359–1280.

♦ Schlegel's Cycling and Fitness Centers, 1913 19th, Forest Grove, OR 97116, (503) 357–9807

McMinnville

♦ Tommy's Bicycle Shop, 624 NE 3rd Street, McMinnville, OR 97128, (503) 472–2010, www.tommysbicycle.com.

REST ROOMS

♦ There are no rest rooms available on this route except at the winery tasting rooms.

MAPS

♦ USGS 7.5-minute quads Carlton and Dundee; *DeLorme Oregon Atlas and Gazetteer,* map 59.

Mount Angel–Silver Falls
State Park Cruise

This tour takes you through the scenic rolling farmland of Marion County. Highlights include the opportunities to explore the Bavarian-style town of Mount Angel and the Mount Angel Abbey, explore the shops in historic Silverton, view magnificent waterfalls, and tour the historic South Falls Lodge at Silver Falls State Park.

This loop tour begins in the small town of Mount Angel, which features Bavarian-style storefronts and is most well known for its annual Oktoberfest, held in mid-September to celebrate the great taste of German-style sausage, sauerkraut, and handcrafted beer. From Engelberg Centennial Park in downtown Mount Angel, you'll pedal east for about a mile and a half to the top of a 300-foot butte and the Mount Angel Abbey. This Benedictine monastery was founded in 1882 and is a rambling campus of red-brick buildings that house a church, retreat house, magnificent library, and museum. Park your bike at the top and take the time to explore this scenic setting. Rest rooms and water are available next to the museum. After you are finished exploring the abbey, sail downhill and continue pedaling east. Over the next 6 miles, you'll travel on rural country roads past fields of grapes, hops, grass seed, and nursery crops. On a clear day you can see the shimmering peak of Mount Hood to the northeast.

After 8.3 miles you'll arrive in the small town of Silverton. This historic town is filled with a variety of unique shops and restaurants. One of Silverton's largest attractions is the Oregon Gardens. This botanical wonderland showcases a broad range of plant species in different garden settings. To take the side trip to the Oregon Gardens, turn onto West Main Street in downtown Silverton,

Start: Engelberg Centennial Park in Mount Angel.

Length: 47.7-mile loop.

Season: Year-round.

Approximate riding time: Four to six hours.

Recommended start time: 10:00 A.M.

Terrain: This route follows major highways and rural country roads in Marion County.

Traffic and hazards: Highway 214 has no shoulder until the last 4.5 miles of the ride. This road is narrow and shady, and it is recommended that you wear very bright clothing. The traffic on Highway 214 can be moderate to heavy during the summer months. The rural roads on this route have light traffic and no shoulder. If you are prone to allergies, you may want to bring medication with you on this ride. Pollen counts can be high in the summer months when farmers are harvesting hay.

Getting there: From I–5 take exit 271 to WOODBURN/SILVERTON/MOUNT ANGEL/HIGHWAY 214. This exit is located approximately 29 miles south of Portland and 18 miles north of Salem. At the stoplight at the end of the off-ramp, reset your odometer to zero. Drive 10.2 miles southeast on Highway 214 to downtown Mount Angel and the intersection with East Charles Street. Turn left onto East Charles Street, and drive 0.1 mile to Engelberg Centennial Park, located on the left side of the road.

and follow the signs to the gardens at 879 West Main Street. (The gardens are open daily from 9:00 A.M. to 6:00 P.M.)

From Silverton you'll have a challenging 14-mile climb with more than 1,300 feet of elevation gain to Silver Falls State Park. On this section of the ride, you'll pedal on Highway 214 as it snakes its way steeply uphill past Christmas tree farms, wide-open pastures, and fragrant hay fields. At 22.1 miles you'll enter Silver Falls State Park. This 8,700-acre park is Oregon's largest state park and features miles of hiking trails that take you past cascading waterfalls. Once you enter the park, you'll ride through towering forest of Douglas fir, western hemlock, red cedar, alder, and maple trees. Sword fern and foxglove cover the hillsides with a colorful carpet of greens and purples. A variety of wildlife can be seen in the park, including deer, beaver, black bear, coyotes, songbirds, and squirrels.

At 25.1 miles you have the option to hop off your bike and check out the historic South Falls Lodge, which offers interpretive displays and houses a snack bar, gift shop, and rest rooms. The lodge was built by the Civilian Conservation Corps in the 1930s and is now listed on the National Register of Historic Places. Adjacent to the lodge is the trailhead for the 7-mile Canyon Trail, which takes you past ten beautiful waterfalls along the north and south forks of Silver Creek. A grassy picnic area is also located here.

Once you are finished sight-seeing, get ready for a fast, exhilarating downhill back to Silverton. Use caution on this section of the route. There are many

The historic Mount Angel Abbey was built in 1928.

blind curves and shady areas where it is difficult for motorists to see you. You'll arrive in Silverton after 42.8 miles, then you'll have an easy cruise on Highway 214 back to Engelberg Centennial Park in Mount Angel. To celebrate all of your hard work, stop by the Mount Angel Brewing Company in downtown Mount Angel to taste some local microbrews and great food.

ADDITIONAL RIDE INFORMATION

♦ Silver Falls State Park, Oregon State Parks and Recreation, 1115 Commercial Street NE, Suite 1, Salem, OR 97301-1002, (800) 551–6949, www. oregonstateparks.org/park_211.php.

LOCAL INFORMATION

♦ Mount Angel Chamber of Commerce, PO Box 221, Mount Angel, OR 97362, (503) 829–6941.
♦ Silverton Chamber of Commerce, 206 South Water Street, Silverton, OR 97381, (503) 873–5615, www.silverton.or.us/chamber.

LOCAL EVENTS/ATTRACTIONS

♦ Mount Angel Oktoberfest, held in mid-September in downtown Mount Angel. (503) 845-6882 or (503) 845–9736, www.oktoberfest.org.

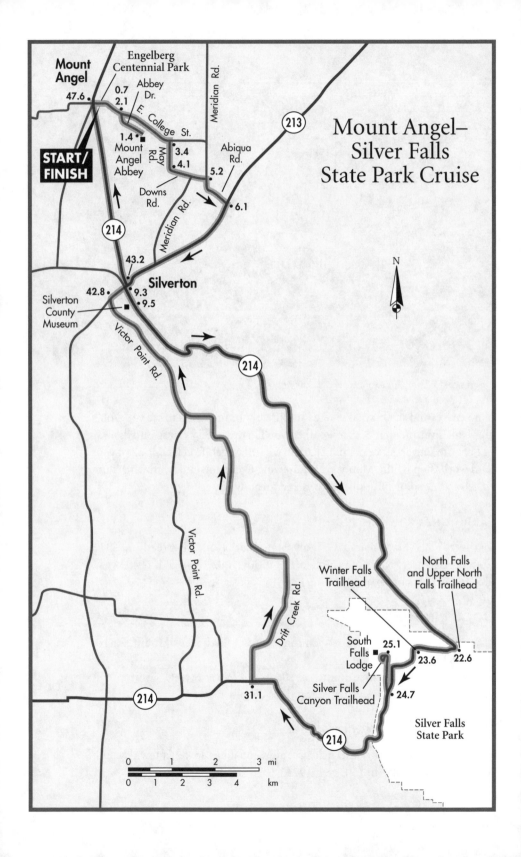

Mount Angel–
Silver Falls
State Park Cruise

Mount Angel

Engelberg Centennial Park

47.6

0.7
2.1

Abbey Dr.

E. College St.

Meridian Rd.

213

N

1.4

Mount Angel Abbey

May Rd.

3.4
4.1

Abiqua Rd.

5.2

Downs Rd.

214

Meridian Rd.

6.1

43.2

Silverton

42.8

9.3

9.5

Silverton County Museum

Victor Point Rd.

214

Victor Point Rd.

Drift Creek Rd.

Winter Falls Trailhead

North Falls and Upper North Falls Trailhead

South Falls Lodge

25.1

23.6

22.6

Silver Falls Canyon Trailhead

24.7

214

31.1

214

Silver Falls State Park

START/ FINISH

214

0   1   2   3 mi

0   1   2   3   4 km

Start by turning left (east) from the park onto East Charles Street. Continue riding on Church Street. (East Charles Street ends).

0.2 Ride by St. Mary's Church on your right. Church Street ends here and turns into East College Street.

0.7 Turn right onto Abbey Drive, and ride uphill under the shade of towering Douglas fir trees.

1.2 At the Y-intersection turn left toward the signed MONASTERY RETREAT HOUSE/ SEMINARY/LIBRARY.

1.4 Arrive at the top of the hill and a main parking area. Explore the Mount Angel Abbey, and admire the far-reaching views of the vast farming country of Marion County. There are rest rooms and water next to the museum (the museum hours are 10:00 to 11:00 A.M. and 1:00 to 5:00 P.M. daily). Once you're finished exploring the abbey, ride back down the hill to the intersection with East . College Street.

2.1 Turn right onto East College Street. On a clear day you can see Mount Hood to the northeast.

3.4 Turn right onto May Road.

4.1 At the stop sign turn left onto Downs Road.

4.6 At the stop sign turn left onto Meridian Road.

5.2 Turn right onto Abiqua Road.

6.1 At the stop sign turn right onto Highway 213.

8.3 Arrive in downtown Silverton. Highway 213 turns into Oak Street.

9.3 At the stop sign turn left onto North Water Street (Highway 214). If you want to stop for lunch or have an espresso, check out Silver Creek Coffee House on the right.

9.5 Pass Silverton County Museum on your right. Now you'll begin a long, challenging climb with more than 1,300 feet of elevation gain to Silver Falls State Park on Highway 214.

22.1 Enter Silver Falls State Park.

(continued)

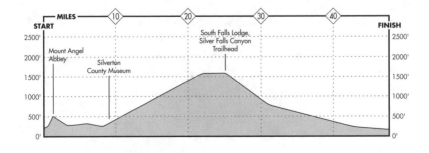

22.6 Pass a parking area on your right that is the trailhead for North Falls and Upper North Falls.

23.0 Pass the North Falls viewpoint on your right. A short trail leads to a great view.

23.6 Pass a trailhead and parking area on your right for Winter Falls.

24.7 Turn right toward South Falls and the historic lodge.

24.9 Ride past the entrance booth (you're on a bike, so you don't need to pay). At the Y-intersection turn left, and follow the signs to the PICNIC AREA/SOUTH FALLS.

25.1 Lock up your bike, and explore the historic lodge, which has rest rooms, a snack bar, a nature store, and an information booth (where you can pick up a park brochure). You also have the option of viewing some of the park's beautiful waterfalls on the 7-mile Canyon Trail, accessed adjacent to the lodge. Once you're finished exploring, ride back out to Highway 214.

25.5 Turn right (south) onto Highway 214. Begin a long, fast descent back to Silverton. Wear bright clothing, and use extreme caution on this descent.

31.1 Turn right onto Drift Creek Road.

42.8 Enter Silverton. (Drift Creek Road becomes Eureka Avenue once you enter Silverton.) Turn right onto Main Street.

43.2 Turn left onto First Avenue (Highway 214), and follow the signs to Mount Angel.

47.6 Turn right onto East Charles Street in downtown Mount Angel.

47.7 Arrive at Engelberg Centennial Park and your starting point.

♦ Mount Angel Abbey and Seminary, One Abbey Drive, Saint Benedict, OR 97373, (503) 845–3030, www.mtangel.edu.

♦ Oregon Gardens, 879 West Main Street, Silverton, OR 97381, (503) 874–8100, www.oregongarden.org. Open 9:00 A.M. to 6:00 P.M. daily. Admission is $6.00 for adults, $5.00 for seniors, $3.00 for children (ages eight to thirteen), and free for children seven and younger.

RESTAURANTS

♦ Mount Angel Brewing Company, 210 Monroe Street, Mount Angel, OR 97362, (503) 845–9624.

♦ Koffee Konnection, 165 Charles Street, Mount Angel, OR 97362, (503) 845–4199.

♦ Silver Creek Coffee House, 111 North Water Street, Silverton, OR 97381, (503) 874–9600.

ACCOMMODATIONS

◆ Abiqua Creek Farms B&B, 16672 Nusom Road, Silverton, OR 97381, (503) 873–6878.
◆ Marvin Gardens Guest House, 511 South Water Street, Silverton, OR 97381, (503) 873–2683.
◆ Silver Falls State Park Campground, Silver Falls State Park, Silver Falls, OR. Contact Oregon State Parks, 1115 Commercial Street NE, Suite 1, Salem, OR 97301-1002, (800) 551–6949, www.oregonstateparks.org/park_211.php.

BIKE SHOPS

◆ Upper Echelon Cycle Shop, 109 South 1st Street, Silverton, OR 97381, (503) 873–2453.

REST ROOMS

◆ Mile 1.4: Mount Angel Abbey.
◆ Mile 25.1: South Falls Lodge.

MAPS

◆ USGS 7.5-minute quads Silverton, Scotts Mills, Stayton, and Drake Crossing; *DeLorme Oregon Atlas and Gazetteer,* maps 54 and 60.

Willamette Mission State Park– Eola Hills Cruise

T his challenging loop tour combines some of the best touring the Willamette Valley has to offer. You'll ride along the scenic Willamette River in the historic Willamette Mission State Park; take a fun ride on the Wheatland Ferry; tour the pastoral setting of Grand Island; then get a great workout when you pedal through the scenic Eola Hills outside of Salem, where you'll have the opportunity to stop at the Strangeland Winery.

This ride begins in historic Willamette Mission State Park, which has expansive lawns and picnic areas, bike paths, walnut and filbert orchards, and picturesque meadowlands. This state park is the location of the Willamette Station of the Methodist Mission, which was established by Reverend Jason Lee in 1834. After his arrival Lee and other missionaries built a one-room school, chapel, kitchen, and living quarters. In addition thirty acres of ground were prepared for planting. After only two years the mission was teaching Indian children and becoming self-sufficient. By 1837 the first white women arrived in the Willamette Valley. One was Anna Maria Pittman, who soon married Jason Lee. In 1840 the main mission was moved from the flood plain to Salem. In 1861 the Willamette River flooded and destroyed most of the original mission. Today none of the original buildings stand, but the Jason Lee Willamette Mission Monument located adjacent to Mission Lake marks the previous location of the original settlement. A hiking trail in the park leads to this monument. Beautiful pink roses growing next to the monument are from some of the original plants that were started at the mission. This park is also home to

Start: Willamette Mission State Park, located approximately 8 miles northwest of Salem.

Length: 35.1-mile loop.

Season: Year-round.

Approximate riding time: Four to six hours.

Recommended start time: 10:00 A.M.

Terrain: This route follows Highway 221 for 5.2 miles, the Lafayette Highway for 1.3 miles, and the Bellview-Hopewell Highway for 3.8 miles. The rest of the route follows rural roads. None of the roads on this route has a shoulder.

Traffic and hazards: Highway 221 is a very busy highway during rush hour and does not have a shoulder. The Lafayette and Bellview-Hopewell Highways have light to moderate traffic and do not have shoulders. The remaining 24.8 miles of the route are on rural roads with no shoulders and light traffic. If you are prone to allergies, bring medication with you on this ride. Pollen counts can be high in the summer when farmers are harvesting hay.

Getting there: From I–5 take exit 263 toward West Brooks and Gervais. (This exit is approximately 8 miles south of Woodburn and 5 miles north of Salem.) Turn west onto Brooklake Road toward Keizer. Drive 1.6 miles on Brooklake Road to the intersection with Wheatland Road. At the stop sign turn right onto Wheatland Road, and drive 2.4 miles to the entrance road to Willamette Mission State Park. Turn left onto the park entrance road, and drive 0.6 mile to the pay booth for the park. (There is a $3.00 day-use fee to enter the park. If an attendant is not in the pay booth, you can purchase a permit from the self-pay machine located at the entrance booth.) Once you pass the pay booth, you'll arrive at a Y-intersection. Turn left toward PARK FACILITIES. Drive 1 mile to a road junction. Continue straight where a sign indicates FILBERT GROVE PICNIC AREA/EQUESTRIAN TRAILHEAD. Drive 0.1 mile and look for a yellow bike sign on the right side of the road. Ten feet past the bike sign, you'll see a gravel parking area on the left side of the road. Park here.

the nation's largest black cottonwood tree. The stately tree is more than 250 years old, more than 156 feet high, and measures 26 feet, 8 inches in circumference.

Begin the tour on a paved bike path that heads north toward the Willamette River, and the Wheatland Ferry landing. Ride the ferry across the slow-moving

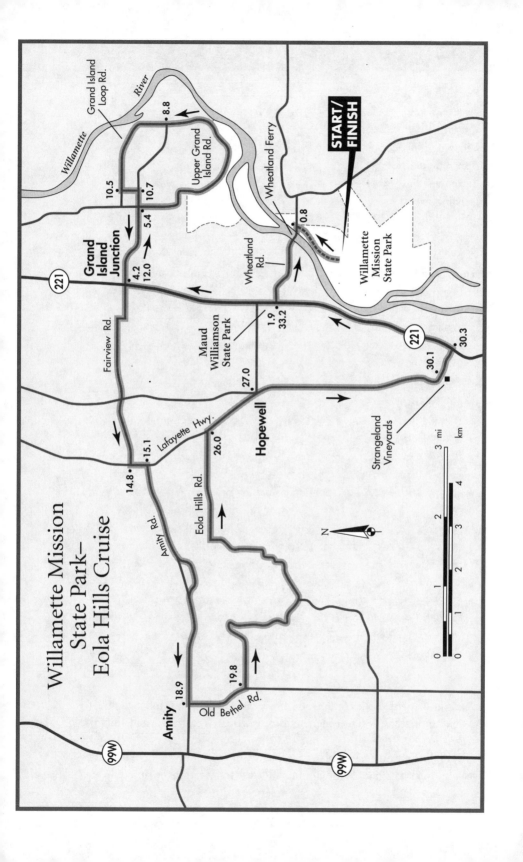

Willamette Mission State Park–Eola Hills Cruise

START/FINISH

Willamette Mission State Park

Willamette River

Grand Island Loop Rd.

8.8

Upper Grand Island Rd.

10.5
10.7

5.4
12.0
4.2

Grand Island Junction

221

Wheatland Ferry

Wheatland Rd.

0.8

1.9
33.2

Maud Williamson State Park

27.0

221

30.1
30.3

Fairview Rd.

Hopewell

Strangeland Vineyards

Lafayette Hwy.

15.1
14.8

26.0

Eola Hills Rd.

Amity Rd.

N

18.9

Amity

19.8

Old Bethel Rd.

99W

99W

3 mi
km

0   1   2   3

0   1   2   3   4

Start by riding north on the paved bike path that is marked with a brown WHEATLAND FERRY sign.

0.8 Arrive at the loading platform for the Wheatland Ferry. Ride the ferry across the Willamette River. (The ferry is open daily from 6:00 A.M. to 9:45 P.M. Cyclists get to ride for free.) Once you reach the other side, start pedaling on Wheatland Road, and travel through the small community of Wheatland.

1.9 At the stop sign turn right onto Highway 221 toward Dayton and McMinnville. The entrance to Maud Williamson State Park is on your left right after you make this turn. This is a shady day-use area that has water, rest rooms, and picnic tables.

4.2 Turn right onto Grand Island Road. If you want to stock up on drinks and snacks, the Grand Island Grocery and Deli is located on the left side of Highway 221 at this intersection.

4.7 Cross a bridge over the river, and begin your scenic tour of Grand Island.

5.4 Turn right onto Upper Grand Island Road. This road is very rough and narrow.

8.0 The road turns to gravel.

8.1 The road turns back to pavement, and you'll pedal past a white metal gate.

8.8 At the Y-intersection turn right onto Grand Island Loop Road.

10.5 At the T-intersection turn left onto Grand Island Road.

10.7 Turn right, and continue riding on Grand Island Road past fields of corn, hay, and pumpkins.

12.0 At the stop sign cross Highway 221 (Salem-Dayton Highway), and continue riding straight on Fairview Road. Use caution at this busy intersection!

14.8 At the stop sign turn left onto Lafayette Highway.

15.1 Turn right onto Amity Road (Bellview-Hopewell Highway), where a sign indicates AMITY/SHERIDAN. After this intersection you'll begin a steep climb.

18.9 Turn left onto Old Bethel Road.

19.8 Turn left onto Eola Hills Road, and start a long, long climb into the Eola Hills wine country.

23.4 Begin a fast descent. Enjoy the far-reaching views of the rural countryside.

(continued)

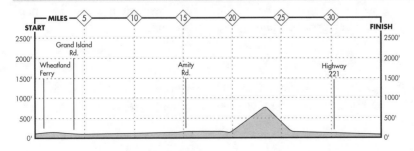

26.0 Turn right onto Lafayette Highway.

27.0 Turn right onto Hopewell Road, and enter the small community of Hopewell.

27.1 Pass the Hopewell Store on your right. There is a phone and portable rest rooms at this store.

30.1 Pass Strangeland Vineyards on your right. The winery is open the first weekend of every month from January through April, and every weekend from noon to 5:00 P.M. from May through December. The winery is closed December 13 through 31.

30.3 At the stop sign turn left onto Highway 221 toward Dayton and McMinnville.

33.2 Turn right onto Wheatland Road.

34.3 Arrive at the Wheatland Ferry. Ride the ferry across the Willamette River. Once you cross the river, turn right onto the Willamette Mission State Park bike path.

35.1 Arrive at your starting pointing at Willamette Mission State Park.

Willamette, then ride through the small town of Wheatland (cyclists get to ride for free). Just shy of 2 miles, you'll pass Maud Williamson State Park on your left. This forested day-use park is a shady oasis and has water, rest rooms, and picnic tables. After 4.2 miles you'll begin pedaling on the quiet rural roads of Grand Island, past century-old farms and fields of corn, fragrant hay, bright orange pumpkins, and other agricultural crops. During the summer and early fall, you'll have a good chance at passing fruit and vegetable stands, where you can try some of the island's bounty. The road around the island is rough but has very light traffic.

After 12 miles you'll end your loop tour of Grand Island, then begin pedaling through the Eola Hills, which are part of a 13-mile ridge that stretches north from Salem toward McMinnville. The climate in these rolling hills is perfect for growing grapes, and many wineries create handcrafted wines in this region. Over the next 14 miles, you'll take part in some steep climbing into these hills that will test your endurance. Luckily there are plenty of distractions, including sweeping views of Willamette Valley farming country and many spectacular Cascade peaks to the northeast. At 30.1 miles you can stop at Strangeland Vineyards on your right. The winery features award-winning pinot noir, pinot gris, chardonnay, and gewürztraminer.

ADDITIONAL RIDE INFORMATION

♦ Willamette Mission State Park, 10991 Wheatland Road NE, Gervais, OR 97026, (800) 551–6949, www.oregonstateparks.org/park_139.php.

♦ Salem Bicycle Club, PO Box 2224, Salem, OR 97308, (503) 363–7725, www.salembicycleclub.org.

♦ Salem Convention and Visitors Association, 1313 Mill Street SE, Salem, OR 97301, (800) 874–7012, www.scva.org.

♦ Bethel Heights Winery, 6060 Bethel Heights Road NW, Salem, OR 97304, (503) 581–2262, www.bethelheights.com. Tasting room hours are Tuesday through Sunday 11:00 A.M. to 5:00 P.M. (June through August); Saturday and Sunday 11:00 A.M. to 5:00 P.M. (March through May, and September through December 23); closed December 24 through February.
♦ Oregon State Fair, held mid-August through Labor Day at the Oregon State Fairgrounds, Salem, OR 97301, (503) 581–2228.
♦ Salem Art Fair and Festival, held the third weekend in July, 600 Mission Street SE, Salem, OR 97302, (503) 581–2228, www.salemart.org.
♦ Strangeland Vineyards, 8500 Hopewell Road NW, Salem, OR 97304, (800) 301–9482, www.open.org/~stanglnd. The winery is open the first weekend of

Enjoying a ride on the Wheatland Ferry.

every month from January through April, and every weekend from noon to 5:00 P.M. from May through December. The winery is closed December 13 through 31.

RESTAURANTS

♦ Davincis, 180 High Street SE, Salem, OR 97301, (503) 399–1413.
♦ Great Harvest Bakery, 339 Court Street NE, Salem, OR 97301, (503) 363–4697.
♦ Indian Palace, 377 Court Street NE, Salem, OR 97301, (503) 371–4808.
♦ Jonathan's Oyster Bar, 445 State Street, Salem, OR 97301, (503) 362–7219.
♦ Willamette Brew Pub, 120 Commerical Street NE, Salem, OR 97301, (503) 363–9779.

ACCOMMODATIONS

♦ Bethel Heights B&B, 6055 Bethel Heights Road NW, Salem, OR 97304, (503) 364–7688. This bed and breakfast is part of the the Bethel Heights winery, which makes handcrafted chardonnay, pinot blanc, pinot gris, and pinot noir.
♦ Willamette Mission State Park, Oregon State Parks and Recreation, 10991 Wheatland Road NE, Gervais, OR 97026, (800) 551–6949, www.oregonstateparks. org/park_139.php.

BIKE SHOPS

♦ Bike N Hike Centers, 887 Commercial Street SE, Salem, OR 97302, (503) 581–2707.
♦ Bike Peddler, 174 Commercial Street NE, Salem, OR 97301, (503) 399–7741.
♦ Luarcas World of Wheels, 170 Chemawa Road North, Salem, OR 97303, (503) 393–0500.
♦ Santiam Bicycle Way of Life, 388 Commercial Street NE, Salem, OR 97301, (503) 363–6602.
♦ Scotts Cycle, 147 Commercial Street SE, Salem, OR 97301, (503) 363–4516.

REST ROOMS

♦ Mile 0.0: Willamette Mission State Park.
♦ Mile 1.9: Maud Williamson State Park.
♦ Mile 27.1: Hopewell Store.

MAPS

♦ USGS 7.5-minute quads Mission Bottom, Dayton, and Amity; *DeLorme Oregon Atlas and Gazetteer,* map 59.

Petes Mountain–Canby Ferry Cruise

This challenging route explores the steep rolling hills of Clackamas County and promises a great workout and extraordinary views of Mount Hood and other Cascade peaks. The ride starts at Willamette Park in the historic community of Willamette, which features many fun shops. After a tough ride up Petes Mountain, you'll cruise downhill to the Canby Ferry—one of the few remaining ferries in Oregon. After crossing the mighty Willamette, you'll pedal on a mostly flat route past Molalla River State Park and through the shimmering green farming country surrounding Canby. You'll complete the final loop of the ride by exploring the hilly countryside of West Linn through a rural area filled with hobby farms and country estates.

This tour begins by taking you through the rolling hills of West Linn. Robert Moore first settled this area in the 1840s. He built a cabin in the hills above Willamette Falls and called the town Robin's Nest. It wasn't long before the town had a lumber and flour mill. In 1845 the town was renamed Linn City after Moore's friend Dr. Lewis F. Linn, a U.S. senator from Missouri. By the 1850s the prosperous town included a post office, newspaper, and boat basin. Robert Moore died in 1857, and not long afterward a fire almost destroyed the entire town. Although Linn City did not survive, the area continued to grow, and the city of West Linn was incorporated in 1913.

From Willamette Falls Park in West Linn, the route climbs more than 650 feet to the top of Petes Mountain on Petes Mountain Road. This road is very narrow and does not have a shoulder. Once you reach this mountain's high point, you'll have spectacular views to the northeast of Mount Hood and the

Start: Willamette Park in West Linn.
Length: 42.7-mile figure eight.
Season: Year-round.
Approximate riding time: Four to five hours.
Recommended start time: 10:00 A.M.
Terrain: City streets and rural roads.
Traffic and hazards: The terrain on this route is very hilly and twisty. The roads do not have shoulders but there is light traffic. Wear bright clothing, and use caution on descents.
Getting there: From I-205 in West Linn, take exit 6 for WEST LINN/10TH STREET. At the end of the off-ramp, turn south onto 10th Street. Go 0.2 mile, and turn right onto Willamette Falls Drive. Travel 0.2 mile south, and turn left onto 12th Street at the BOAT RAMP sign. Head steeply downhill for 0.2 mile, and arrive at Willamette Park. Park next to the rest rooms at the intersection of 12th and Volpp Streets.

surrounding forested foothills. After the summit the route has many fun ups and downs until you reach the Canby Ferry just shy of 7 miles. The ferry is open from 6:45 A.M. to 9:15 P.M. seven days a week, and cyclists ride for free. High-water conditions occasionally close this ferry. The first ferry to cross at this location began operating in 1914, and the ferryman's wages were $10 per month. Over the years several different ferries were put into use and retired. The *M. J. Lee II* is the current ferry in use and was christened in July 1997. It can haul nine vehicles and has a cruising speed of 6.4 miles per hour. This pleasant cruising speed gives you time to enjoy views of the meandering Willamette River.

The route continues south, and at 8.3 miles you'll arrive at 566-acre Molalla River State Park. This quiet park is located at the confluence of the Pudding, Molalla, and Willamette Rivers. The river system creates wetlands and forest that are prime wildlife habitat. The park is home to a large great blue heron rookery that has been at this location since 1910. Ducks, geese, and double-crested cormorants can be seen in the wetlands. You may also see bald eagles perched high in the trees above the Willamette River. There is a gravel hiking trail that heads about three-quarters of a mile upstream along the Willamette. You can also hike a three-quarter-mile trail that heads around a pond ecosystem.

From the park the route continues south and takes you past fields of vegetables crops and colorful flowers until you reach downtown Canby. From here the route continues south on the Canby-Marquam Highway through classic Willamette Valley farming country. Over the next 17 miles, you'll complete a large, fairly flat loop that takes you past shimmering green fields filled with grazing sheep and cattle, nursery crops, and Christmas trees. The route takes you back through Canby, then across the Canby Ferry for a second fun ferry ride. After crossing the ferry get ready for more hill climbing as you begin the second loop. This loop takes you on a roller-coaster ride past sweeping meadows, pastures, horse farms, and expensive executive homes. Homesteader Road promises a bit of a rough ride, but the remainder of this loop is mostly smooth.

The Tualatin River.

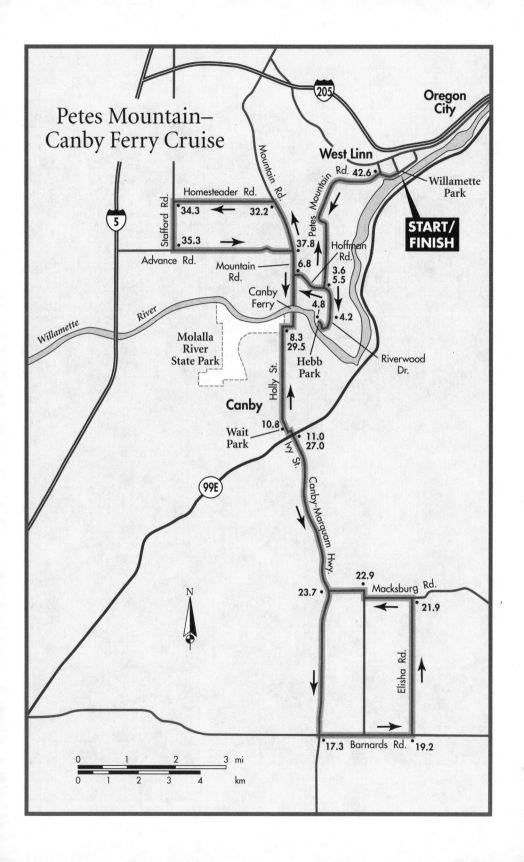

Petes Mountain–Canby Ferry Cruise

Oregon City

West Linn

Willamette Park

START/FINISH

Rd. 42.6

Homesteader Rd.

34.3   ← 32.2

35.3   →

Stafford Rd.

Mountain Rd.

Petes Mountain Rd.

Advance Rd.

37.8

6.8

Mountain Rd.

Hoffman Rd.

3.6
5.5

Canby Ferry

4.8

4.2

Willamette River

Molalla River State Park

8.3
29.5

Hebb Park

Riverwood Dr.

Holly St.

Canby

Wait Park

10.8

11.0
27.0

Ivy St.

99E

Canby-Marquam Hwy.

N

22.9

23.7

Macksburg Rd.

21.9

Elisha Rd.

17.3 Barnards Rd. 19.2

| 0 | 1 | 2 | 3 mi |

| 0 | 1 | 2 | 3 | 4 km |

Start by turning right onto Volpp Street.

0.1 Turn left onto Tualatin Avenue.

0.2 Tualatin Avenue turns into Petes Mountain Road. Begin a very steep climb.

1.4 Reach the summit of Petes Mountain. On a clear day you can see Mount Hood and the surrounding foothills to the northeast.

3.6 Turn left onto Riverwood Drive toward HEBB PARK. (Hoffman Road goes right at this junction).

4.1 Turn right onto Riverwood Drive toward HEBB PARK. (Peach Cove Road goes left at this junction).

4.2 Turn right on Hebb Park Road.

4.8 Arrive at Hebb Park on the Willamette River. Rest rooms and water are available here. After taking a break, turn around and ride out of the park on Hebb Park Road. Retrace your route back to the intersection of Riverwood Drive and Hoffman Road.

5.5 Turn left onto Hoffman Road toward WILSONVILLE/HOFFMAN ROAD.

6.8 Turn left onto Mountain Road toward the CANBY FERRY.

7.5 Arrive at the Canby Ferry. Ride the ferry across the river (cyclists ride for free). Ride up a short steep hill (this road eventually turns into Holly Street).

8.0 Turn right into Molalla River State Park.

8.3 Arrive at rest rooms and the Molalla River State Park day-use area. Take a break, then head back out the entrance road to Holly Street.

8.6 Turn right onto Holly Street.

10.8 Pass Wait Park on the right.

10.9 Turn left onto 1st Street in Canby.

11.0 Turn right onto Ivy Street. Cross the railroad tracks and Highway 99, and continue riding south out of town on Ivy Street. Ivy Street turns into the Canby-Marquam Highway.

13.3 Pass the Lone Elder Store on the right.

17.3 Turn left onto Barnards Road. Enjoy great views of Mount Hood on this section of the route.

(continued)

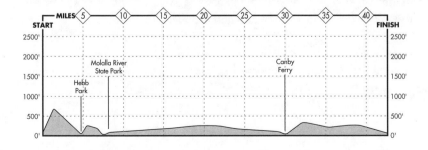

19.2 Turn left onto Elisha Road. Note this road is very rough.

21.9 Turn left onto Macksburg Road.

22.9 The road curves sharply to the right and becomes Dryland Road, then curves to the left and turns into Macksburg Road.

23.7 Turn right onto the Canby-Marquam Highway, and follow this road into downtown Canby. This highway turns into Ivy Street once you reenter Canby.

27.0 Cross Highway 99, and cross the railroad tracks.

27.1 Turn left onto 1st Street.

27.2 Turn right onto Holly Street.

29.5 Pass the entrance road to Molalla River State Park on the left.

30.0 Reach the Canby Ferry. Cross the river on the ferry. After crossing the river ride up a short steep hill on Mountain Road.

32.2 Turn left onto Homesteader Road. Note this is a rough road.

34.3 Turn left onto Stafford Road.

35.3 Turn left onto Advance Road.

37.8 Turn right onto Mountain Road.

38.3 Turn left onto Hoffman Road.

39.0 Take a sharp left onto Petes Mountain Road.

41.2 Begin a steep descent on Petes Mountain Road. Watch your speed on this narrow, shoulderless road.

42.5 Petes Mountain Road turns into Tualatin Avenue.

42.6 Take a sharp right onto 12th Avenue.

42.7 Arrive at Willamette Park.

Watch your speed on some of the descents on this loop. Parts of the route drop quickly into steep ravines, then surge steeply back uphill. At 39 miles the second loop ends, and you'll travel on an exhilarating descent on Petes Mountain Road back to your starting point at Willamette Park.

LOCAL INFORMATION

♦ Canby Chamber of Commerce, 140 NE 2nd Avenue, PO Box 35, Canby, OR 97013, (503) 266–4600, www.canby.com/chamber.

♦ Oregon State Parks and Recreation, 1115 Commercial Street NE, Suite 1, Salem, OR 97301-1002, (800) 551–6949, www.oregonstateparks.org.

♦ West Linn Parks and Recreation Department, 22500 Salamo Road, West Linn, OR 97068, (503) 557–4700, www.ci.west-linn.or.us/Parks/Parksindex.htm.

LOCAL EVENTS/ATTRACTIONS

♦ Canby Wine, Art, and Jazz Festival, held in June, 140 NE 2nd Avenue, Canby, OR 97013, (503) 266–1136.

RESTAURANTS

♦ Hart & Soul Bake-Shop & Eatery, 224 NW 1st Avenue, Canby, OR 97013, (503) 263–2305.
♦ Willamette Coffee House, 2120 8th Court, West Linn, OR 97068, (503) 722–1708.

ACCOMMODATIONS

♦ Riverbend House B&B, 949 Willamette Falls Drive, West Linn, OR 97068, (503) 557–1662.

BIKE SHOPS

♦ Bikes N More, 200 Northwest 1st Avenue, Canby, OR 97013, (503) 266–9535.

REST ROOMS

♦ Mile 4.8: Hebb Park.
♦ Mile 8.3: Molalla River State Park.
♦ Mile 29.5: Molalla River State Park.

MAPS

♦ USGS 7.5-minute quads Oregon City, Canby, and Yoder; *DeLorme Oregon Atlas and Gazetteer,* map 60.

16

Covered Bridges Cruise

O n this tour you can view five of Oregon's rare covered bridges. The ride begins in the sleepy town of Scio and loops through rolling farming country of Linn County.

Larwood Bridge.

This tour gives you a rare glimpse at five of Oregon's remaining fifty-two covered bridges, almost all of which were built between 1910 and 1950. You will see the Shimanek, Hannah, Larwood, Hoffman, and Gilkey bridges. These charming bridges are a pride to local communities and are also a unique part of Oregon's history. When these bridges were built, wood was plentiful and was the material of choice. The bridges were covered to keep the ever-present Oregon rain from rotting the wood. Covering the bridges increased their life span by three to five times. Bridge designs were provided to each county by the state. Most of the bridges built used the Howe truss design. Basically a truss is a bridge support that is made in the shape of a triangle. The Howe truss was developed by William Howe in 1840. This truss uses metal rods to add extra support to the bridge. When tension is applied to the metal rods, it keeps the bridge from sagging. Today wood has been replaced with the more durable materials of concrete and steel. As more of Oregon's original bridges were torn down or replaced, many local communities stepped in to restore and preserve the remaining bridges. Oregon is ranked fifth in the United States for number of covered bridges.

This tour begins at Chapin Park in downtown Scio, which was established in 1860 and is thought to be named after the community of Scio, Ohio. Be sure to bring plenty of water with you because there aren't any water stops on this route. You'll head east out of town and travel almost 3 miles through flat farmland to the red-and-white-trimmed Shimanek Bridge, which spans Thomas Creek. This bridge is 130 feet long and was built in 1966. It is the fifth bridge to be built at this location. The original was built in 1861 and was not covered, so it did not last. The other three bridges were damaged by floods and bad storms. From here you'll pedal uphill (with more than 600 feet of elevation gain) for several more miles past open fields of wheat, corn, and Christmas trees, and pastures filled with cattle and horses.

Your next covered bridge stop is

at the Hannah Bridge at 13.4 miles. This 105-foot-long bright white bridge was built in 1936 and spans Thomas Creek. From here you'll pedal south and then east through more rolling farmland to the 105-foot Larwood Bridge, which spans Crabtree Creek at 26.7 miles. This white, airy covered bridge was built in 1939. You may want to stop and have lunch at the Larwood Wayside just after you cross the bridge. This shady wayside has picnic tables and rest rooms (but

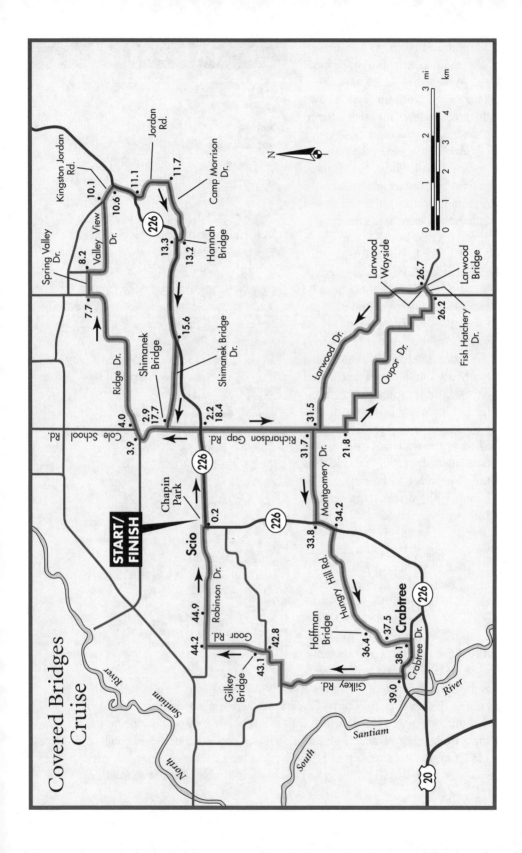

Covered Bridges Cruise

Start by turning left onto 1st Street.

0.1 Turn left onto Main Street.

0.2 Turn left (east) onto Highway 226 toward Mill City and Lyons.

2.2 Turn left (north) onto Richardson Gap Road.

2.9 Arrive at the Shimanek Bridge, which spans Thomas Creek. This red-and-white–trimmed bridge was built in 1966. After the bridge begin a steep ascent.

3.9 Richardson Gap Road turns into Ridge Drive.

4.0 You'll arrive at a Y-intersection. Stay right, and continue riding uphill on Ridge Drive (Cole School Road continues left at this intersection.)

7.7 Turn right onto Spring Valley Drive.

8.2 Turn right onto Valley View Drive.

10.1 At the stop sign turn right onto Kingston-Jordan Drive.

10.6 At the stop sign turn right onto Highway 226. Use caution when turning onto this busy highway.

11.1 Turn left (south) onto Jordan Road, then climb a very steep hill after you cross the bridge.

11.7 At the T-intersection turn right onto Camp Morrison Drive.

13.2 Arrive at the Hannah Bridge, which spans Thomas Creek. This bridge was built in 1936.

13.3 At the T-intersection turn left (west) onto Highway 226.

15.6 Turn right onto Shimanek Bridge Drive. This road surface is loose and gravelly.

17.7 At the stop sign turn left (south) onto Richardson Gap Road, then cross the Shimanek Bridge.

18.4 Cross Highway 226, and continue riding straight on Richardson Gap Road.

21.8 Turn left (east) onto Oupor Drive. Keep an eye out for blackberries, which ripen in mid-August.

23.1 Turn left, and continue riding on Oupor Drive.

26.2 At the T-intersection and stop sign, turn left (east) onto Fish Hatchery Drive.

26.5 At a Y-intersection continue left on Fish Hatchery Drive.

(continued)

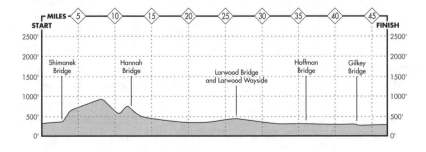

26.7 Cross the Larwood Bridge, which spans Crabtree Creek. After you cross the bridge, you may want to stop at the Larwood Wayside on the left. Rest rooms and picnic tables are available here, as well as a great swimming hole. No water is available.

26.8 You'll arrive at a T-intersection. Turn left onto Larwood Drive.

31.5 At the stop sign turn right onto Richardson Gap Road.

31.7 Turn left onto Montgomery Drive.

33.8 At the stop sign and T-intersection, turn left onto Highway 226.

34.2 Turn right onto Hungry Hill Road.

36.4 Reach the Hoffman Bridge, which spans Crabtree Creek. This bridge was built in 1936.

37.5 Stop and look for a train before you cross the railroad tracks.

38.1 At the T-intersection and stop sign, turn right onto Crabtree Drive.

39.0 At the stop sign turn right onto Gilkey Road.

41.8 At the stop sign and T-intersection, turn right, and continue riding on Gilkey Road.

42.3 At the Y-intersection go left, and continue riding on Gilkey Road.

42.8 At a road intersection continue straight on Goar Road (Gilkey Road goes right).

43.1 Arrive at the Gilkey Bridge, which spans Thomas Creek. This bridge was built in 1939. There are great swimming opportunities on this part of the creek.

44.2 At the T-intersection turn right onto Robinson Drive toward Scio.

44.9 Stop and look for a train before you cross the railroad tracks.

46.6 Arrive in Scio. Robinson Drive turns into First Avenue

46.8 At the stop sign cross Main Street, and continue riding straight on First Avenue.

47.0 Arrive at Chapin Park on the right.

no water). There is also a great swimming hole here where the Roaring River flows into Crabtree Creek.

From here you'll head west and then north to complete another loop with two more bridges. The riding is mostly flat until you reach Hungry Hill Road, which climbs gradually until you reach the Hoffman Bridge at mile 36.4. This 90-foot-long white bridge was built in 1936, spans Crabtree Creek, and features mystical gothic windows. A few miles past this bridge, you'll pass the town of Crabtree.

After Crabtree the route turns north and follows Gilkey Road over flat terrain past fragrant fields of mint, corn, and hay. The 120-foot-long Gilkey Bridge is the last covered bridge on the route, and it spans Thomas Creek. Built in 1939 this bridge underwent a major renovation in 1998. As you cross the bridge, you'll more than likely see kids cooling off in the creek or fishing along the banks. After this bridge the route continues another 4 miles north on a flat route past more farmland to your starting point at Chapin Park in Scio.

LOCAL INFORMATION

♦ Salem Convention and Visitors Association, 1313 Mill Street SE, Salem, OR 97301, (800) 874–7012, www.scva.org.

LOCAL EVENTS/ATTRACTIONS

♦ Oregon State Fair, held mid-August through Labor Day at the Oregon State Fairgrounds, Salem. Contact the fair at 2330 17th Street NE, Salem, OR 97303-3201, (503) 947-3247, www.fair.state.or.us.

♦ Salem Art Fair and Festival, held the third weekend in July, 600 Mission Street SE, Salem, OR 97302, (503) 581–2228, www.salemart.org.

♦ Strawberry Century Bicycle Ride, held the second weekend in June, Lebanon, OR. Contact Santiam Slow Spokes, c/o Lebanon Community Hospital, PO Box 739, Lebanon, OR 97355, (541) 926–3234.

RESTAURANTS

♦ Plantation Inn, 237 North 2nd Street, Jefferson, OR 97352, (541) 327–3343.

ACCOMMODATIONS

♦ Marquee House B&B, 333 Wyatt Court NE, Salem, OR 97301, (800) 949–0837, www.oregonlin.com/marquee.

♦ Vista Park B&B, 480 Vista Avenue SE, Salem, OR 97302, (888) 588–0699, www.vistapark.com.

BIKE SHOPS

♦ Bike N Hike Centers, 887 Commercial Street SE, Salem, OR 97302, (503) 581–2707.

♦ Bike Peddler, 174 Commercial Street NE, Salem, OR 97301, (503) 399–7741.

♦ Luarcas World of Wheels, 170 Chemawa Road North, Salem, OR 97303, (503) 393–0500.

♦ Santiam Bicycle Way of Life, 388 Commercial Street NE, Salem, OR 97301, (503) 363–6602.

♦ Scotts Cycle, 147 Commercial Street SE, Salem, OR 97301, (503) 363–4516.

REST ROOMS

♦ Mile 26.7: Larwood Wayside.

MAPS

♦ USGS 7.5-minute quads Scio, Jordan, and Crabtree; *DeLorme Oregon Atlas and Gazetteer,* map 54.

Sandy River Gorge–
Troutdale Cruise

T his tough hilly ride takes you into the beautiful Sandy River
Gorge. The tour begins at Lewis and Clark State Park and
climbs more than 1,000 feet to a high point at Roslyn Lake. After a hard
day of riding, take a break from the saddle and explore Troutdale, which
features a variety of unique shops, restaurants, and museums.
Afterward, it's a short ride back to your starting point at Lewis and
Clark State Park.

This hilly tour begins at Lewis and Clark State Park, named after explorers
Meriwether Lewis and William Clark, who passed through this area in 1805.
You'll warm up by riding a gentle ascent next to the smooth-flowing Sandy
River. This gorgeous river is fed by melting glaciers on Mount Hood and flows
northwest about 50 miles to where it joins the Columbia River near Troutdale.
The river is a popular salmon fishery, with the biggest salmon run in the spring.
Where the route hugs the banks of the river, keep an eye out for osprey hunt-
ing for trout. These magnificent fishing raptors have black and white plumage
and striking amber eyes. They have a wing span of about 6 feet and weigh about
four pounds. They are often seen perched in trees high above the river.

After 4 miles you'll enter the small community of Springdale. If you need
to fuel up for the ride, be sure to stop at Mom's Café and Bakery. After 6.5 miles
you'll turn onto Gordon Creek Road. This narrow road drops steeply into the
Sandy River Gorge after about 7 miles. The road surface is rough in spots, and
you should watch your speed when you descend into the canyon. Once you're

in the canyon, there are many opportunities for close-up river views. Over the next 10 miles, you'll have to negotiate many ups and downs as the route travels past second-growth forest and small farms. At 16.6 miles you'll cross the fast-flowing Bull Run River. This river is a major tributary of the Lower Sandy River and is the source the Bull Run Reservoir, which stores Portland's drinking water.

At just past 17 miles, the route takes you by pretty Roslyn Lake. There is a small park on the lakeshore, and it's a good place to stop for lunch. Watch for waterfowl feeding in the lake. You may also see anglers trying their luck for rainbow trout. At 19.8 miles take a break at Dodge Park before you cross the Sandy River. After crossing the river the route climbs steeply on a hilly course past Christmas tree farms, horse farms, and nurseries. After about 8 more miles, you'll enter Troutdale and ride through a more congested area until you reach downtown at just past 32 miles. Be sure to stop and explore the restaurants, museums, and shops. Cross the Sandy River, then ride back at your starting point at Lewis and Clark State Park.

THE BASICS

Start: From Lewis and Clark State Park, located 2 miles east of Troutdale on the Historic Columbia River Highway.

Length: 33-mile loop.

Season: Year-round (roads can by icy during the winter months).

Approximate riding time: Four to six hours.

Recommended start time: 10:00 A.M.

Terrain: Rural roads and city streets.

Traffic and hazards: Most of the roads on this ride do not have a shoulder, are narrow, and have hairpin curves. Use caution on descents, and wear bright colors so motorists can more easily see you. This ride is best completed at midday or on a weekend. Avoid this ride during morning and evening rush hour.

Getting there: From the intersection of I–205 and I–84 in Portland, drive 9 miles east on I–84 to exit 18 for LEWIS AND CLARK STATE PARK. At the end of the off-ramp, turn left onto the Columbia River Highway toward LEWIS AND CLARK STATE PARK/OXBOW REGIONAL PARK. Continue 0.2 mile, and turn left into Lewis and Clark State Park.

ADDITIONAL RIDE INFORMATION

♦ Columbia River Gorge National Scenic Area, 902 Wasco Avenue, Suite 200, Hood River, OR 97031, (541) 386–2333, www.fs.fed.us/r6/columbia.
♦ Oregon State Parks and Recreation, 1115 Commercial Street NE, Suite 1, Salem, OR 97301-1002, (800) 551–6949, www.oregonstateparks.org.
♦ Portland Wheelmen Touring Club, P.O. Box 2972, Portland, OR 97208-2972, 503-257-PWTC, www.pwtc.com.

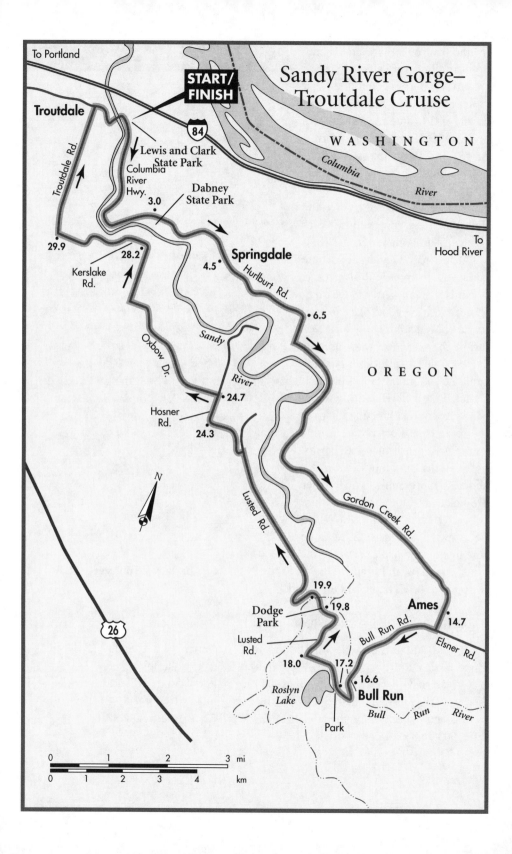

Sandy River Gorge–Troutdale Cruise

To Portland

START/ FINISH

I-84

Troutdale

Troutdale Rd.

Lewis and Clark State Park

Columbia River Hwy.

3.0

Dabney State Park

29.9

28.2

Kerslake Rd.

4.5

Springdale

Hurlburt Rd.

6.5

Sandy

River

Oxbow Dr.

24.7

Hosner Rd.

24.3

N

Lusted Rd.

Gordon Creek Rd.

19.9

19.8

Dodge Park

Lusted Rd.

18.0

17.2

Park

Roslyn Lake

16.6

Bull Run

Bull Run Rd.

Ames

14.7

Elsner Rd.

Bull   Run   River

26

W A S H I N G T O N

Columbia

River

To Hood River

O R E G O N

| 0 | 1 | 2 | 3 mi |
| 0 | 1 | 2 | 3 | 4 km |

Start by turning left from the Lewis and Clark State Park entrance onto the Columbia River Highway.

0.2 Turn left at the stop sign toward HISTORIC HIGHWAY/CORBETT.

3.0 Pass Dabney State Park on your left. Rest rooms and water are available here.

3.3 Stay to the right, following signs to Multnomah Falls.

3.9 Enter the small community of Springdale.

4.2 Pass Mom's Garden Bakery and Café on the right.

4.3 Go right at a Y-intersection where a sign indicates HISTORIC HIGHWAY, CORBETT, MULT-NOMAH FALLS, and continue on the Columbia River Highway.

4.5 Turn right onto Hurlburt Road.

6.5 Turn right onto Gordon Creek Road.

14.7 Take a sharp left onto Bull Run Road (Elsner Road goes right at this junction).

16.6 Cross a bridge over the Bull Run River.

17.2 Turn right onto Ten Eyck Road toward Sandy. Right after this turn you'll pass a small park on the left next to Roslyn Lake. This is a good place to stop for lunch.

18.0 Take a sharp right onto Lusted Road.

19.8 Take a sharp right, and continue riding on Lusted Road. You'll pass Dodge Park on your right (rest rooms and water are available here) after this road junction.

19.9 Cross the Sandy River, and begin a steep climb.

24.3 Turn right onto Hosner Road.

24.7 Turn left onto Oxbow Drive.

27.1 Turn right onto 302nd Avenue.

28.2 The road curves to the left and turns into Kerslake Road.

28.9 Turn left onto Sweetbriar Road.

29.9 Turn right onto Troutdale Road.

30.6 Pass Stark Street Espresso on the left.

30.8 Pass Cedarplace Inn B&B on the left.

31.5 Turn right onto Sandy Avenue.

31.7 Turn right onto Harlow Street (this turns into 3rd Street).

32.1 Take a sharp right, and continue on Harlow Street.

(continued)

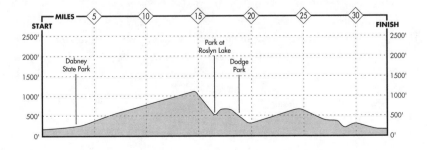

32.2 Turn right onto the Historic Columbia River Highway. You have the option of stopping and exploring the shops and restaurants in downtown Troutdale.

32.3 Pass the Depot Rail Museum on the left.

32.7 Pass Glen Otto Park on the right, and cross the Sandy River.

32.8 Turn left onto the Columbia River Highway.

33.0 Arrive at Lewis and Clark State Park on the right.

LOCAL INFORMATION

♦ Troutdale Chamber of Commerce, 338 East Columbia River Highway, Troutdale, OR 97060, (503) 669–7473, www.troutdalechamber.org.

LOCAL EVENTS/ATTRACTIONS

♦ Depot Rail Museum, 473 East Historic Columbia River Highway, Troutdale, OR 97060, (503) 661–2164.

♦ Harlow House Museum, 726 East Historic Columbia River Highway, Troutdale, OR 97060, (503) 661–2164.

RESTAURANTS

♦ Black Rabbit Restaurant at McMenamin's Edgefield, 2126 SW Halsey Street, Troutdale, OR 97060, (503) 492–3086.

♦ Mom's Garden Bakery and Café, 32030 East Historic Columbia River Highway, Springdale, OR 97060, (503) 695–3285.

♦ Tad's Chicken'n Dumplins, 1325 East Columbia River Highway, Troutdale, OR 97060, (503) 666–5337.

ACCOMMODATIONS

♦ Cedarplace Inn B&B, 2611 South Troutdale Road, Troutdale, OR 97060, (800) 267–4744, www.cedarplaceinn.com/accommodations.html.

♦ McMenamin's Edgefield, 2126 SW Halsey Street, Troutdale, OR 97060, (503) 669–8610. This 103-room European-style hotel features comfy rooms, a winery, brewery, movie theater, and restaurant. Room rates here are $85–$120, or you can opt for a hostel room for only $20 per person. Room prices include breakfast (except if you are staying in the men's or women's hostel dormitory).

The Sandy River is a favorite fishing spot.

BIKE SHOPS

♦ Bike Gallery, 2332 East Powell Boulevard, Gresham, OR 97080, (503) 669–5190.

♦ Gateway Bicycles, 11905 NE Halsey Street, Portland, OR 97220, (503) 254–0800, www.gatewaybicycles.com.

♦ Gresham Bicycle & Fitness Center, 567 NE 8th Street, Gresham, OR 97030, (503) 661–2453.

REST ROOMS

♦ Mile 0.0: Lewis and Clark State Park.
♦ Mile 3.0: Dabney State Park.
♦ Mile 19.8: Dodge Park.

MAPS

♦ USGS 7.5-minute quads Washougal, Camas, Sandy, and Bull Run; *DeLorme Oregon Atlas and Gazetteer,* maps 61 and 67.

18

Banks–Vernonia State Park Ramble

This fun family ride takes you on a paved multiuse trail through a fern-filled forest in rural Columbia County. The ride begins in Anderson Park in the small town of Vernonia and takes you on a scenic 14-mile out-and-back ride along the banks of the quiet Nehalem River and bubbling Beaver Creek.

This route takes you on a 14-mile out-and-back paved section of the 21-mile Banks/Vernonia State Park Seven miles of the northern half and more than 5 miles on the southern half of the trail are paved. The rest of the trail is gravel. This multiuse trail follows the old railway line from the community of Vernonia south to the small town of Banks. There are seven access points along this trail (starting at Anderson Park in Vernonia and ending in Banks). Beginning in the 1920s the original railway line carried lumber from the Oregon-American mill in Vernonia to the city

Smooth sailing on the Banks—Vernonia State Park Trail.

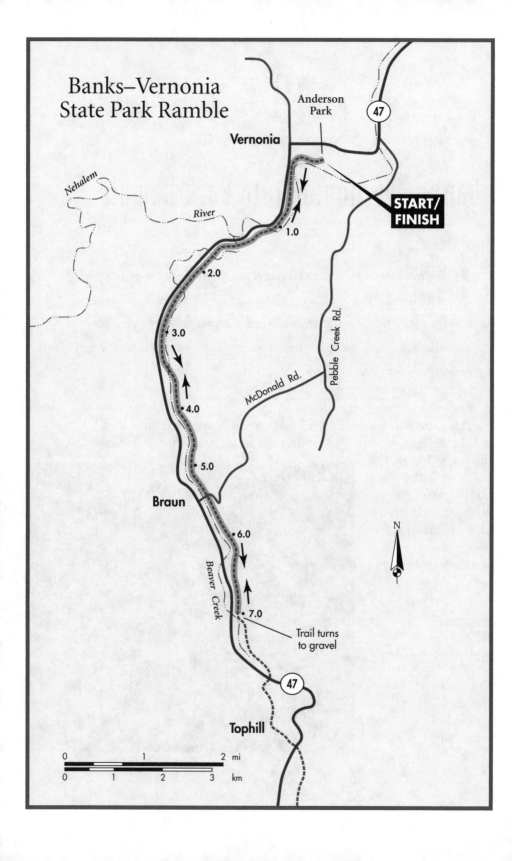

Banks–Vernonia
State Park Ramble

Anderson
Park

47

Vernonia

Nehalem

River

START/
FINISH

1.0

2.0

Pebble Creek Rd.

3.0

McDonald Rd.

4.0

5.0

Braun

N

6.0

Beaver Creek

7.0

Trail turns
to gravel

47

Tophill

0   1   2 mi
0   1   2   3 km

of Portland. In 1957 the lumber mill closed, and the railway line was subsequently forced to shut down. In 1974 the state highway department purchased the rights to use the land and officially transferred this right-of-way to the Oregon Parks and Recreation in 1990.

The tour begins in shady Anderson Park in Vernonia, which is located on the banks of the beautiful Nehalem River. A campground, picnic area, rest rooms, and showers can be found at this quiet park. From the park the route heads south through a shady Douglas fir forest. The paved path parallels busy Highway 47 but offers many distractions to keep your mind off the highway noise. Over the next 7 miles you'll ride over many picturesque wood bridges on the Nehalem River and Beaver Creek. The route parallels the Nehalem River for the first mile, then parallels bubbling Beaver Creek for about the next 5 miles. Use caution when crossing these

THE BASICS

Start: Anderson Park in Vernonia.
Length: 14 miles out and back.
Season: Year-round.
Approximate riding time: Two hours.
Recommended start time: 11:00 A.M.
Terrain: Paved multiuse path.
Traffic and hazards: Use caution when crossing wood bridges, which can be mossy and slick. Watch for tree debris and wet leaves from storms. When you're riding next to houses, keep an eye out for loose dogs—they are often protective of their owners' property and may try to chase you.
Getting there: From the intersection of I–405 and U.S. Highway 26 in Portland, head west on U.S. Highway 26 for about 28 miles to the junction with Highway 47. Turn north onto Highway 47 toward Vernonia. Go 14 miles to downtown Vernonia, and turn right onto Bridge Street. Continue 0.2 mile on Bridge Street, and turn right onto Jefferson Street. Go 0.4 mile and arrive at Anderson Park.

MILES AND DIRECTIONS

Start by turning south (right) onto the paved multiuse path
1.0 Cross the Nehalem River.
7.0 The paved path ends. Turn around and retrace the route to your starting point at Anderson Park.

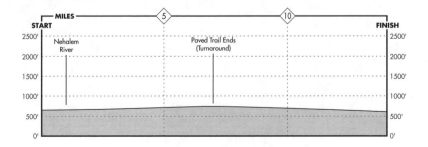

wood bridges during rainy weather. They are covered with moss and become very slick when it's wet out. After 7 miles the path turns to gravel. This is your turnaround point. Retrace the route back to your starting point at Anderson Park in Vernonia.

LOCAL INFORMATION

♦ Oregon State Parks and Recreation, 1115 Commercial Street NE, Suite 1, Salem, OR 97301-1002, (800) 551–6949, www.oregonstateparks.org.

LOCAL EVENTS/ATTRACTIONS

♦ The Washington County Museum (PCC Rock Creek Campus), 17677 NW Springville Road, Portland, OR 97229, (503) 645–5353.

RESTAURANTS

♦ Cornelius Pass Roadhouse, 4045 NW Cornelius Pass Road, Portland, OR 97124, (503) 640-6174.

ACCOMMODATIONS

♦ Vernonia Inn, 900 Madison Avenue, Vernonia, OR 97064, (541) 429–4006.

BIKE SHOPS

♦ Bike N Hike, 156 SE 4th Avenue, Hillsboro, OR 97123, (503) 681–0594.

REST ROOMS

♦ Mile 0.0: Anderson Park.

MAPS

♦ USGS 7.5-minute quad Vernonia; *DeLorme Oregon Atlas and Gazetteer,* map 65.

North Plains Ramble

Т his ride takes you on a tour of the beautiful rolling hills of rural Washington County. Century-old farms, nurseries, and wineries are some of the many sights along this hilly route. You'll also have the chance to sample some of Oregon's award-winning microbrews and burgers at the Rogue Brew Pub in North Plains and the Helvetia Tavern in Helvetia.

Rural Washington County offers premier road riding, and this route takes you on a tour through some of its most beautiful scenery. Washington County rests on an ancient bed of basalt lava located on the western edge of the Columbia Plateau. Twenty million years ago this area was covered with lava that flowed down the Columbia River basin from eastern Oregon. After the last ice age, water flooded the area and upon receding deposited sand, gravel, and a layer of topsoil throughout the region. These rich deposits, combined with the region's fairly mild temperatures, are perfect for growing specialty crops, such as grass seed, hazelnuts, berries, hops, wine grapes, and nursery products.

The route starts at the Rogue Brew Pub, which serves local microbrews, wines, and delicious burgers. You'll pedal north for 3 miles on Shadybrook Road. This quiet rural road winds through picturesque countryside filled with grazing sheep and cattle. It serves as a good warm-up for the hill climb that begins when you turn onto Mason Hill Road at 4.3 miles. Mason Hill Road climbs more than 250 feet past fields of grapes, century-old farms, and executive homes. As you climb higher you'll have unsurpassed views of the northern Tualatin Valley, and the route becomes more forested. After just less than a mile of hill climbing, you'll turn southeast onto Jackson Quarry Road and begin a fun, twisting descent through pockets of shady Douglas fir forest.

After a few miles of descending, the route turns east onto Helvetia Road and winds through more spectacular farming country. This area was settled by Swiss and German immigrants in the late 1800s. Before prohibition, it had a burgeoning wine industry and was known as Grape Hill. Near the halfway point in the ride, have lunch at the Helvetia Tavern, which features mouthwatering burgers and fries. From here you'll finish by riding through more rural countryside back to your starting point in North Plains.

LOCAL INFORMATION

♦ Washington County Visitors Association, 5075 SW Griffith Drive, #120, Beaverton, OR 97005, (800) 537–3149, www.wcva.org.

LOCAL EVENTS/ATTRACTIONS

♦ Helvetia Winery, 22485 NW Yungen Road, Hillsboro, OR 97124, www. helvetiawinery.com.

Scenic Helvetia hill country.

Start: North Plains.

Length: 18.5-mile loop.

Season: Year-round.

Approximate riding time: Two to three hours.

Recommended start time: 11:00 A.M.

Terrain: Rural roads.

Traffic and hazards: Use caution on the three railroad crossings on this route. West Union Road can be very busy. Avoid riding this route during morning and evening rush hour.

Getting there: From the intersection of I–405 and Highway 26 in Portland, head west on Highway 26 for about 18 miles to exit 57 signed for NORTH PLAINS. At the end of the off-ramp, turn right (north) onto Glencoe Road, and continue 0.4 mile to the intersection with Commercial Street. Turn left onto Commercial Street, go 0.8 mile, and park in front of the Rogue Brew Pub on the left side of the road.

RESTAURANTS

♦ Helvetia Tavern, 10275 NW Helvetia Road, Hillsboro, OR 97124, (503) 647–5286.

♦ Rogue Brew Pub & Eatery, 31500 NW Commercial Street, North Plains, OR 97133, (503) 647–5268, www.roguepub.com.

ACCOMMODATIONS

♦ The Yankee Tinker B&B, 5480 SW 183rd Avenue, Beaverton, OR 97007, (503) 649–0932, www.yankeetinker.com.

BIKE SHOPS

♦ Bike N Hike, 156 SE 4th Avenue, Hillsboro, OR 97123, (503) 681–0594.

REST ROOMS

♦ Mile 0.0: Rogue Ale Brew Pub.
♦ Mile 9.0: Helvetia Tavern.

MAPS

♦ USGS 7.5-minute quads Hillsboro, and Dixie Mountain; *DeLorme Oregon Atlas and Gazetteer,* map 66.

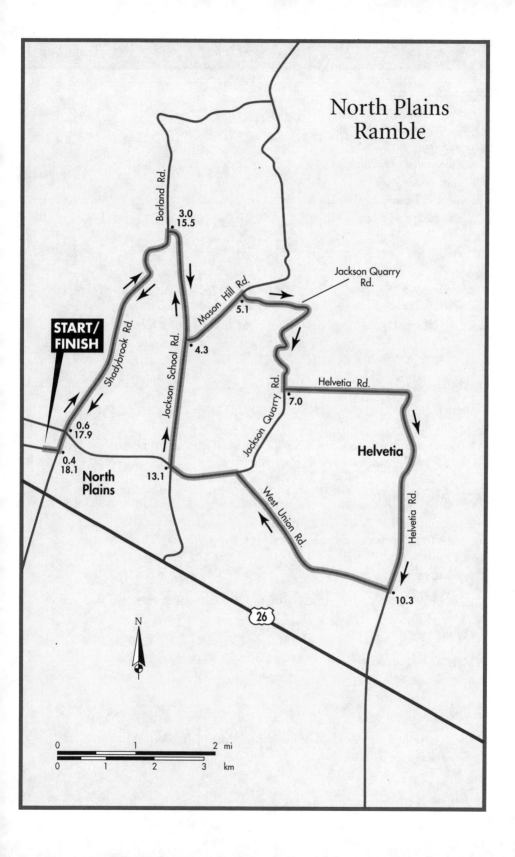

North Plains Ramble

Borland Rd.

3.0
15.5

Jackson Quarry Rd.

Mason Hill Rd.

5.1

**START/
FINISH**

Shadybrook Rd.

Jackson School Rd.

4.3

Helvetia Rd.

7.0

Jackson Quarry Rd.

Helvetia

0.6
17.9

0.4
18.1

**North
Plains**

13.1

West Union Rd.

Helvetia Rd.

10.3

26

N

0		1		2 mi

| 0 | 1 | 2 | 3 km |

Start by turning right onto Commercial Street.

0.4 Turn left onto Glencoe Road.

0.5 Cross the railroad tracks.

0.6 Turn right onto Shadybrook Road.

1.5 Turn right, and keep riding on Shadybrook Road (Pumpkin Ridge Road goes left).

3.0 Turn right onto Jackson School Road.

4.3 Turn left onto Mason Hill Road, and begin climbing steeply.

5.1 Turn right onto Jackson Quarry Road, and begin a steep descent.

7.0 Turn left onto Helvetia Road.

9.0 Pass Helvetia Tavern on the right.

10.3 Turn right onto West Union Road.

13.1 Turn right onto Jackson School Road.

13.4 Cross the railroad tracks.

15.5 Turn left onto Shadybrook Road.

17.9 Shadybrook Road merges with Glencoe Road.

18.0 Cross the railroad tracks.

18.1 Turn right onto Commercial Street

18.5 Arrive back at the Rogue Ale Brew Pub.

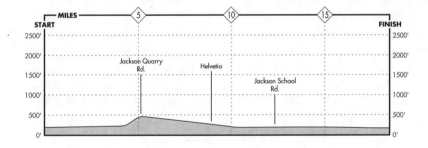

Brownsville–Coburg Covered Bridges Cruise

Thisᵗ loop route begins in the historic town of Brownsville and takes you through the picturesque Crawfordsville Valley past two historic covered bridges. It then travels through thick-forested hills and returns via Coburg back to your starting point in Brownsville.

This scenic tour starts at Pioneer Park in the small community of Brownsville, tucked away in picturesque Crawfordsville Valley between Salem and Eugene. It was originally settled in 1846 by three pioneer families: the Kirks, Browns, and Blakelys. To find out more about the history of these families and other settlers, visit the Linn County Museum in downtown Brownsville. The museum also has a free walking-tour map so you can view many of the historic buildings and houses in the community. If you need to fuel up before you head out, stop for a hearty breakfast and fresh coffee at the Saddle Butte Coffee Company.

The route heads east out of town on Northern Drive. Northern Drive travels past many historic houses, then takes you into the misty Crawfordsville Valley past fields of sheep and cattle. The Calapooia River sweeps through this sleepy valley. Just shy of 8 miles, be sure to stop and view the Crawfordsville covered bridge. This historic white bridge was built in 1932 and spans the meandering Calapooia River. It was the backdrop to the 1976 movie *The Flood*. The route continues east and takes you through Crawfordsville, where you can stock up on snacks and drinks at the Crawfordsville Market. The route then swings south onto Brush Creek Road, begins climbing past thick second-growth forest for the next 6 miles, and then winds downhill. If you want to take a break from the saddle, stop at Shotgun Creek Park at 20.2 miles. This is a quiet spot along the banks of bubbling Shotgun Creek.

Your next stop is the Earnest covered bridge built in 1938. This bright white bridge spans the Mohawk River and was featured in the 1987 civil war movie *Shenandoah*. From here you'll pedal through rolling hills for the next 10 miles as the route travels through the communities of Marcola and Mohawk. After 31.4 miles you'll turn west onto McKenzie View Drive. This scenic road travels past expensive homes and hobby farms and promises grand views of the McKenzie River. If you want to stay and explore this area more, stop and spend the night at the McKenzie View B&B at mile 33.1 (be sure to call ahead for availability). This impressive B&B has six acres of grounds along the shores of the McKenzie River. As you continue the route swings north and hooks up with Coburg Road, which takes you through the sleepy town of Coburg. The route continues north on flat terrain through miles of green fields filled with grazing sheep, cows, and horses. Just shy of 50 miles, the route turns east onto Diamond Hill Drive, then swings north on Gap Road and takes you through more scenic farm country and back to your starting point at Brownsville. Just before you end the ride, take time to explore the historic Italian villa–style Moyer House, which was built by John and Elizabeth Moyer in 1881. The exterior of the house features fancy carved finials, corner boards, frieze boards, and eave's brackets. The house is open for tours on weekends.

THE BASICS

Start: Pioneer Park in Brownsville.

Length: 61-mile loop.

Season: Year-round.

Approximate riding time: Five to seven hours.

Recommended start time: 9:00 A.M.

Terrain: Major highway combined with rural roads.

Traffic and hazards: Watch for moderate to heavy traffic on Highway 228. Donna Road and McKenzie View Drive are very narrow and twisty. Watch for cars on blind curves, and use caution on descents.

Getting there: From Salem at exit 253, DETROIT LAKE/HIGHWAY 22, drive south on I-5 for 36.5 miles to exit 216, HALSEY/BROWNSVILLE/HIGHWAY 228. At the end of the off-ramp, turn left (east) onto Highway 228, and drive 3.9 miles to downtown Brownsville. Turn left onto Main Street toward PIONEER PARK/CITY CENTER. Go 0.4 mile on Main Street and turn left onto Park Avenue. Proceed 0.2 mile on Park Avenue to Pioneer Park.

From Eugene, drive approximately 23 miles north on I-5 to exit 216, HALSEY/BROWNSVILLE/HIGHWAY 228. At the end of the off-ramp, turn right (east) onto Highway 228, and drive 3.9 miles to downtown Brownsville. Turn left onto Main Street toward PIONEER PARK/CITY CENTER. Go 0.4 mile on Main Street, and turn left onto Park Avenue. Proceed 0.2 mile on Park Avenue to Pioneer Park.

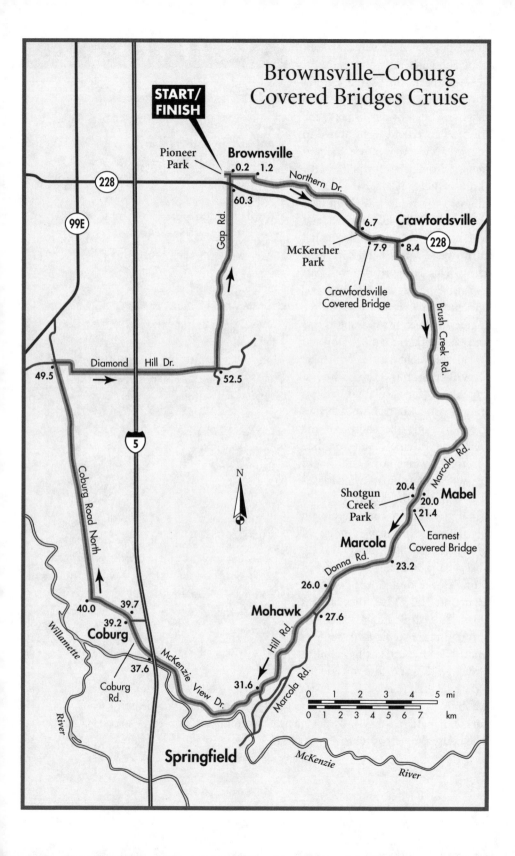

Brownsville–Coburg
Covered Bridges Cruise

START/FINISH

Pioneer Park

Brownsville
0.2   1.2

Northern Dr.

60.3

228

99E

6.7   **Crawfordsville**

McKercher Park

7.9   8.4   228

Crawfordsville Covered Bridge

Brush Creek Rd.

Diamond   Hill   Dr.

49.5

52.5

Gap Rd.

5

N

Marcola Rd.

Shotgun Creek Park   20.4

20.0   **Mabel**

21.4

Earnest Covered Bridge

Marcola

Coburg Road North

Donna Rd.

23.2

26.0

40.0   39.7   **Mohawk**   27.6

39.2

Coburg

37.6

McKenzie View Dr.

Coburg Rd.

Hill Rd.

31.6

Marcola Rd.

0   1   2   3   4   5 mi
0   1   2   3   4   5   6   7   km

Springfield

Willamette   River

McKenzie   River

Start by riding out of the Pioneer Park on Park Avenue.

0.2 Turn right onto Main Street.

0.3 Turn left onto Kirk Avenue.

1.2 Stay to the right on Northern Drive.

6.7 At the stop sign and T-intersection, turn left onto Highway 228.

7.0 Pass McKercher Park on your right. Rest rooms are available at the park.

7.9 Pass the Crawfordsville covered bridge on your right. This bridge was built in 1932 and spans the Calapooia River.

8.0 Pass the Crawfordsville Market on your right.

8.4 Turn right onto Brush Creek Road toward MARCOLA.

20.0 You'll arrive in Mabel.

20.4 Pass Shotgun Creek Park on your right.

21.4 Turn left onto Paschelke Road to view the Earnest covered bridge. This bridge was built in 1938 and spans the Mohawk River. After viewing the bridge continue riding on Brush Creek Road.

23.2 Enter Marcola.

26.0 Turn right onto Donna Road.

27.6 Turn right onto Hill Road. This turnoff is just past Mohawk General Store.

31.6 Turn right onto McKenzie View Drive toward Coburg.

33.1 Pass the McKenzie View B&B on your left.

37.6 At stop sign and T-intersection, turn right onto Coburg Road.

39.2 Enter Coburg.

39.6 Pass the Coburg Café on the right.

39.7 Turn left onto Van Duyn Street. Van Duyn Street eventually turns into Coburg Road.

40.0 Turn right onto Coburg Road North.

49.5 At the stop sign and T-intersection, turn right onto Diamond Hill Drive.

52.5 Stay to the left. Diamond Hill Drive turns into Gap Road. (When you enter Brownsville, Gap Road turns into Washburn Street.)

(continued)

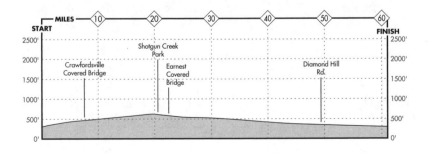

60.3 At the stop sign turn right onto Highway 228.

60.4 Turn left onto Main Street.

60.8 Turn left onto Park Street. This turnoff is 200 yards past the historic Moyer House.

61.0 Arrive at Pioneer Park.

LOCAL INFORMATION

♦ Brownsville Chamber of Commerce, PO Box 278, Brownsville, OR 97327, (541) 466–5311, www.brownsvilleoregon.org.

LOCAL EVENTS/ATTRACTIONS

♦ Antique Fair, held in mid-August, PO Box 278, Brownsville, OR 97327, (541) 466–5311.

♦ Linn County Historical Museum, 101 Park, PO Box 607, Brownsville, OR 97327, (541) 466–3390, www.lchm-friends.peak.org/WEBSIT~1/Page_1x. html. The museum and Moyer House are open 11:00 A.M. to 4:00 P.M. on Saturday, and 1:00 to 4:00 P.M. on Sunday.

♦ Oktoberfest, held in October, PO Box 278, Brownsville, OR 97327, (541) 466–5311.

♦ Pioneer Picnic, held in June, PO Box 278, Brownsville, OR 97327, (541) 466–5311.

RESTAURANTS

♦ Saddle Butte Coffee Co., PO Box 896, Brownsville, OR 97327, (541) 466–3559.

ACCOMMODATIONS

♦ Atavista Farm B&B, 35580 Highway 228, Brownsville, OR 97327, (541) 466–5566, home.centurytel.net/Atavista/.

♦ McKenzie View B&B, 34922 McKenzie View Drive, Springfield, OR 97478, (541) 726–6968, www.mckenzie-view.com.

BIKE SHOPS

Salem

♦ Bike N Hike Centers, 887 Commercial Street SE, Salem, OR 97302, (503) 581–2707.

The Italian villa–style Moyer House, built in 1881.

- Bike Peddler, 174 Commercial Street NE, Salem, OR 97301, (503) 399–7741.
- Santiam Bicycle Way of Life, 388 Commercial Street NE, Salem, OR 97301, (503) 363–6602.
- Scotts Cycle, 147 Commercial Street SE, Salem, OR 97301, (503) 363–4516.

Eugene
- Bike Barn, 465 Coburg Road, Eugene, OR 97401, (541) 342–5757.
- Blue Heron Bicycles, 877 East 13th Avenue, Eugene, OR 97401, (541) 343–2488.
- Eugene Bicycle Works, 455 West 1st Avenue, Eugene, OR 97401, (541) 683–3397.
- Hutch's Bicycle Store Eugene, 960 Charnelton Street, Eugene, OR 97401, (541) 345–7521.
- Mike's Bike Shop, 930 River Road, Eugene, OR 97404, (541) 461–0016. Paul's Bicycle Way of Life, 152 West 5th Avenue, Eugene, OR 97401, (541) 344–4105.

REST ROOMS

- Mile 0.0: Pioneer Park.
- Mile 7.0: McKercher Park.

MAPS

- USGS 7.5-minute quads Brownsville, Crawfordsville, Marcola, Mohawk, Springfield, Eugene East, Coburg, Indian Head, and Union Point; *DeLorme Oregon Atlas and Gazetteer,* maps 47 and 48.

Fern Ridge Reservoir— Coast Foothills Ramble

his loop tour begins at Fern Ridge Reservoir and takes you through the coast foothills west of Eugene. The route travels on peaceful rural roads past green pastures filled with grazing cattle, sheep, llamas, and horses. This moderately hilly ride also promises outstanding views of the shimmering green Willamette Valley and Cascade peaks to the east. During the summer months you can cool off in the refreshing waters of Fern Hill Reservoir.

This tour starts at scenic Orchard Point Park, located on the north end of Fern Ridge Reservoir. The park has rest rooms, water, and picnic facilities, as well as a boat launch. The reservoir is a popular outdoor attraction for fishing, boating, sailing, and swimming during the summer months. This man-made lake has about 30 miles of shoreline and an average water depth of 11 feet. The Long Tom

Fern Ridge Reservoir.

Start: Orchard Point Park, Eugene.

Length: 34.1-mile loop.

Season: Year-round.

Approximate riding time: Three to four hours.

Recommended start time: 10:00 A.M.

Terrain: Major highways and rural roads.

Traffic and hazards: Watch for traffic on Highway 36 and when you cross the Territorial Highway. Wear bright colors, and watch your speed on descents—some of the rural roads on this route are narrow and twisty.

Getting there: From I-5 in Eugene take exit 194B for EUGENE HIGHWAY 105/126. Head west for 1.4 miles, and take exit 2 for COBURG ROAD/DOWNTOWN. Go 2 miles and follow signs for HIGHWAY 126 WEST/FLORENCE (you are now on 6th Avenue). Proceed 1 mile, then turn left onto Garfield Street toward VENETA/FLORENCE/ELMIRA. Go 0.4 mile, and turn right onto 126 West toward VENETA/FLORENCE/ELMIRA. Head west on Highway 126 for 4.3 miles, then turn right (north) onto Green Hill Road. Travel 3.5 miles on Green Hill Road, then turn left (west) onto Clear Lake Road. Go 3.8 miles on Clear Lake Road, and turn left into Orchard Point Park. Note that there is a $3.00 parking fee at this park from Memorial Day weekend through Labor Day weekend.

River feeds the reservoir from the north, and several other creeks flow into the reservoir. Fishing enthusiasts enjoy catching panfish, crappie, bluegill, and largemouth bass. Wildlife and more than 250 species of birds inhabit the area during different seasons of the year, including blue herons, ducks, swans, geese, egrets, osprey, bald eagles, and a variety of shorebirds.

This route explores the rural countryside of the coast foothills located west of the lake. The terrain is mainly on backroads with no shoulder but very light traffic. The route has several fun ups and downs and small sections that are on busier highways. You'll pedal past large pastures filled with sheep, goats, cattle, horses, and llamas against a backdrop of pine-scented forest. At the route's high points, you'll have endless views of Eugene, the vast Willamette Valley, and the Cascade Mountains to the east. As you pedal the route, keep a sharp eye out for an abundance of hawks hunting the open fields. These keen-eyed raptors are often seen perching in trees, on fence posts, and on phone poles looking for their next meal. Red-tailed hawks are one of the more common hawks you'll see. These heavy-bodied birds can be identified by their distinctive reddish brown tail and cinnamon-brown and white undersides. If you want to explore this area more, you can camp at Richardson Park. The campground is open from mid-April through mid-October.

LOCAL INFORMATION

♦ Lane County Parks, 90064 Coburg Road, Eugene, OR 97408, (541) 682–4414, www.co.lane.or.us/parks/laneParks.htm.

LOCAL EVENTS/ATTRACTIONS

♦ Lane County Fair, held in August, Eugene, OR (541) 682–4292.
♦ Oregon Bach Festival, held in June, 1257 University of Oregon, Eugene, OR 97403–1257, (800) 457–1486, www.bachfest.uoregon.edu.

RESTAURANTS

♦ High Street Brewery and Café, 1243 High Street, Eugene, OR 97401, (541) 345–4905.
♦ Keystone Café, 395 West 5th Avenue, Eugene, OR 97401, (541) 342–2075.
♦ Steelhead Brewery, 188 East 5th Avenue, Eugene, OR 97401, (541) 686–2739.

ACCOMMODATIONS

♦ The Oval Door B&B, 988 Lawrence Street, Eugene, OR 97401, (800) 882–3160, www.ovaldoor.com.
♦ Richardson Park, Fern Ridge Reservoir, Eugene, OR 97408, (541) 682–2000, www.co.lane.or.us/parks/richard.htm. The campground is open from mid-April through mid-October.

BIKE SHOPS

♦ Bike Barn, 465 Coburg Road, Eugene, OR 97401, (541) 342–5757.
♦ Blue Heron Bicycles, 877 East 13th Avenue, Eugene, OR 97401, (541) 343–2488.
♦ Eugene Bicycle Works, 455 West 1st Avenue, Eugene, OR 97401, (541) 683–3397.
♦ Hutch's Bicycle Store Eugene, 960 Charnelton Street, Eugene, OR 97401, (541) 345–7521.
♦ Mike's Bike Shop, 930 River Road, Eugene, OR 97404, (541) 461–0016.
♦ Paul's Bicycle Way of Life, 152 West 5th Avenue, Eugene, OR 97401, (541) 344–4105.

REST ROOMS

♦ Mile 0.0: Orchard Point Park.
♦ Mile 2.4: Richardson Park.

MAPS

♦ USGS 7.5-minute quads Veneta, Cheshire, and Junction City; *DeLorme Oregon Atlas and Gazetteer,* map 47.

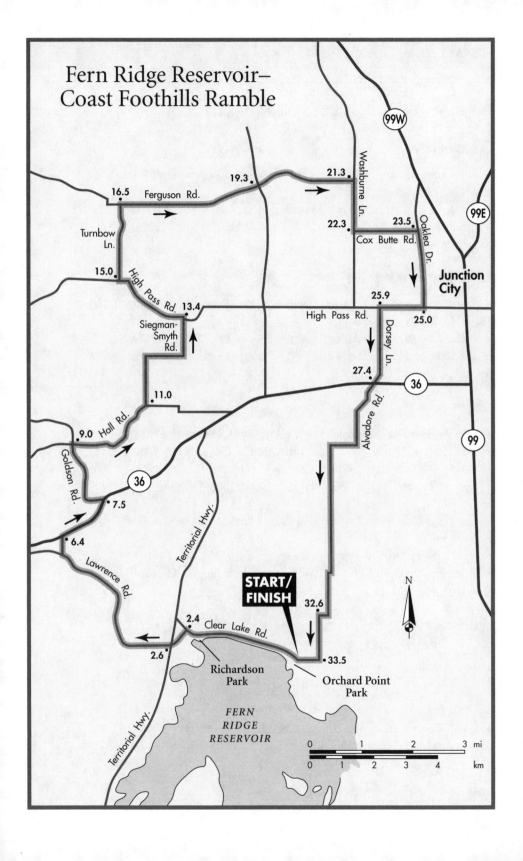

Fern Ridge Reservoir–
Coast Foothills Ramble

99W

99E

16.5 Ferguson Rd. 19.3 21.3 Washburne Ln.

Turnbow Ln.

22.3 23.5 Oaklea Dr.

Cox Butte Rd.

Junction City

15.0 High Pass Rd. 13.4

25.9

Siegman-Smyth Rd.

High Pass Rd.

25.0

11.0

Dorsey Ln.

27.4 36

Hall Rd.

9.0

Alvadore Rd.

Goldson Rd.

36 99

7.5

6.4

Lawrence Rd.

Territorial Hwy.

START/
FINISH

32.6

N

2.4 Clear Lake Rd.

2.6

33.5

Richardson Park

Orchard Point Park

FERN
RIDGE
RESERVOIR

Territorial Hwy.

0   1   2   3 mi

0   1   2   3   4 km

Start by turning left onto Clear Lake Road.

2.4 Pass Richardson Park on the left. Campsites and rest rooms are available at this park.

2.6 Cross Territorial Highway, and continue pedaling on Lawrence Road.

6.4 Turn right onto Highway 36.

7.5 Turn left onto Goldson Road. Begin climbing steeply.

9.0 Turn right onto Hall Road.

11.0 Turn left onto Siegman-Smyth Road.

13.4 Turn left onto High Pass Road.

15.0 Turn right onto Turnbow Lane.

16.5 Turn right onto Ferguson Road.

19.3 Cross the Territorial Highway, and continue pedaling on Ferguson Road.

21.3 Turn right onto Washburne Lane.

22.3 Turn left onto Cox Butte Road.

23.5 Turn right onto Oaklea Drive.

25.0 Turn right onto High Pass Road.

25.9 Turn left onto Dorsey Lane.

27.4 At the stop sign and intersection with Highway 36, continue straight onto Alvadore Road.

32.6 Arrive at a Y-junction. Stay to the left, and continue riding on Alvadore Road.

33.5 Turn right onto Clear Lake Road.

34.1 Turn left into Orchard Point Park.

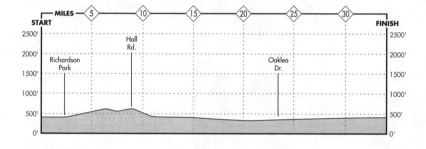

Willamette River Ramble

T his short loop tour is a great introduction to the extensive bike-ways in Eugene. The route begins at Alton Baker Park down-town and takes you through cottonwood forest and picturesque parks along the banks of the Willamette River. This is a great family ride with plenty of opportunities to stop and explore the many beautiful parks in Eugene.

Eugene is one of the most bike-friendly cities in Oregon and is host to more than 28 miles of dedicated bike paths and more than 78 miles of on-street bicycle lanes. This short tour will give you a good introduction to this city, which prides itself on alternative transportation. The tour starts at scenic Alton Baker Park located on the banks of the Willamette River in downtown Eugene. The park has rest rooms; water; a pond; picnic tables; and running, walking, and biking paths. From the park the route heads southeast along the banks of the Willamette River. You'll pedal past shady cotton-

Willamette River.

woods, and you'll have plenty of scenic views of the wide Willamette. After 2 short miles you'll cross the Willamette River on the Knickerbocker Bike Bridge. This bridge is one of four dedicated bike bridges in the city. After crossing the bridge the route turns northwest. You'll pedal through some business parks, and you'll have to ride a short distance on some quiet city streets before you meet the South Bank Trail at 3.3 miles.

After you turn onto the South Bank Trail, the route continues on its northwest journey along the banks of the Willamette. You'll sail past the smooth greens of Skinner Butte Park, and after 5.3 miles you'll arrive at the Owen Rose Gardens. Colorful varieties of roses can be seen here, with the peak blooming period in May and June. The park is also home to a famous cherry tree

THE BASICS

Start: Alton Baker Park, Eugene.
Length: 7.7-mile loop.
Season: Year-round.
Approximate riding time: One hour.
Recommended start time: 9:00 A.M.
Terrain: Dedicated bike/pedestrian path and quiet city streets.
Traffic and hazards: Watch for pedestrians and runners on this popular route.
Getting there: From the intersection of 7th Street and Pearl Street in downtown Eugene, turn left onto 7th Street and follow signs to Coburg Road. Go 0.5 mile, and cross the Ferry Street Bridge over the Willamette River. After crossing the bridge turn right onto Centennial Boulevard, and go 0.2 mile to the intersection with Club Road. Turn right onto Club Road, continue 0.1 mile, and turn left into Alton Baker Park.

that is thought to be more than 100 years old. At 5.9 miles you'll pedal across the Greenway Bike Bridge. (If you are craving more mileage, don't cross the bridge here; instead, continue north on the bike path for about another 2.5 miles, then head back to the bridge.) After crossing the bridge the route turns southeast, takes you past the Valley River Shopping Mall, and continues along the shores of the Willamette River until you reach Alton Baker Park at 7.7 miles.

LOCAL INFORMATION

♦ Eugene Parks, 1820 Roosevelt Boulevard, Eugene, OR 97401, (541) 682–4800, www.ci.eugene.or.us/PW/PARKS/index.htm.

LOCAL EVENTS/ATTRACTIONS

♦ Lane County Fair, held in August, 796 West 13th Avenue, Eugene, OR 97402 (541) 682–4292.
♦ Oregon Bach Festival, held in June, 1257 University of Oregon, Eugene, OR 97403–1257, (800) 457–1486, www.bachfest.uoregon.edu.

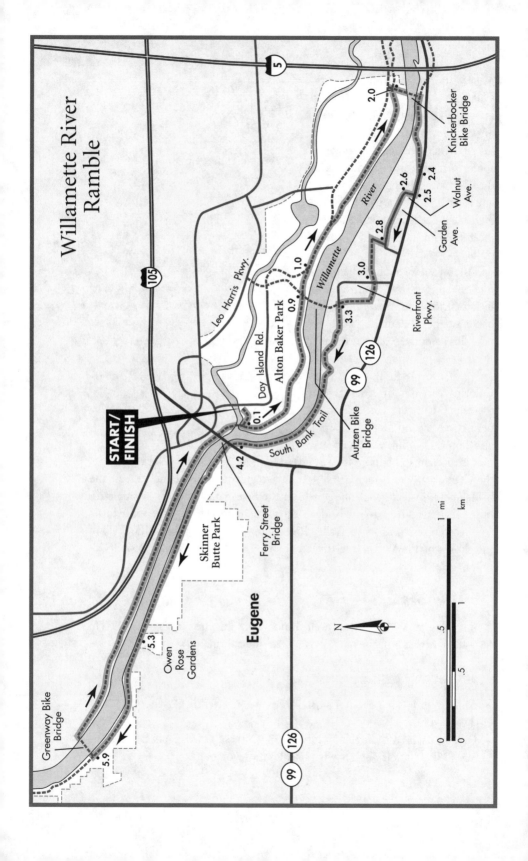

Willamette River Ramble

Knickerbocker Bike Bridge

2.0

Walnut Ave.

2.6
2.5 2.4

Garden Ave.

2.8

3.0

Riverfront Pkwy.

Willamette River

126

99

Autzen Bike Bridge

South Bank Trail

3.3

Leo Harris Pkwy.

1.0

0.9

Day Island Rd.

Alton Baker Park

0.1

START/FINISH

4.2

Ferry Street Bridge

Skinner Butte Park

Eugene

Owen Rose Gardens

5.3

Greenway Bike Bridge

5.9

105

126

99

N

1 mi

km

.5

.5

1

1

0

0

Start by picking up the paved path that goes around the edge of a large pond and heads toward the river.

0.1 Turn left (south) onto the paved path that parallels the Willamette River.

0.9 Ride under the Autzen Bike Bridge. After going under the bridge, the path forks. Go right.

1.0 The paved path joins a paved road.

1.3 Turn right onto the narrower bike path.

2.0 Turn right and cross the Knickerbocker Bike Bridge. After crossing the bridge turn right (north), and continue following the paved path as it parallels the river.

2.4 The bike path parallels Highway 99.

2.5 Turn right onto Walnut Avenue.

2.6 Turn left onto Garden Avenue.

2.8 Turn right and continue riding onto Garden Avenue.

2.9 Turn left onto the signed MILL RACE paved path.

3.1 Cross Riverfront Parkway, and continue riding on the paved bike path, where a sign states RIVERBANK TRAILS. Ride about 200 yards, and take a very sharp right turn on a wide, paved path toward the river.

3.3 Turn left onto the signed SOUTH BANK TRAIL.

4.2 Ride under a bike bridge and the Ferry Street Bridge.

5.0 Pass rest rooms and a water fountain on the left.

5.3 Pass the Owen Rose Gardens on the left. Be sure to check out the old cherry tree next to the rose garden.

5.9 Turn right, and cross the Greenway Bike Bridge. After crossing the bridge turn right (south), and follow the paved bike path back to your starting point at Alton Baker Park.

7.7 Arrive at Alton Baker Park.

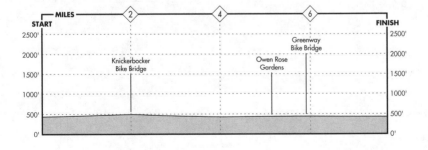

♦ High Street Brewery and Café, 1243 High Street, Eugene, OR 97401, (541) 345–4905.

♦ Keystone Café, 395 West 5th Avenue, Eugene, OR 97401, (541) 342–2075.

♦ Steelhead Brewery, 188 East 5th Avenue, Eugene, OR 97401, (541) 686–2739.

ACCOMMODATIONS

♦ The Oval Door B&B, 988 Lawrence Street, Eugene, OR 97401, (800) 882–3160, www.ovaldoor.com.

BIKE SHOPS

♦ Bike Barn, 465 Coburg Road, Eugene, OR 97401, (541) 342–5757.

♦ Blue Heron Bicycles, 877 East 13th Avenue, Eugene, OR 97401, (541) 343–2488.

♦ Eugene Bicycle Works, 455 West 1st Avenue, Eugene, OR 97401, (541) 683–3397.

♦ Hutch's Bicycle Store Eugene, 960 Charnelton Street, Eugene, OR 97401, (541) 345–7521.

♦ Mike's Bike Shop, 930 River Road, Eugene, OR 97404, (541) 461–0016.

♦ Paul's Bicycle Way of Life, 152 West 5th Avenue, Eugene, OR 97401, (541) 344–4105.

REST ROOMS

♦ Mile 0.0: Alton Baker Park.

♦ Mile 5.0: Rest rooms and water.

MAPS

♦ USGS 7.5-minute quad Eugene East; *DeLorme Oregon Atlas and Gazetteer*, map 47.

Jasper State Park—
Covered Bridges Ramble

T his tour begins in Jasper State Park, located off Highway 58 southeast of Eugene. The route travels through scenic farming country filled with friendly small towns and picturesque covered bridges.

This tour begins in the green paradise of Jasper State Park. Shade trees, grassy lawns, picnic tables, and rest rooms make this a good starting point for your ride. The route starts out parallel to the Middle Fork of the Willamette River, which is lined with stately cottonwood trees. The Middle Fork is the largest tributary on the upper Willamette and joins the Coast Fork of the Willamette south of Eugene. Enjoy the views of the river, but also look out for logging trucks. Just shy of 5 miles, the route takes you past the Pengra covered bridge. This stately white bridge was built in 1938 and spans Fall Creek. It replaced an older bridge that was built at the same location in 1904. The present bridge fell into near ruin but was restored and reopened in 1994. This bridge has the longest timbers of any covered bridge in Oregon.

The route continues southeast on Jasper-Lowell Road and soon enters the community of Fall Creek, where you have the option of stocking up on drinks and snacks at the Fall Creek Market. After you pedal another 3 miles, you'll cross the Unity covered bridge. This picturesque bridge spans Fall Creek and was built in 1936. It features a large window on its east side, which allows motorists to see oncoming traffic. At 11.4 miles you'll arrive at Lowell City Park, which features the miniature 1988 Cannon Street covered bridge. The community of Lowell was named when Amos D. Hyland came to the area in the 1850s from Lowell, Maine. This park is a good spot to take a break and eat lunch.

Start: Jasper State Park, Jasper.

Length: 27.1-mile loop.

Season: Year-round.

Approximate riding time: Three to four hours.

Recommended start time: 11:00 A.M.

Terrain: Major highway and rural roads.

Traffic and hazards: Watch for log trucks.

Getting there: From I–5 in Eugene take exit 188A for HIGHWAY 58/OAKRIDGE. Turn east onto Highway 58, and proceed 5.3 miles to Parkway Road. Turn left onto Parkway Road toward JASPER/JASPER PARK/SPRINGFIELD. Go 2.1 miles on Parkway Road, then turn right onto Jasper Park Drive. Continue 0.1 mile on Jasper Park Drive to Jasper State Park. A $3.00 day-use parking permit is required at this state park.

The route continues south and crosses the Dexter Reservoir. Just after 12 miles you can stop at a paved parking area and soak in views of the reservoir and Lowell covered bridge. This 165-foot-long bridge was built in 1945. This roadside stop is also a popular spot for anglers. After viewing the bridge you'll turn onto busy Highway 58. Use caution when riding on this high-traffic road. Soon enough you'll leave the busy highway behind when you turn onto Lost Creek Road. The route continues in a southwest direction through rural countryside until you reach the Parvin covered bridge at 15.4 miles. This 75-foot-long bridge spans Lost Creek and was built in 1921. From here the route continues northwest, and for the next 12 miles you'll pedal on quiet roads past farms and orchards until you complete the loop at Jasper State Park.

LOCAL INFORMATION

♦ Oregon State Parks and Recreation, 1115 Commercial Street NE, Suite 1, Salem, OR 97301-1002, (800) 551–6949, www.oregonstateparks.org.

LOCAL EVENTS/ATTRACTIONS

♦ Lane County Fair, held in August, 796 West 13th Avenue, Eugene, OR 97402 (541) 682–4292.

♦ Oregon Bach Festival, held in June, 1257 University of Oregon, Eugene, OR 97403-1257, (800) 457–1486, www.bachfest.uoregon.edu.

RESTAURANTS

♦ My Place Restaurant, 38382 Dexter Road, Dexter, OR 97431, (541) 937–1949.

ACCOMMODATIONS

♦ The Campbell House, A City Inn, 252 Pearl Street, Eugene, OR 97401, (541) 343–1119 or (800) 264–2519, www.campbellhouse.com.

Pengra covered bridge.

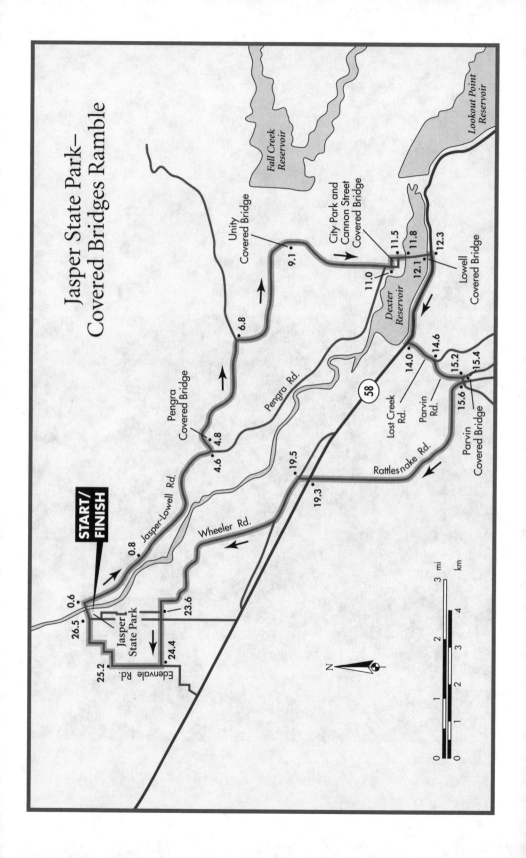

Jasper State Park–
Covered Bridges Ramble

Fall Creek
Reservoir

Lookout Point
Reservoir

Unity
Covered Bridge

City Park and
Cannon Street
Covered Bridge

9.1

11.5
11.8
11.0
12.1
12.3

Dexter
Reservoir

Lowell
Covered Bridge

6.8

Pengra
Covered Bridge

Pengra Rd.

58

14.0
14.6
15.2
15.4

Lost Creek
Rd.

Parvin
Rd.

4.6
4.8

15.6

Parvin
Covered Bridge

19.5

Rattlesnake Rd.

19.3

Jasper-Lowell Rd.

START/
FINISH

0.8

Wheeler Rd.

0.6

26.5

23.6

Jasper
State Park

24.4

25.2

Edenvale Rd.

N

0   1   2   3 mi

0   1   2   3   4 km

Start by riding out of Jasper State Park on Jasper Park Drive.

0.1 Turn right onto Jasper Park Road.

0.6 Turn right onto Jasper Road, and cross the Middle Fork River.

0.8 Turn right onto Jasper-Lowell Road toward FALL CREEK DAM/LOWELL.

0.9 Pass the Jasper Store on the left.

4.6 Stay to the left on Jasper-Lowell Road (Pengra Road heads right).

4.8 Turn right onto Place Road to view the Pengra covered bridge. After viewing the bridge turn around and turn right onto Jasper-Lowell Road.

6.5 Pass the Fall Creek Market on the right.

6.8 Turn right onto Jasper-Lowell Road, and cross over Fall Creek.

9.1 Cross the Unity covered bridge, then arrive at a four-way junction. Continue straight on Jasper-Lowell Road.

11.0 Turn left onto Jasper-Lowell Road (Pengra Road goes right).

11.4 Pass Lowell City Park on the right, where you can view the miniature Cannon Street covered bridge. Picnic tables and rest rooms are also available here.

11.5 Turn right onto Jasper Park Road toward Highway 58.

11.8 The route begins to cross the Dexter Reservoir.

12.1 Pass a paved parking area on the right, where you can stop to view the Lowell covered bridge.

12.3 Turn right onto Highway 58.

14.0 Turn left onto Lost Creek Road toward Dexter.

14.6 Go under a railroad bridge, then turn right onto Parvin Road.

15.2 Cross Rattlesnake Road, and continue riding on Parvin Road.

15.4 Cross the Parvin covered bridge. After crossing the bridge turn right onto Lost Valley Lane.

15.6 Turn left onto Rattlesnake Road.

19.3 Cross Highway 58, and continue riding on Rattlesnake Road.

19.5 Turn left onto Wheeler Road.

23.6 Cross Jasper Park Road, and continue riding on Wheeler Road.

(continued)

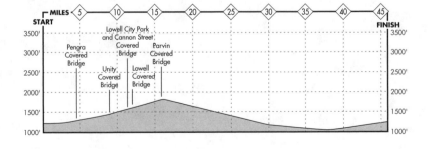

24.4 Turn right onto Edenvale Road.

25.2 Turn right, and continue riding on Edenvale Road (Ridgeway Road goes left at this junction).

26.5 Cross Jasper Park Road, and continue riding on Jasper Park Road.

27.0 Turn left onto Jasper Park Drive.

27.1 Arrive at Jasper State Park.

BIKE SHOPS

♦ Bike Barn, 465 Coburg Road, Eugene, OR 97401, (541) 342–5757.

♦ Blue Heron Bicycles, 877 East 13th Avenue, Eugene, OR 97401, (541) 343–2488.

♦ Eugene Bicycle Works, 455 West 1st Avenue, Eugene, OR 97401, (541) 683–3397.

♦ Hutch's Bicycle Store Eugene, 960 Charnelton Street, Eugene, OR 97401, (541) 345–7521.

♦ Mike's Bike Shop, 930 River Road, Eugene, OR 97404, (541) 461–0016.

♦ Paul's Bicycle Way of Life, 152 West 5th Avenue, Eugene, OR 97401, (541) 344–4105.

REST ROOMS

♦ Mile 0.0: Jasper State Park.

♦ Mile 11.4: Lowell City Park.

MAPS

♦ USGS 7.5-minute quads Jasper and Lowell; *DeLorme Oregon Atlas and Gazetteer,* map 42.

24

Row River Ramble

This fun and easy tour starts in Cottage Grove, adjacent to rambling Mosby Creek. The tour is a paved multiuse trail that follows the course of the Row River and takes you next to Dorena Lake. The route has many trailheads and places to stop and enjoy the views of Dorena Lake and the surrounding farming country. As an added bonus you can view the historic Mosby Creek covered bridge and the Dorena covered bridge.

This unique rail-trail is owned and managed by the Bureau of Land Management. The original rail line was started in 1902, and steam engines carried logs, ore, supplies, and passengers along the route, which stretched to the town of Disston. This tour starts at the Mosby Creek Trailhead, which has rest rooms and water. From the parking area this paved trail heads to the northeast. Just before crossing a picturesque bridge over Mosby Creek, check out the Mosby Creek covered bridge, which is located just off the trail on the right. This bright white covered bridge was built in 1920, and extensive

Dorena Lake.

Start: From the Mosby Creek Trailhead in Cottage Grove, about 18 miles south of Eugene and 50 miles north of Roseburg off of I–5.

Length: 25.2 miles out and back.

Season: Year-round.

Approximate riding time: Two to three hours.

Recommended start time: 10:00 A.M.

Terrain: Paved multiuse path.

Traffic and hazards: Watch for tree debris and wet leaves from storms. When you're riding next to farms, keep an eye out for loose dogs—they are often protective of their owners' property and may try to chase you.

Getting there: From I–5 in Cottage Grove, take exit 174 toward Dorena Lake. At the end of the off-ramp, turn east onto Row River Road. Drive 1 mile east on Row River Road, then turn right onto Currin Conn Road. Immediately after this turn take a quick left onto Mosby Creek Road. Go 2 miles southeast on Mosby Creek Road, then turn left onto Layng Road. Just after this turn take a quick left into the Mosby Creek Trailhead parking lot.

restoration work was completed in 1990. After 1.3 miles you'll cross the Row River. This swift-moving river once was used to float logs to more than twenty mills that operated along its banks. After crossing the river the route turns southeast and takes you past oak woodlands, wetlands, and small farms.

At 3.4 miles you'll arrive at Dorena Trailhead, which is located on the northwest edge of Dorena Reservoir. From here you can view the 150-foot-high earthen dam that was built to prevent floods and provide irrigation and recreation for the surrounding communities. Over the next 5 miles, the trail hugs the northern shore of Dorena Lake and takes you through a shady Douglas fir forest with many open areas to view the lake.

A variety of creeks empty into the Dorena Lake, including Rat, Smith, Teeter, Cedar, and King. These wetland ecosystems provide food and shelter for geese, ducks, blue herons, and osprey. Wild camas (an edible blue-flowered lily) also grows in this area. The root of this plant was a major part of the Native American's diet. When you reach the Bake Stewart Park Trailhead at 8.3 miles, you'll leave the lake behind and continue pedaling through oak woodlands and past many small farms with cattle and horses. Once you reach the small town of Dorena at 9.5 miles you have the option of turning right off the trail to view the Dorena covered bridge. This 1949 bridge spans the Row River. It was retired in 1973 and overhauled in 1996.

As the route continues, look for songbirds and listen for the loud croaking sounds of resident frogs. Red-tailed hawks are a common sight. This section of the trail is thick with blackberries that ripen in mid- to late August. At 11 miles you'll reach the Hawley Butte Trailhead. Here you can get drinks and snacks at the River Store, across the road from the bicycle path. From this point you'll pedal another 2.1 miles to the signed trail's end. Turn around and retrace the route back to your starting point at the Mosby Creek Trailhead.

ADDITIONAL RIDE INFORMATION

♦ Bureau of Land Management, Eugene District, 751 South Danebo, Eugene, OR 97402 (541) 683–6600, www.edo.or.blm.gov/Rec/Row_Trail.htm.

LOCAL INFORMATION

♦ Cottage Grove Chamber of Commerce, 330 Highway 99 South, Suite B, Cottage Grove, OR 97424, (541) 942–2411, www.cgchamber.com.

LOCAL EVENTS/ATTRACTIONS

♦ Bohemia Mining Days, held in mid-July, 330 Highway 99 South, Suite B, Cottage Grove, OR 97424, (541) 942–6125.
♦ Fall Harvest Festival, held in October, 330 Highway 99 South, Suite B, Cottage Grove, OR 97424, (541) 942–2411.

RESTAURANTS

♦ Vintage Inn Restaurant, 1590 Gateway Boulevard, Cottage Grove, OR 97424, (541) 942–7144.

ACCOMMODATIONS

♦ Apple Inn Bed and Breakfast, 30697 Kenady Lane, Cottage Grove, OR 97424, (800) 942–2393, www.appleinnbb.com.

BIKE SHOPS

♦ Bike Barn, 465 Coburg Road, Eugene, OR 97401, (541) 342–5757.
♦ Blue Heron Bicycles, 877 East 13th Avenue, Eugene, OR 97401, (541) 343–2488.
♦ Eugene Bicycle Works, 455 West 1st Avenue, Eugene, OR 97401, (541) 683–3397.
♦ Hutch's Bicycle Store Eugene, 960 Charnelton Street, Eugene, OR 97401, (541) 345–7521.
♦ Mike's Bike Shop, 930 River Road, Eugene, OR 97404, (541) 461–0016.
♦ Paul's Bicycle Way of Life, 152 West 5th Avenue, Eugene, OR 97401, (541) 344–4105.

REST ROOMS

♦ Mile 0.0: Mosby Creek Trailhead.
♦ Mile 3.5: Dorena Trailhead.
♦ Mile 5.3: Harms Park.
♦ Mile 7.7: Rest room.

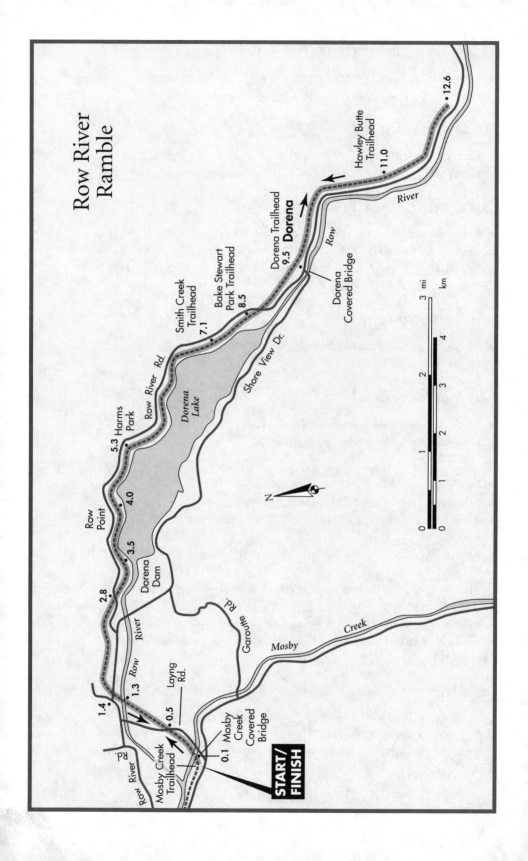

Start by riding northeast on the paved path from the Mosby Creek Trailhead.

0.1 Stop and check out the Mosby Creek covered bridge, located about 200 yards to the right of the paved path. After viewing the bridge cross Mosby Creek.

0.5 Cross Layng Road.

1.3 Cross the Row River.

1.4 Cross Row River Road.

2.8 Cross Row River Road.

3.5 Dorena Trailhead. Enjoy the views of Dorena Dam and Dorena Lake. Rest rooms (no water) are available here.

4.0 Row Point Trailhead.

5.3 Harms Park. Rest rooms (no water) and picnic tables are available here.

7.1 Smith Creek Trailhead.

7.7 Pass a rest room on the right (no water).

8.5 Bake Stewart Park Trailhead. Just after the trailhead cross Row River Road.

9.5 Dorena Trailhead. You have the option here of turning right on a dirt road, then turning right on Row River Road to view the Dorena covered bridge.

11.0 Hawley Butte Trailhead. If you want drinks and snacks, you can exit the paved path here by turning left onto Row River Road and stocking up at the River Store.

12.6 Arrive at the end of the trail marked by a TRAIL'S END sign. Turn around and retrace the route back to the trailhead.

25.2 Arrive at the Mosby Creek Trailhead.

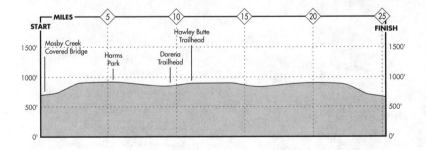

MAPS

♦ USGS 7.5-minute quads Cottage Grove, Dorena Lake, and Culp Creek; *DeLorme Oregon Atlas and Gazetteer,* maps 41 and 42.

25

Oakland Ramble

This loop tour starts in the charming nineteenth-century town of Oakland and takes you through a picturesque landscape of rolling hills and oak woodlands. When you are finished with your tour, you can learn about Oakland's history in the Oakland Museum and have lunch at Tolly's Restaurant, which features an old-time soda fountain.

Oakland is a small town that has maintained its nineteenth-century charm. It was established in 1851 by Dr. Dorsey S. Baker. The town was relocated to its present site in 1872 when the O&C Railroad reached this location.

You'll begin your tour at the small grassy park adjacent to First Street. Almost immediately you'll turn onto Locust Street, which takes you right through the center of a downtown filled with the original brick buildings that date back to the 1890s. The Oakland Museum is located on your right and is open from 1:00 P.M. to 4:00 P.M. daily (except holidays). This small museum chronicles the history of the area.

After riding through downtown Oakland, the route heads northeast into the countryside on Driver Valley Road. This narrow, twisty road takes you past farms and cattle ranches and through thick white oak

Downtown Oakland.

woodlands. These stout hardwood trees are draped with thick tangles of glowing moss that glisten in the morning mist. They grow abundantly on the rolling grassy hills that characterize this part of Oregon. Native Americans toasted the acorns produced by the white oak. It is thought that Native Americans purposefully perpepuated the oak woodlands by performing controlled burning. White oaks are resistant to fire, and oak seedlings readily sprout after a fire.

You'll ride through this rolling countryside for 16 miles. Watch for deer that graze on the open grassy slopes and for red-tailed hawks hunting for their next meal. When you return to Oakland, be sure to stop at Tolly's Restaurant. This establishment features an old-time soda fountain and is filled with glistening wood floors and tables. It is a great place to stop and eat lunch after your ride.

LOCAL INFORMATION

♦ Oakland Chamber of Commerce, 117 3rd Street, Oakland, OR 97462, (541) 459–4531.

♦ Roseburg Visitors and Convention Bureau, 410 SE Spruce Street, Roseburg, OR 97470, (800) 444–9584, www.visitroseburg.com.

LOCAL EVENTS/ATTRACTIONS

♦ Oakland Museum, 130 Locust Street, Oakland, OR 97462, (541) 459–3087. Open 1:00 P.M. to 4:00 P.M. daily. Admission is free.

RESTAURANTS

♦ Tolly's Restaurant, 115 NE Locust Street, Oakland, OR 97462, (541) 459–3796.

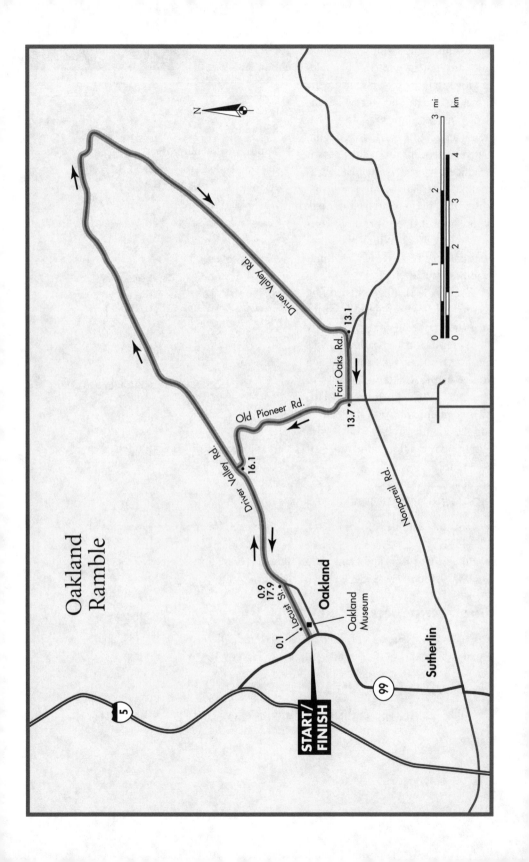

Oakland Ramble

N

Oakland

Sutherlin

START/FINISH

Oakland Museum

Locust St.

Driver Valley Rd.

Old Pioneer Rd.

Fair Oaks Rd.

Driver Valley Rd.

Nonpareil Rd.

5

99

0.1

0.9
17.9

16.1

13.7

13.1

0   1   2   3 mi

0   1   2   3   4 km

Start by turning left onto First Street. Then take a quick right onto Locust Street.

0.1 Pass the Oakland Museum on the right.

0.3 Pass the historic library on the left.

0.9 At a road junction with a yield sign, turn right onto the unsigned Driver Valley Road.

13.1 Veer right at the road junction. Driver Valley Road turns into Fair Oaks Road.

13.7 Turn right at Old Pioneer Road.

16.1 Turn left onto Driver Valley Road.

17.9 Turn left onto Locust Street.

18.8 Turn left onto First Street, and take a quick right into the gravel lot and your starting point.

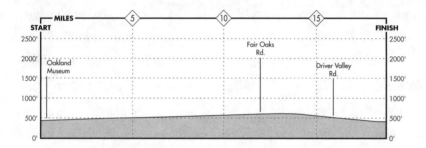

ACCOMMODATIONS

♦ Beckley House B&B, 338 SE Second Street, Oakland, OR 97462, (541) 459–9320.

BIKE SHOPS

♦ The Cycles La Moure, 1217 Northeast Walnut Street, Roseburg, OR 97470, (541) 957–1020.

REST ROOMS

♦ There are no rest rooms on this route.

MAPS

♦ USGS 7.5-minute quads Sutherlin and NonPareil; *DeLorme Oregon Atlas and Gazetteer,* map 35.

Diamond Lake–Crater Lake Challenge

T his strenuous tour takes you around the deep blue waters of Diamond Lake and Crater Lake. The route begins at the South Shore Picnic Area at Diamond Lake. From the picnic area you'll climb more than 2,000 feet to the rim of spectacular Crater Lake in Crater Lake National Park. Once you reach the rim of Crater Lake, you'll ride on the very hilly 33-mile Rim Drive, which circles the lake. Despite the strenuous and challenging hills on this road, there are many fabulous viewpoints where you can enjoy the beauty and magnificent geology of this area. Once you complete the loop, you can look forward to a long, fast descent back to Diamond Lake. If you are feeling like a more leisurely ride, you may want to take an optional 15-mile tour around Diamond Lake.

This strenuous route begins at the South Shore Picnic Area at the 3,200-acre Diamond Lake in Umpqua National Forest. This deep blue lake is popular with anglers and boaters as well as cyclists. Before you begin this tour, make sure you have plenty of food and water to last the entire day (it is recommended that you bring a minimum of four liters of water per person) because there are very few opportunities to stock up on this tour. Also, be sure to wear bright clothing to increase your visibility, and bring extra layers for both the windy weather that can occur on rim of the lake and the chilly descent back to Diamond Lake.

The first part of the tour you'll ride on a forest service road and major highways to the entrance to Crater Lake National Park at 3.8 miles. The entrance fee is $5.00 per biker. After the entrance booth you'll pedal uphill through a thick forest canopy until you reach the open expanse of Pumice Desert, starting at

Start: The South Shore Picnic Area at Diamond Lake.

Length: 57.6-mile loop.

Season: Mid- to late June through October.

Approximate riding time: Ten to twelve hours.

Recommended start time: 7:00 A.M.

Terrain: This route follows major highways and rural roads in the Umpqua National Forest and Crater Lake National Park.

Traffic and hazards: Highway 230 and Highway 138 have a 3-foot shoulder with moderate traffic, including logging trucks. The Crater Lake Entrance Road has a 2-foot shoulder for the first 1.5 miles. This road can have moderate to heavy traffic during the summer. Rim Drive is very narrow with no shoulder; it can be uneven and rough due to rock falls during the spring thaw. Try to avoid situations in which you are riding abreast of two passing vehicles. Be aware of RVs. Watch your speed on the long down-hill sections. Keep a firm grip on your handlebars through these rough sections. Wear bright clothing—many areas on the road are shady. Bring extra layers for and cold conditions on the crater rim. If you are not used to altitude, you may experience headaches or shortness of breath. Opportunities to obtain water on this tour are few. Be sure to carry a minimum of four liters of water per person. This is a very strenuous tour and should only be attempted by experienced and fit cyclists.

Getting there: From Bend at the intersection of Franklin Avenue and Highway 97, drive 76 miles south on Highway 97 to the intersection with Highway 138. Turn right (east) onto Highway 138, and drive 15 miles to the intersection with Highway 230. Turn left onto Highway 230 toward DIAMOND LAKE SOUTH SHORE/MEDFORD. Drive 0.1 mile on Highway 230, and turn right onto Forest Road (FR) 4795, where a sign indicates DIAMOND LAKE RECREATION AREA. Drive 0.7 mile toward THIELSEN VIEW CAMPGROUND/ BROKEN ARROW CAMPGROUND. At the next road junction, turn left, and drive 0.2 mile on FR 4795 (unsigned) to the South Shore Picnic Area parking lot located on the right side of the road.

From Roseburg drive approximately 80 miles west on Highway 138 to the intersection with Highway 230. Turn right onto Highway 230 toward DIAMOND LAKE SOUTH SHORE/MEDFORD. Drive 0.1 mile on Highway 230, and turn right onto Forest Road (FR) 4795, where a sign indicates DIAMOND LAKE RECREATION AREA. Drive 0.7 mile toward THIELSEN VIEW CAMPGROUND/BROKEN ARROW CAMPGROUND. At the next road junction, turn left, and drive 0.2 mile on FR 4795 (unsigned) to the South Shore Picnic Area parking lot located on the right side of the road.

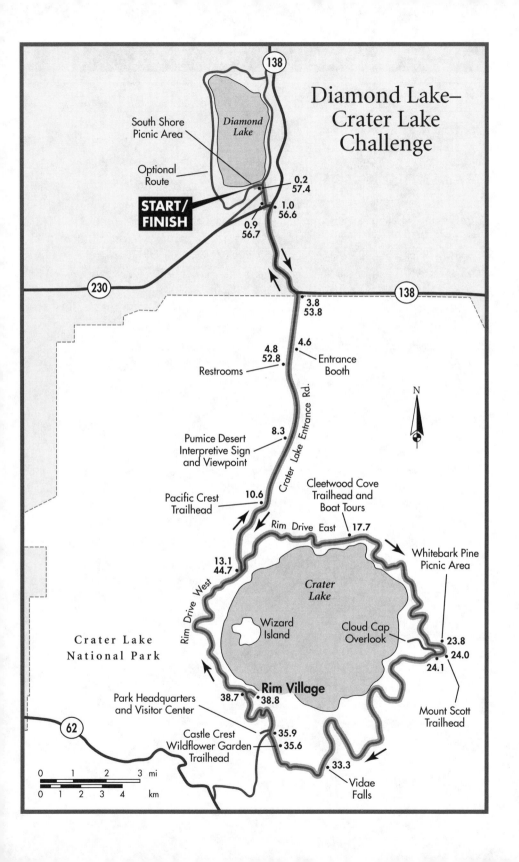

Diamond Lake–Crater Lake Challenge

138

Diamond Lake

South Shore
Picnic Area

Optional
Route

0.2
57.4

**START/
FINISH**

1.0
56.6

0.9
56.7

230

138

3.8
53.8

4.6

4.8
52.8

Restrooms

Entrance
Booth

Crater Lake Entrance Rd.

N

8.3

Pumice Desert
Interpretive Sign
and Viewpoint

Cleetwood Cove
Trailhead and
Boat Tours

Pacific Crest
Trailhead

10.6

Rim Drive East

17.7

Whitebark Pine
Picnic Area

13.1
44.7

Rim Drive West

*Crater
Lake*

Wizard
Island

Cloud Cap
Overlook

23.8

24.0

24.1

**Crater Lake
National Park**

Mount Scott
Trailhead

Rim Village

Park Headquarters
and Visitor Center

38.7

38.8

62

Castle Crest
Wildflower Garden
Trailhead

35.9

35.6

33.3

Vidae
Falls

0   1   2   3 mi
0   1   2   3   4 km

MILES AND DIRECTIONS

Start by turning left out of the South Shore Picnic Area onto Forest Road (FR) 4795.

0.2 At the stop sign and T-intersection, turn right onto unsigned FR 4795.

0.9 At the stop sign and T-intersection, turn left onto Highway 230.

1.0 At the T-intersection and stop sign, turn right onto Highway 138 East toward CRATER LAKE AND BEND.

3.8 You'll arrive at a Y-intersection. Turn right onto the Crater Lake Entrance Road.

4.6 Pass the entrance booth to Crater Lake on your left. The entrance fee is $5.00 per biker. (The entrance fee for cars is $10.00)

4.8 You'll pass rest rooms on your right (no water).

7.7 Arrive at the edge of the Pumice Desert.

8.3 Arrive at a concrete pullout on your left and an interpretive sign describing the Pumice Desert.

10.6 Pass the Pacific Crest Trailhead on your right.

13.1 Turn left onto the Rim Drive East toward CLEETWOOD TRAIL/BOAT TOURS. Just past this turn is a great viewpoint of the lake on your right.

17.7 Pass the Cleetwood Cove Trailhead on your right. (There are rest rooms available at this trailhead.) You have the option of hiking 2 miles round-trip to the lakeshore. Note that this hike has 700 feet of elevation gain. Or, you can take a narrated boat tour to Wizard Island.

23.8 Pass the Whitebark Pine Picnic Area on your left. Vault toilets are available here (no water).

24.0 Pass the Mount Scott Trailhead on your left. You have the option here of hiking 5 miles out and back to the summit of Mount Scott.

24.1 Turn left toward Highway 62. (The turnoff to Cloud Cap Overlook goes right at this intersection.)

33.3 Pass Vidae Falls on your right.

35.6 Pass Castle Crest Wildflower Garden Trailhead on your right.

35.9 At the stop sign and T-intersection, turn right toward VISITOR INFORMATION/RIM VILLAGE. Pedal a short distance, then turn left into the visitors center parking area.

(continued)

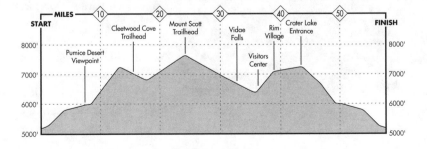

Rest rooms and water are available here during operating hours. After you're finished exploring, head back to the main road, and turn left.

38.7 At the Y-intersection go right toward RIM VILLAGE.

38.8 Arrive at Rim Village, which has rest rooms and water, restaurants, and a gift shop. Crater Lake Lodge is also adjacent to the Rim Village Complex. When you're finished taking a break, head back toward Rim Drive.

38.9 Turn right onto Rim Drive West toward Highway 138.

44.7 Continue straight toward Highway 138. After a few miles you'll begin a long, fun downhill.

52.8 Pass rest rooms on your left (no water).

53.8 Turn left onto Highway 138, and continue your fast downhill descent.

56.6 Turn left onto Highway 230 toward DIAMOND LAKE SOUTH SHORE/MEDFORD.

56.7 Turn right onto FR 4795, where a sign indicates DIAMOND LAKE RECREATION AREA.

57.4 Turn left, and continue riding FR 4795 toward THIELSEN VIEW CAMPGROUND/BROKEN ARROW CAMPGROUND.

57.6 Turn right into the South Shore Picnic Area on your right. Rest rooms are available here.

7.7 miles. This wide-open treeless plain is made up of pumice and ash deposits from Mount Mazama, which exploded about 7,700 years ago. In some areas the ash deposits are 50 feet deep. To learn more about this unique desert, pull off the road at a viewpoint and interpretive sign at 8.3 miles. From here you can admire the striking razor-edge summit of 9,182-foot Mount Thielsen, which rises majestically to the north.

As you continue on the tour, the climbing becomes more steep and intense until you reach Rim Drive at 13.1 miles. From this intersection you'll have the opportunity to take your first glimpse of the spectacular beauty of 1,932-foot-deep Crater Lake—the deepest lake in North America. Crater Lake is located in the immense caldera of the now-

Riding through the Pumice Desert with the knife edge summit of Mount Thielsen in the background.

extinct Mount Mazama. Mount Mazama once reached a height of 12,000 feet and spewed pumice, cinder, and ash for more than half a million years. Catastrophic eruptions from this volcano began approximately 7,700 years ago, spreading ash deposits over 5,000 square miles. During this time the volcano collapsed on itself, creating the deep caldera. Over a period of 5,000 years after this collapse, the lake formed when springs, snow, and rain filled the caldera. Wizard Island, located in the caldera, is a secondary volcano that rises 764 feet above the lake.

The ride continues to challenge you as you circle the lake in a clockwise direction on Rim Drive. This narrow, twisty road is very hilly and rough in some sections and has no shoulder. Use extreme caution when RVs pass you, and watch your speed on descents where rough spots in the road are

Crater Lake is the sapphire gem of southern Oregon.

hidden by shade. Despite these challenges Rim Drive has dozens of spectacular viewpoints where you can pull off the road and soak in the immense beauty of the sapphire-colored lake. After 17.7 miles you have the option of taking a 2-mile round-trip hike to the shore of Crater Lake on the Cleetwood Cove Trail. From this trail you can also take a narrated boat tour around the lake and to Wizard Island. Tickets are sold at the parking lot opposite the trailhead. Tours are generally offered from June through mid-September from 10:00 A.M. to 4:30 P.M. After pushing pedals for 24 miles, you'll have another chance to take a break from the saddle at the Mount Scott Trailhead. A 5-mile round-trip hike can be taken to the summit of 8,929-foot Mount Scott—the highest peak surrounding the lake. If you decide to hike this trail, keep in mind that it has 1,500 feet of elevation gain.

Continue your hilly journey around the lake, making sure to take the time to stop at the many viewpoints accessed off Rim Drive. After 35.6 miles you may want to take an easy stroll on the 0.5-mile Castle Crest Wildflower Garden Loop Trail. This trail has a showy display of wildflowers during July. Not far past this trailhead, you can stop at the visitor information building to learn more about the secrets of Crater Lake National Park. After 38.8 miles you'll arrive at Rim Village, which has a gift shop, rest rooms, snack bar, and access to historic Crater Lake Lodge (you can also refill your water bottles here). After you finish your 33-mile Rim Drive loop, you'll be rewarded by a long, downhill cruise back to Diamond Lake.

If you do not want to tackle this tough ride, there are other cycling opportunities available to you. You can take an excellent 15-mile ride around Diamond Lake on paved FR 4795. You can also ride on the paved sections of the Diamond Lake Bicycle Path, which can be accessed from different points along FR 4795. If you still want to ride around Crater Lake (but do not want attempt the ride from Diamond Lake), you can drive to the Crater Rim and ride 33 miles around the lake on Rim Drive.

LOCAL INFORMATION

◆ Crater Lake National Park, PO Box 7, Crater Lake, OR 97604-0007, (541) 594–2211, www.nps.gov/crla.
◆ Umpqua National Forest, Diamond Lake Ranger District, 2020 Toketee Road, Idleyld Park, OR 97447, (541) 498–2531, www.fs.fed.us/r6/umpqua

RESTAURANTS

◆ Crater Lake Lodge, 1211 Avenue C, White City, OR 97503, (541) 830–8700. Open mid-May through October.
◆ Diamond Lake Resort, HC 30, Box 1, Diamond Lake, OR 97731, (800) 733–7593.

ACCOMMODATIONS

◆ Crater Lake Lodge, 1211 Avenue C, White City, OR 97503, (541) 830–8700. Open mid-May through October. Call for current rates.
◆ Diamond Lake Resort, HC 30, Box 1, Diamond Lake, OR 97731, (800) 733–7593. Call for current rates.

BIKE SHOPS

Bend
◆ Bend Cyclery, 853 NW Bond Street, Bend, OR 97701, (541) 385–5256.
◆ Century Cycles, 1135 NW Galveston, Bend, OR 97701, (541) 389–4224, www.centurycycles.org.

♦ Hutch's Bicycle Store, 725 NW Columbia Street, Bend, OR 97701, (541) 382–9253, www.hutchsbicycles.com.

♦ Pine Mountain Sports, 133 SW Century Drive, Bend, OR 97701, (541) 385–8080.

♦ Sunnyside Sports, 930 NW Newport Avenue, Bend, OR 97701, (541) 382–8018, www.kmx.com/sunnyside.

Roseburg

♦ The Cycles La Moure, 1217 NE Walnut Street, Roseburg, OR 97470, (541) 957–1020.

♦ Schwinn Cyclery Garden Valley, 662 NE Garden Valley Boulevard, Roseburg, OR 97470, (541) 672–3721.

REST ROOMS

♦ Mile 0.0: South Shore Picnic Area at Diamond Lake.
♦ Mile 4.8: Entrance to Crater Lake National Park.
♦ Mile 17.7: Cleetwood Cove Trailhead.
♦ Mile 23.8: Whitebark Pine Picnic Area.
♦ Mile 38.8: Rim Village

MAPS

♦ USGS 7.5-minute quads Diamond Lake, Pumice Desert West, Pumice Desert East, Crater Lake West, and Crater Lake East; *DeLorme Oregon Atlas and Gazetteer,* maps 29 and 37.

Three Capes Scenic Cruise

This loop route takes you on a tour of the north Oregon coast. It begins in the small town of Pacific City, which is home to the famous dory fishing boats. You'll pedal north on the Three Capes Scenic Highway, which takes you past Cape Lookout State Park and Cape Meares State Park. Miles of trails and ocean views are present at both of these parks. Cape Meares State Park also features a historic lighthouse. The route takes you past many small coastal communities that are worth exploring, including Tierra Del Mar, Netarts, Oceanside, Cape Meares, and Tillamook.

This tour begins at Cape Kiwanda State Park in Pacific City, which is blessed with a scenic beach, a massive sand dune and sandstone cliff, and a rocky offshore island called Haystack Rock. The beach is famous for its fleet of dory fishing boats, which are launched directly into the surf during the summer months. If you want to experience the thrill of launching into the surf on a dory boat and fishing off Haystack Rock, a local guide from the Haystack Fishing Club can take you out along this scenic stretch of coast. The sheltered beach is also popular with surfers and boogie boarders. On the north side of the dune, you may see hang gliders in action.

From the Cape Kiwanda parking area, you'll ride north through the small community of Tierra Del Mar, and at 11.6 miles you'll pass the Cape Lookout Trailhead. It is highly recommended that you stop and hike this 5-mile out-and-back trail, which takes you to a high viewpoint at the tip of Cape Lookout. From here you may see migrating gray whales (between December and June). After 14.3 miles you'll arrive at the entrance to Cape Lookout State Park. This

Start: Cape Kiwanda public parking lot in Pacific City.

Length: 59.5-mile loop.

Season: Year-round.

Approximate riding time: Five to seven hours.

Recommended start time: 9:00 A.M.

Terrain: This route travels on major highways and rural roads.

Traffic and hazards: The Three Capes Scenic Highway does not have a shoulder, is very narrow, and often has a rough surface. During the winter months the Three Capes Scenic Highway often has plant debris on the road from winter storms. U.S. Highway 101 has a 3-foot shoulder and moderate to heavy traffic. The weather on the Oregon coast is often wet, windy, and cold. Be sure to bring rain gear and extra insulating layers.

Getting there: From the intersection of Highway 18 and U.S. Highway 101 in Lincoln City, turn north onto U.S. Highway 101. Travel 14.6 miles, and turn left (west) onto Brooten Road toward CAPE KIWANDA RECREATION AREA/PACIFIC CITY. Go 2.8 miles onto Brooten Road, then turn left onto Pacific Avenue toward NETARTS/OCEANSIDE. Continue 0.3 mile on Pacific Avenue, and turn right onto Cape Kiwanda Drive. Go 1 mile, then turn left into the Cape Kiwanda public parking area adjacent to the Pelican Pub and Brewery restaurant.

From Tillamook travel 25 miles south on U.S. Highway 101, and turn right (west) onto Brooten Road toward CAPE KIWANDA RECREATION AREA/PACIFIC CITY. Go 2.8 miles on Brooten Road, then turn left onto Pacific Avenue toward NETARTS/OCEANSIDE. Continue 0.3 mile on Pacific Avenue, and turn right on Cape Kiwanda Drive. Go 1 mile, then turn left into the Cape Kiwanda public parking area adjacent to the Pelican Pub and Brewery restaurant.

2,014-acre park has a campground and many miles of trails to explore.

At 19.3 miles you'll pass Bayshore RV Park and Marina, which is located on the shores of beautiful Netarts Bay. If you want to go crabbing, the marina rents crabbing boats and crab rings; they also have crab cooking facilities. As you continue north the road hugs the shoreline of Netarts Bay. After 3 more miles you'll arrive at the small cliffside town of Oceanside. Be sure to stop at the Symons State Scenic Viewpoint to soak in the views of Three Arch Rocks a half mile offshore. More than 200,000 seabirds nest on these rocky sea islands.

After 25.6 scenic miles you'll arrive at Cape Meares State Park, which has many hiking trails and is home to the 38-foot-tall Cape Meares lighthouse. This

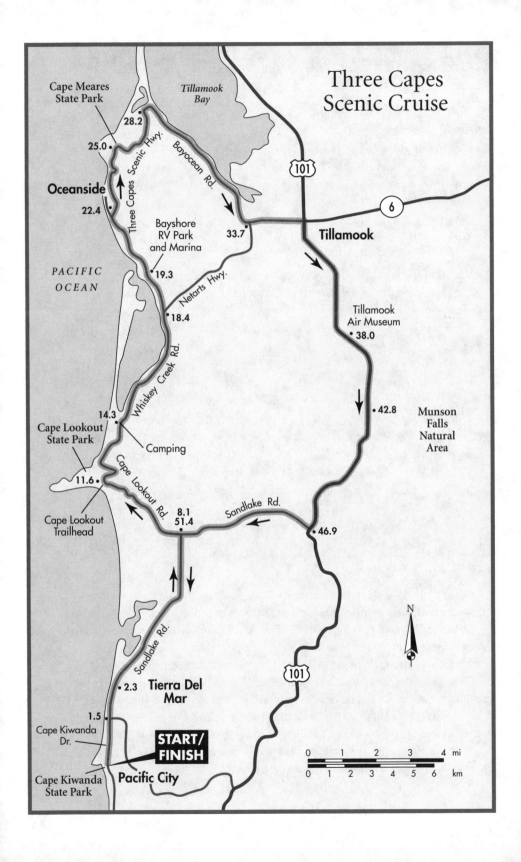

Three Capes Scenic Cruise

Cape Meares State Park

Tillamook Bay

28.2

25.0

Three Capes Scenic Hwy.

Bayocean Rd.

Oceanside

22.4

Bayshore RV Park and Marina

33.7

US 101

Tillamook

6

PACIFIC OCEAN

19.3

Netarts Hwy.

18.4

Tillamook Air Museum
38.0

42.8

Munson Falls Natural Area

Whiskey Creek Rd.

14.3

Cape Lookout State Park

Camping

Cape Lookout Rd.

11.6

Cape Lookout Trailhead

8.1
51.4

Sandlake Rd.

46.9

N

Sandlake Rd.

US 101

2.3

Tierra Del Mar

1.5

Cape Kiwanda Dr.

START/ FINISH

Pacific City

Cape Kiwanda State Park

0   1   2   3   4 mi
0 1 2 3 4 5 6 km

Start by turning left (north) onto Cape Kiwanda Drive toward Netarts and Tillamook.

1.5 At a stop sign continue straight on Sandlake Road toward CAPE LOOKOUT STATE PARK/NETARTS/OCEANSIDE.

2.3 Enter Tierra Del Mar.

8.1 At the stop sign and T-intersection, turn left onto Cape Lookout Road toward Cape Lookout State Park, Netarts, and Oceanside. (Sandlake Road goes right at this junction.)

9.2 Pass a pullout and interpretive sign on the left. You may run into patches of sand on the road that blow over the road from the nearby dunes. The route begins to climb.

11.6 Pass the Cape Lookout Trailhead on the left.

13.2 Pass Anderson's Viewpoint on your left.

14.3 Pass the entrance to Cape Lookout State Park on the left. Rest rooms, water, and campsites are present in the state park.

16.9 Pass the Whiskey Creek Fish Hatchery on the left.

18.4 At the road junction go left on Netarts Drive toward Netarts and Oceanside.

19.3 Pass Bayshore RV Park and Marina on your right. You can rent boats and crabbing gear at this marina. At the stop sign and T-intersection, turn left and follow signs for the Three Capes Scenic Highway.

20.2 Pass Netarts Grocery on the left.

22.4 At the road junction turn right, and continue on the Three Capes Scenic Highway toward Cape Meares State Park and Cape Meares. The road begins climbing steeply after this junction. *Note:* You have the option of turning left at this intersection and exploring the small town of Oceanside. If you decide to check out Oceanside, a great place to stop for lunch is Roseanna's Oceanside Café.

25.0 Turn left onto the entrance road to Cape Meares State Park.

25.6 Arrive at a large parking area. Hop off your bike, and walk 0.25 mile down a paved path to view the historic Cape Meares lighthouse. Rest rooms and

(continued)

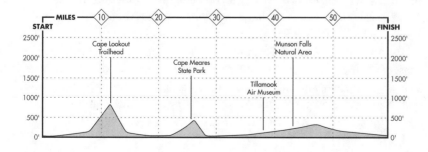

water are available at this stop. After exploring the park head back out the entrance.

26.2 At the stop sign turn left (north) onto the Three Capes Scenic Highway. Begin a steep descent. Watch your speed—the road surface is very rough.

28.2 At the stop sign and T-intersection, turn right onto Bayocean Road toward Tillamook.

33.7 At the stop sign and T-intersection, turn left toward Tillamook. The road now has a 2-foot shoulder.

35.0 Enter downtown Tillamook. At the stoplight turn right (south) onto U.S. Highway 101 toward Hebo and Newport.

38.0 Pass the turnoff to the Tillamook Air Museum on the left.

40.5 Pass a rest area with rest rooms and water on the right.

42.8 Pass the Munson Falls Natural Area on the left.

46.9 Turn right onto Sandlake Road toward Cape Kiwanda and Pacific City. Ride with caution—the road surface is very rough.

51.4 At the stop sign turn left toward Pacific City and continue riding south on Sandlake Road.

57.4 Pass a beach access point on the right.

58.0 At the stop sign continue straight toward Pacific City.

59.5 Turn right into the Cape Kiwanda public parking area.

historic lighthouse was built in 1890 and is the shortest lighthouse on the Oregon coast. From the parking area a 0.25-mile paved path leads to this picturesque beacon. Along the way there are several viewpoints with interpretive signs where you can view nesting seabirds, such as double-crested cormorants, Brandt's cormorants, pigeon guillemots, common murres, and tufted puffins. A gift shop is located in the lighthouse and is open daily from June through September and on the weekends during October, March, and April.

The route continues north for another 3 miles and heads southeast on Bayocean Road along the shores of quiet Tillamook Bay toward Tillamook. At 35 miles you'll reach downtown Tillamook and turn south onto U.S. Highway 101. Use caution as you ride on the highway through town because there is no shoulder. A popular Tillamook attraction you should check out is the Tillamook Air Museum, located about 3 miles south of town. This impressive museum houses more than two dozen vintage aircraft, World War II artifacts, a theater, gift shop, and café. At 42.8 miles you'll pass the turnoff to Munson Falls Natural Area. You have the option of taking a 2.4-mile round-trip detour (part of this is gravel road) to view 266-foot Munson Falls—the tallest water-

Cape Meares lighthouse, Cape Meares State Park.

fall in the Coast Mountain range. From the trailhead a 0.6-mile out-and-back trail takes you to a viewpoint of these impressive falls.

The route continues south on U.S. Highway 101 for about 9 more miles, then heads west on the more rural Sandlake Road. The route then turns southwest and winds through more scenic coastal forest until you reach your starting point at Cape Kiwanda.

ADDITIONAL RIDE INFORMATION

◆ Oregon State Parks and Recreation, 1115 Commercial Street NE, Suite 1, Salem, OR 97301-1002, (800) 551–6949, www.oregonstateparks.org.

LOCAL INFORMATION

◆ Pacific City Chamber of Commerce, PO Box 331, Pacific City, OR 97135, (503) 965–6161, www.pacificcity.net.
◆ Tillamook Chamber of Commerce, 3705 U.S. Highway 101 North, Tillamook, OR 97223, (503) 842–7525, www.tillamookchamber.org.

LOCAL EVENTS/ATTRACTIONS

◆ Blue Heron French Cheese Company, 2001 Blue Heron Drive, Tillamook, OR 97141, (800) 275-0639, www.blueheronoregon.com.
◆ Bayshore RV Park and Marina, PO Box 218, Bilyeu Avenue, Netarts, OR 97143, (503) 842–7774. This marina rents crabbing boats and crab rings.
◆ Cape Kiwanda State Recreation Area, Oregon State Parks, 1115 Commercial Street NE, Suite 1, Salem, OR 97301-1002, (800) 551–6949, www.oregonstateparks.org/park_183.php.
◆ Cape Lookout State Park, Oregon State Parks, 1115 Commercial Street NE, Suite 1, Salem, OR 97301-1002, (800) 551–6949, www.oregonstateparks.org/park_186.php.
◆ Cape Meares State Park & Lighthouse, 1115 Commercial Street NE, Suite 1, Salem, OR 97301, (800) 551–6949, www.oregonstateparks.org/park_181.php.
◆ Haystack Fishing Club, PO Box 935, Pacific City, OR 97135, (888) 965–7555, www.oregoncoast.com/haystack.
◆ Tillamook Cheese Factory, 4175 Highway 101 North, Tillamook, OR 97141, (503) 842–4481, www.tillamookcheese.com.
◆ Tillamook Air Museum, 6030 Hangar Road, Tillamook, OR 97141, (503) 842–1130, www.tillamookair.com.
◆ Whale Watch Week, held in January on the entire Oregon coast. Contact Oregon State Parks, PO Box 693, Waldport, OR 97344, (541) 563–2002, www.whalespoken.org.

RESTAURANTS

Pacific City

♦ Grateful Bread Bakery, 34805 Brooten Road, Pacific City, OR 97135, (503) 965–7337.

♦ Pelican Public and Brewery, 33180 Cape Kiwanda Drive, Pacific City, OR 97135, (503) 965–7007, www.pelicanbrewery.com.

Oceanside

♦ Roseanna's Oceanside Café, 1490 Pacific Street, Oceanside, OR 97134, (503) 842–7351.

Tillamook

♦ La Mexicana Restaurant, 2203 3rd Street, Tillamook, OR 97141, (503) 842–2101.

ACCOMMODATIONS

♦ Cape Lookout State Park Campground, Oregon State Parks, 1115 Commercial Street NE, Suite 1, Salem OR 97301-1002, (800) 551–6949, www.oregonstateparks.org/park_186.php.

♦ Eagle's View Bed and Breakfast, 37975 Brooten Road, Pacific City, OR 97135, (888) 846–3292, moriah.com/eaglesview.

♦ Inn at Cape Kiwanda, 33105 Cape Kiwanda Drive, Pacific City, OR 97135, (888) 965–7001, www.InnAtCapeKiwanda.com.

♦ Inn at Pacific City, 35215 Brooten Road, Pacific City, OR 97135, (888) 722–2489, www.innatpacificcity.com.

♦ Sea Rose B&B, 1685 Maxwell Mountain Road, Oceanside, OR 97134, (503) 842–6126.

BIKE SHOPS

♦ There are no bike shops in this area.

REST ROOMS

♦ Mile 0.0: Cape Kiwanda public parking area.
♦ Mile 14.3: Cape Lookout State Park and Campground.
♦ Mile 25.6: Cape Meares State Park.
♦ Mile 38: Tillamook Air Museum.
♦ Mile 40.5: Rest area.

MAPS

♦ USGS 7.5-minute quads Nestucca Bay, Sand Lake, Netarts, Tillamook, Beaver, and Hebo; *DeLorme Oregon Atlas and Gazetteer,* maps 58 and 64.

Sunset Bay–Shore Acres–
Bandon Challenge

Enjoy the beauty of the Oregon coast on this gorgeous route that takes you on a tour of five state parks, past the Coquille River Lighthouse and the South Slough Marine Estuarine Preserve. You can also tour the unique shops in downtown Bandon and stay in one of Bandon's many fun bed-and-breakfast inns.

This classic coast tour begins in the sheltered cove of Sunset Bay State Park. A sandy beach, grassy picnic areas, hiking trails, and the offshore Cape Arago lighthouse are some of the many fun distractions at this park. It also has a campground that is open year-round. From the park you'll head south on the Cape Arago Highway to explore Shore Acres State Park and Cape Arago State Park.

Shore Acres State Park lies on a rugged section of coastline that features dramatic sandstone cliffs and rocky offshore islands. You can admire this stretch of coastline from an enclosed observation tower. This park

Coquille River lighthouse.

was once part of the Louis Simpson estate. Simpson was a lumberman and ship builder, and he built a huge estate here in 1905. The park is also well known for its spectacular flower gardens.

The route continues south to Cape Arago State Park, which is located on a high rocky headland. This park is an important breeding area for sea lions, who raise their pups in the sheltered coves. Offshore you'll hear the raucous calls of a large colony of sea lions off Simpson Reef.

After exploring this park you'll turn around and head north on the Cape Arago Highway, then turn south onto Seven Devils Road toward Bandon. This windy road passes through second-growth forest and some not-so-pretty clearcuts. At 12.2 miles take a break from the saddle, and explore the South Slough Marine Estuarine Preserve and Interpretive Center. The preserve covers 4,700 acres. Visit the interpretive center, which has exhibits explaining estuarine ecology, and displays describing the plants and animals that live here. You can also explore the estuary on a variety of nature trails.

Your next stop is Bullards Beach

THE BASICS

Start: Sunset Bay State Park, located 12.3 miles southwest of Coos Bay on the Cape Arago Highway.
Length: 80.4-mile loop.
Season: Year-round.
Approximate riding time: One to two days.
Recommended start time: 9:00 A.M.
Terrain: This route travels on major highways and rural roads.
Traffic and hazards: The Cape Arago Highway does not have a shoulder and is very narrow. During the winter months the there is often plant debris on the road from storms. All other rural roads have light traffic and no shoulder. U.S. Highway 101 has a 3-foot shoulder and moderate to heavy traffic. The weather on the Oregon coast is often wet, windy, and cold. Be sure to bring rain gear and extra insulating layers.
Getting there: From the intersection of U.S. Highway 101 and Commercial Street in downtown Coos Bay, turn west onto Commercial Avenue toward Charleston and Sunset Bay. Go 3.7 miles, and arrive at a stoplight. Turn left onto the Cape Arago Highway toward Charleston and Sunset Bay. Travel 8.6 miles on the Cape Arago Highway to the entrance to Sunset Bay State Park on the right.

State Park and the Coquille River lighthouse. This solar-powered lighthouse was built in 1896 and is perched on the north bank of the Coquille River. Be sure to take a short walk from the parking area to view it. There is also beach access from this location. Bullards Beach State Park has a campground if you want to stay overnight. If you don't want to spend the night in a tent, you may want to stay in one of the campground's thirteen yurts. A yurt is a circular tent-like structure that has a wooden floor and is 16 feet in diameter. Each yurt is outfitted with three beds, an electric heater, lights, and a lockable door.

From Bullards Beach State Park, you'll ride back to U.S. Highway 101, then

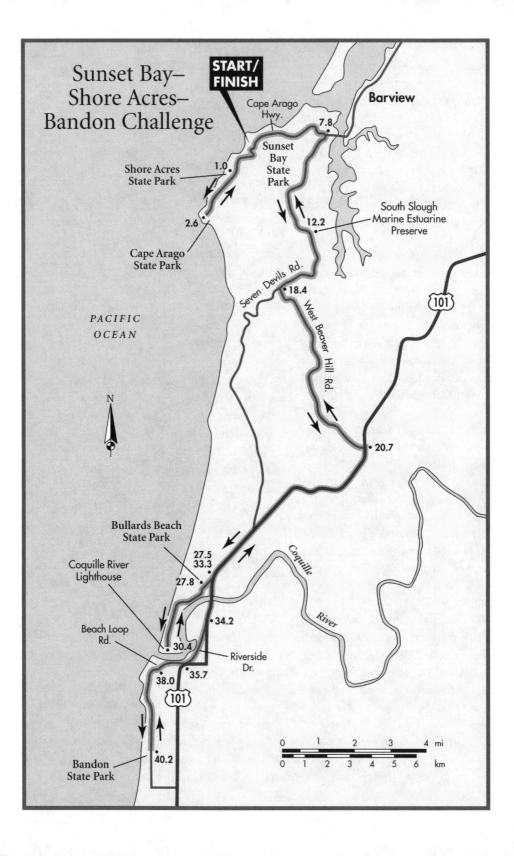

Sunset Bay–
Shore Acres–
Bandon Challenge

START/
FINISH

Barview

Cape Arago
Hwy.

7.8

Sunset
Bay
State
Park

Shore Acres
State Park

1.0

2.6

South Slough
Marine Estuarine
Preserve

12.2

Cape Arago
State Park

Seven Devils Rd.

18.4

West Beaver Hill Rd.

PACIFIC
OCEAN

N

20.7

Coquille

Bullards Beach
State Park

27.5
33.3

Coquille River
Lighthouse

27.8

River

34.2

Beach Loop
Rd.

30.4

Riverside
Dr.

38.0

35.7

101

Bandon
State Park

40.2

0   1   2   3   4 mi

0 1 2 3 4 5 6 km

101

Start by turning right (south) onto the Cape Arago Highway.

1.0 Pass the entrance to Shore Acres State Park. Rest rooms and water are available here.

2.6 Arrive at Cape Arago State Park, where there are rest rooms and water. After you have finished exploring, turn around and head north on the Cape Arago Highway.

7.8 Turn right onto Seven Devils Road toward Bandon.

12.2 Pass the South Slough Marine Estuarine Preserve on the left. Rest rooms are available at the interpretive center.

18.4 Stay to the left on West Beaver Hill Road.

20.7 At the stop sign turn right onto U.S. Highway 101 South.

27.5 Turn right at the Bullards Beach State Park sign.

27.8 Pass the entrance to the Bullards Beach Campground on the right.

28.8 At the road junction turn left toward the Coquille River lighthouse.

30.4 Arrive at the Coquille River lighthouse parking area. Rest rooms are available (no water). Explore the lighthouse and beach, then turn around and head back to U.S. Highway 101.

33.3 Turn right (south) onto U.S. Highway 101.

33.5 Cross a bridge over the Coquille River. Use caution.

34.2 Turn right onto Riverside Drive.

35.7 Turn right onto First Street in downtown Bandon.

38.0 Turn right onto Beach Loop Road.

39.7 Pass an entrance to Bandon State Park on the right.

40.2 Pass the Bandon State Park day-use area on the right. This is your turnaround point. Retrace the route back to your starting point at Sunset Bay State Park.

80.4 Arrive at Sunset Bay State Park.

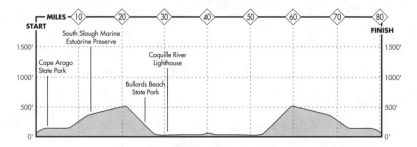

turn south until you arrive in downtown Bandon at mile 35.7. Bandon was founded by Irish baron George Bennett and originally was an important shipping center for dairy and wool products, lumber, and fish. Stop and explore the many shops and restaurants in Bandon's Old Towne. Bandon is also home to many cozy bed-and-breakfast inns that welcome cyclists. From downtown Bandon the route continues south for 5 more miles past impressive offshore sea stacks and dramatic rocky coastline, which are part of Bandon State Park. There are several viewpoints and access points along this 5-mile stretch—take your time and enjoy the spectacular views. After 40.2 miles you'll turn around and retrace the route back to your starting point.

ADDITIONAL RIDE INFORMATION

♦ Oregon State Parks and Recreation, 1115 Commercial Street NE, Suite 1, Salem, OR 97301-1002, (800) 551–6949, www.oregonstateparks.org.

LOCAL INFORMATION

♦ Bandon Chamber of Commerce, 300 SE Second Street, Bandon, OR 97411, (541) 347–9616.
♦ Coos Bay–North Bend Convention Promotions & Convention Bureau, 500 Central, Room 10, Coos Bay, OR 97420, (541) 269–8921.

LOCAL EVENTS/ATTRACTIONS

♦ Bandon Cheese Factory, 680 Second Street, Bandon, OR 97411, (800) 548–8961.
♦ Bandon Cranberry Festival, held in September, 300 SE Second Street, Bandon, OR 97411, (541) 347–9616.
♦ Bandon Wine and Seafood Festival, held in May, 300 SE Second Street, Bandon, OR 97411, (541) 347–9616.
♦ Charleston Merchants' Annual Crab Feed, held in Febuary, Charleston Marina, Charleston, OR 97420, (800) 824–8486.
♦ Oregon Coast Music Festival, held in July, Coos Bay, OR 97420 (541) 267–0938.

RESTAURANTS

♦ Blue Heron Bistro, 110 West Commercial, Coos Bay, OR 97420, (541) 267–3933.
♦ Sea Star Bistro, 375 Second Street, Bandon, OR 97411, (541) 347–9632.

ACCOMMODATIONS

♦ Beach Street B&B, 200 Beach Street, Bandon, OR 97411, (888) 335–1076.
♦ Bullards Beach State Park Campground, Oregon State Parks, 1115 Commercial Street NE, Suite 1, Salem, OR 97301-1002, (800) 551–6949, www.oregonstateparks.org/park_71.php.

♦ Lighthouse B&B, 650 Jetty Road SW, Bandon, OR 97411, (541) 347–9316, www.lighthouselodging.com.
♦ Sunset Bay State Park Campground, Oregon State Parks, 1115 Commerical Street NE, Suite 1, Salem, OR 97301-1002, (800) 551–6949, www.oregonstateparks.org/park_100.php.
♦ This Olde House B&B, 202 Alder Avenue, Coos Bay, OR 97420, (541) 267–5224, www.bnbweb.com/thisoldehouse.html.

BIKE SHOPS

♦ There are no bike shops in this area.

REST ROOMS

♦ Mile 0: Sunset Bay State Park.
♦ Mile 1:0 Shore Acres State Park.
♦ Mile 2.6: Cape Arago State Park.
♦ Mile 12.2: South Slough Marine Estuarine Reserve Interpretive Center.
♦ Mile 30.4: Coquille River lighthouse.

MAPS

♦ USGS 7.5-minute quads Cape Arago, Charleston, Riverton, Bullards, and Bandon; *DeLorme Oregon Atlas and Gazetteer,* map 33.

29

Gold Hill Cruise

*T*his challenging tour takes you through scenic valleys and rolling hills in the Rogue River Valley in southern Oregon. Along the way you can view the mighty Rogue River; Upper and Lower Table Rocks; 9,495-foot Mount McLoughlin; and the Wimer covered bridge. This route is also close to Ashland, which is host to the famous Oregon Shakespeare Festival.

This tour begins in the small town of Gold Hill in the Rogue River Valley in southern Oregon. From Gold Hill the route heads north on Highway 234 and parallels the Rogue River through an oak and pine forest. At 2.4 miles be sure to stop at the Gold Nugget Wayside. Here you'll find several interpretive signs describing the geology and history of the area and hike on a trail that leads down to the river's edge. The Takelma people lived in this wooded valley for generations before white settlers arrived on the scene. These Native Americans were made up of two

Rogue River.

different groups: the Dagelma and the Latgawa. These two tribes lived off the bounty of this river valley by hunting elk and deer, fishing for salmon, and gathering grass seeds, acorns, and camas roots. This peaceful life was shattered when gold was discovered in the sands of the Rogue River in 1849. With this discovery thousands of miners with gold fever came here with dreams of striking it rich. Settlers also arrived on the scene via the Scott-Applegate Trail. The Takelmas didn't appreciate this new influx of outsiders arriving in their peaceful valley. After a period they refused to allow settlers passage through their land, and they attacked everyone who tried. In an effort to relieve tensions, the U.S. Army negotiated an end to the attacks with the Table Rock Treaty of 1853. Peace lasted only two years— until miners attacked a Takelma settlement and killed many women and children. The Takelma took revenge and killed sixteen people in a nearby mining camp. These incidents started the Rogue River War.

Throughout the winter months of 1855, the Takelmas held their position against the U.S. Army. Eventually they surrendered and were relocated to the Grande Ronde Indian Reservation, located about 60 miles southwest of Portland on the South Yamhill River.

The route continues north through a wide-open valley filled with farms and cattle ranches. On a clear day you can see 9,495-foot Mount McLoughlin to the east. This majestic peak has gone by a variety of names. Early on settlers dubbed it Mount Pit (also spelled Pitt), borrowing on the nearby Pit River moniker derived from the game-trapping pits that Native Americans dug out along its banks. Snowy Butte and Big Butte were also tossed around from time to time, but in 1905 Congress officially named the mountain after Dr. John McLoughlin, a valued administrator in the Hudson's Bay Company from 1824 to 1849.

At 8.6 miles you'll continue your northward journey on Meadows Road. This road winds past farms and ranches and then climbs higher into thick oak

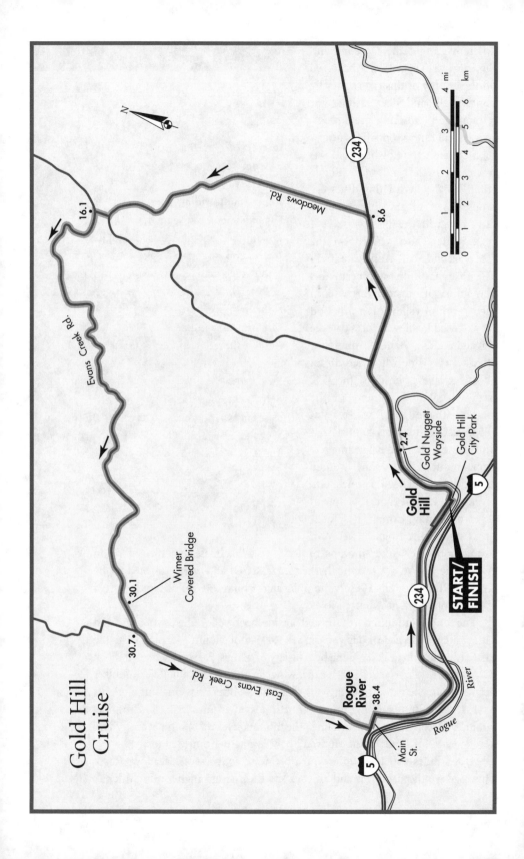

Gold Hill
Cruise

N

234

Meadows Rd.

8.6

16.1

Evans Creek Rd.

30.1

Wimer
Covered Bridge

30.7

East Evans Creek Rd.

Gold Nugget Wayside

2.4

Gold Hill
City Park

Gold Hill

5

234

START/
FINISH

Rogue
River

38.4

Main St.

5

Rogue River

0   1   2   3   4 mi

0   1   2   3   4   5   6 km

Start by turning left onto 4th Street. Ride across railroad tracks, and turn right where a sign indicates SAMS VALLEY HIGHWAY 234/CRATER LAKE.

2.4 Pass the Gold Nugget Wayside on your right. Rest rooms and interpretive signs are located here. A hiking trail leads down to the Rogue River.

8.6 Turn left onto Meadows Road.

16.1 Turn left onto Evans Creek Road toward Wimer.

30.1 Pass the Wimer Market and the Wimer covered bridge on the left.

30.7 Turn left onto East Evans Creek Road.

37.0 Enter the town of Rogue River.

38.0 Turn left onto Main Street.

38.4 Main Street curves right and turns into River Road.

43.0 Cross railroad tracks.

43.7 Pass the Del Rio Winery on the left.

43.8 Continue straight onto Highway 234 South toward Gold Hill.

45.9 Turn left onto 4th Street, and pedal a short distance to the city park and your starting point.

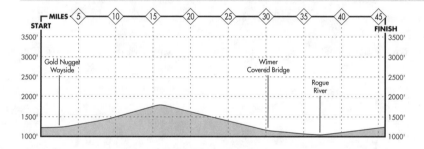

and pine forest. From this road you'll also have good views of Upper and Lower Table Rocks.

At just past 16 miles, you'll turn south onto Evans Creek Road and begin a fun descent to the small community of Wimer. This is a good spot to take a break and stock up on food and snacks at the Wimer Market next to the Wimer covered bridge. The 85-foot-long bridge was built in 1927 and spans Evans Creek. Over the next 11 miles the route winds through Evans Creek Canyon. At 37 miles you'll arrive in the town of Rogue River, which is host to more stores and restaurants that are happy to feed hungry cyclists. From here you'll follow River Road back to your starting point in Gold Hill.

LOCAL INFORMATION

♦ Grants Pass Visitors and Convention Bureau, 1995 NW Vine Street, Grants Pass, OR 97528, (800) 547–5927, www.visitgrantspass.org.

◆ Medford Visitor Information Center, 1314 Center Drive, Suite E, Medford, OR 97501, (541) 776–4021.

LOCAL EVENTS/ATTRACTIONS

◆ Oregon Shakespeare Festival, 15 South Pioneer Street, Ashland, OR 97520, (541) 482–4331, www.orshakes.org.

RESTAURANTS

◆ Abbys Legendary Pizza, 121 Pine Street, Rogue River, OR 97537, (541) 582–4203.
◆ Ranch Cafe, 8005 East Evans Creek Road, Rogue River, OR 97537, (541) 582–2538.

ACCOMMODATIONS

◆ Willowbrook Inn B&B, 628 Foots Creek Road, Gold Hill, OR 97525, (541) 582–0075, www.chatlink.com/~willowbr.

BIKE SHOPS

◆ Moores Bicycle Shop, 720 Crater Lake Avenue, Medford, OR 97504, (541) 772–9253.
◆ Dick's Bicycle Shop, 824 Rogue River Highway, Grants Pass, OR 97527, (541) 474–2867.
◆ Don's Bike Center, 211 SW G Street, Grants Pass, OR 97526, (541) 471–3494.

REST ROOMS

◆ Mile 0.0: Gold Hill City Park.
◆ Mile 2.4: Gold Nugget Wayside.

MAPS

◆ USGS 7.5-minute quads Gold Hill, Sams Valley, Boswell Mountain, Wimer, and Rogue River; *DeLorme Oregon Atlas and Gazetteer,* maps 19, 20, 27, and 28.

Maupin–Shaniko Challenge

This two-day cycling adventure tests your fitness and toughness as it passes through the remote wheat-farming country of Wasco County. The ride begins at White River Falls State Park and takes you into the scenic Deschutes River Canyon, where you'll have the opportunity to see Native Americans fishing for salmon at roaring Sherars Falls. The route travels along the Deschutes River, passes through the small community of Maupin, and then takes you on an uphill odyssey through remote farming country to the small historic town of Shaniko. At Shaniko you can stay in the historic hotel and tour many other unique historic buildings. On day two you'll complete the loop by riding through more open country and then soaring back to the Deschutes River Canyon and cranking out of the canyon back to your starting point.

White River Falls State Park is the starting point for this adventurous ride. Be sure to check out the roaring falls, which plunge 90 feet over a basalt ledge into the canyon. You can also take a 0.25-mile hike to the canyon floor to check out the historic Tygh Valley Power Plant, built in 1901 by the Wasco Warehouse Milling Company. It was originally built to power a flour mill that ground the wheat provided by local farmers. In 1910 the plant was purchased by Pacific Power and Light and provided power to Sherman and Wasco Counties until 1969.

The tour begins with a fun descent into the Deschutes River Canyon. After 3.4 miles you'll arrive at the tumultuous torrent of Sherars Falls. These falls are

Start: White River Falls State Park, located 35 miles southeast of The Dalles off Highway 216.
Length: 83.1-mile loop.
Season: Year-round (the roads can be icy during the winter months).
Approximate riding time: Two days.
Recommended start time: 7:00 A.M. (It is recommended you leave at this time in order to avoid the sweltering summertime temperatures on Bakeoven Road.)
Terrain: This route travels on major highways and rural roads.
Traffic and hazards: Highway 216 has no shoulder and light traffic. U.S. Highway 97 has a 3-foot shoulder, moderate to heavy traffic, and quite a bit of truck traffic. This is a very strenuous route and should only be attempted by experienced and fit cyclists. Summertime temperatures on this route can exceed 100 degrees. It is recommended that you attempt this route in the spring or fall to avoid the extreme heat. There are also few opportunities to obtain water. Bring a minimum of four to five liters of water per rider.
Getting there: From I–84 in The Dalles, take exit 87 toward Dufur and Bend. At the end of the off-ramp, turn south onto Highway 197, and travel 29.4 miles to the junction with Highway 216. Turn left (east) onto Highway 216, and proceed 4.2 miles to the entrance to White River Falls State Park. Turn right onto the entrance road, and go 0.2 mile on a dirt road to a large parking area. Note: White River Falls State Park is a day-use-only park. Once you have explored the park and stocked up on water, you'll need to head back out to Highway 216 and park your vehicle along the highway. Do not leave your vehicle parked overnight in the park's main parking area, or you may be cited.

named after Joseph Sherar. He bought the bridge crossing the river in 1871 for $7,040. He was responsible for many road improvements into this area and established and operated a stage and railroad station at the falls until the early 1900s. These falls are an important salmon fishery for the Confederated Tribes of Warm Springs, and you'll likely see tribe members fishing for salmon off rickety wooden platforms perched at the edge of the falls. Each year about 600 fall chinook salmon are netted at this location and are distributed among tribal members. The falls race through a deep lava chute, concentrating the fish into a smaller area as they swim upstream to spawn. The fishermen catch the powerful salmon by dipping nets into the fast-moving water.

After the falls you'll ride to the moody Deschutes River. During the summer months watch for rafters bobbing through the rapids. Check out the Oak Springs rapid at mile 8.1 for the best rafting action.

About 4 miles later you'll arrive at the small high-desert metropolis of Maupin, which has restaurants and other services. Be sure to stock up on water at Maupin City Park before you continue on the next section of the ride, which promises plenty of hill climbing as well as heat (if you are riding in the summer).

Just on the outskirts of Maupin, you'll turn onto Bakeoven Road. For the next 27 miles, you'll climb more than 2,600 feet through isolated, wide-open country filled with miles

Historic Power Plant at White River Falls State Park.

and miles of wheat fields and open plateaus. This ascent is tough and hot, and you'll find out soon enough that this road was aptly named.

After 39 miles you'll arrive in the historic town of Shaniko. In its heyday (from 1900 to 1911) Shaniko was known as the "Wool Capital of the World." It was a railway town and had 600 residents; many historic buildings are still here, including the large wooden water tank on the edge of town. Water was stored in a large reservoir and pumped to the large water tanks; water for the reservoir came from natural springs.

Plan on spending the night at the historic Shaniko Hotel (be sure to call ahead for availability). After you're settled in check out the antique shops, the historic buildings, and the Shaniko Museum—and be sure to have an ice cream at the one and only ice cream shop in town.

On the second day of the tour, you'll head north on U.S. Highway 97 for 20 miles past vast wheat ranches, where you'll have phenomenal views of Mount Hood to the west. Soon you'll turn off the busy highway and travel on quiet rural roads through more open farming country, until you reach Highway 216 at mile 68.1. Over the next 10 miles, this narrow, windy highway takes you on a steep descent into the gorgeous Deschutes River Canyon. At mile 79.4 you'll cross Sherars Bridge over the Deschutes River and then pedal on a steep ascent back to your starting point at White River Falls State Park at mile 83.1.

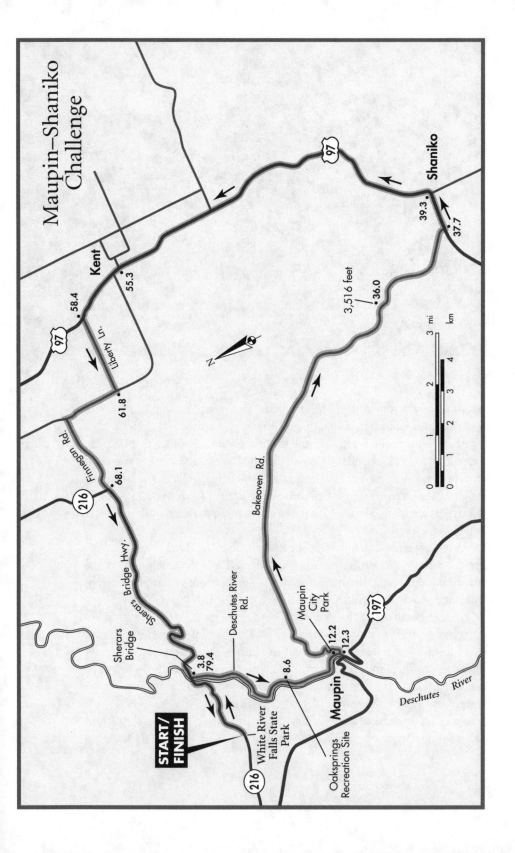

Maupin–Shaniko
Challenge

Start from the intersection of Highway 216 and the entrance road to White River Falls State Park. Pedal east on Highway 216.

1.0 Begin a steep descent through a narrow canyon.

3.2 The road parallels the Deschutes River.

3.4 Pass Sherars Falls on the right.

3.5 Pass a rest room and parking area on your right.

3.8 Cross Sherars Bridge over the Deschutes River.

4.0 Turn right onto the Deschutes River Access Road toward Maupin.

5.8 Pass Sandy Beach Boat Ramp on the right where there are rest rooms.

6.5 Cross a cattle guard. Pass the White River Recreation Site on the right. Rest rooms are present here (no water). Campsites are available for $5.00 per night.

8.1 Pass a viewpoint for Oak Springs Rapids on the right.

8.6 Pass the Oak Springs Recreation Site on the right. Rest rooms and campsites are present here (no water).

8.8 Cross a cattle guard.

9.0 Pass the Blue Hole Recreation Site with rest rooms (no water) on the right.

10.6 Pass the Gray Eagle Recreation Site, which has rest rooms and picnic tables (no water).

11.4 Pass the Oasis Recreation Site on the right, which has rest rooms and campsites (no water).

12.2 Pass Maupin City Park on the right. Rest rooms, picnic tables, and water are present here. It is recommended that you stock up on water at this park—there aren't any other water stops until you reach Shaniko at 39.3 miles.

12.3 At the stop sign, turn left onto Bakeoven Road. Begin a very steep, difficult climb. (If you want to stock up on snacks and drinks, turn right at this intersection, and head into downtown Maupin.)

36.0 Reach the 3,516-foot summit of Bakeoven Road.

(continued)

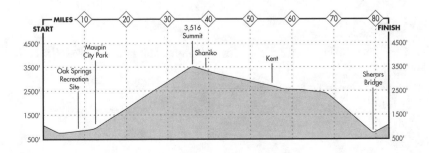

37.7 At the stop sign and T-intersection, turn left onto U.S. Highway 97 toward Shaniko. There is a 3-foot shoulder on this highway but moderate to heavy traffic. Be cautious of truck traffic.

39.1 Enter Shaniko. It is recommended that you spend the night at the Shaniko Historic Hotel (call ahead for availability). Be sure to stock up on water/drinks before you continue.

39.3 At the road junction stay to the left, and continue pedaling on U.S. Highway 97. From this point you'll have outstanding views of Mount Hood to the west.

55.3 Enter Kent (no services or water).

58.4 Turn left onto Liberty Lane. Enjoy more great views of Mount Hood.

61.8 At the stop sign and T-intersection, turn right onto Finnegan Road.

68.1 At the stop sign turn left onto Highway 216.

74.8 Begin a very steep, windy descent into the Deschutes River Canyon.

78.6 Cross the Deschutes River.

79.4 Cross Sherars Bridge over the Deschutes River, and begin a steep climb through a narrow canyon.

83.1 Arrive at the entrance road to White River Falls State Park.

ADDITIONAL RIDE INFORMATION

♦ Oregon State Parks and Recreation, 1115 Commercial Street NE, Suite 1, Salem, OR 97301, (800) 551–6949, www.oregonstateparks.org/park_36.php.

LOCAL INFORMATION

♦ The Dalles Chamber of Commerce, 404 West Second Street, The Dalles, OR 97058, (800) 255–3385, www.thedalleschamber.com.

LOCAL EVENTS/ATTRACTIONS

♦ Wasco County Fair, held the third week in August, 404 West Second Street, The Dalles, OR, 97058 (800) 255–3385.

RESTAURANTS

♦ Deschutes River Inn, 509 Deschutes Avenue, Maupin, OR 97037, (541) 395–2468.

♦ Oasis Resort, 609 U.S. Highway 197 South, Maupin, OR 97037, (541) 395–2611.

- Shaniko Café, located inside the Shaniko Historic Hotel, PO Box 86, Shaniko, OR 97057, (541) 489–3441.

ACCOMMODATIONS

- The Shaniko Historic Hotel, PO Box 86, Shaniko, OR 97057, (541) 489–3441 or (800) 483–3441, www.shaniko.com/lodgingx.html.

BIKE SHOPS

- Life Cycles The Dalles, 418 East 2nd Street, The Dalles, OR 97058, (541) 296–9588.

REST ROOMS

- Mile 0.0: White River Falls State Park.
- Mile 3.4: Sherars Falls.
- Mile 5.8: Sandy Beach Boat Ramp.
- Mile 6.5: White River Recreation Site.
- Mile 8.6: Oak Springs Recreation Site.
- Mile 9.0: Blue Hole Recreation Site.
- Mile 10.6: Gray Eagle Recreation Site.
- Mile 11.4: Oasis Recreation Site.
- Mile 12.4: Maupin City Park.
- Mile 39.1: Shaniko Hotel.

MAPS

- USGS 7.5-minute quads Maupin, Sherars Bridge, Dead Dog Canyon, Bronx Canyon, Shaniko, Grass Valley, and Sinamox; *DeLorme Oregon Atlas and Gazetteer,* maps 63 and 84.

Smith Rock State Park–
Sisters Challenge

Explore the magnificent volcano country of central Oregon on this challenging, scenic route. This tour begins in Smith Rock State Park and takes you southwest on rural roads to the small western-style town of Sisters, which is filled with fun shops, restaurants, and beautiful alpine scenery. From Sisters you'll climb steeply on the McKenzie Highway to a spectacular viewpoint of the central Oregon Cascades at Dee Wright Observatory. From the observatory you'll have a fast and thrilling descent back to Sisters, then you'll head east on Highway 126 toward Redmond. Along this part of the route you'll pass through beautiful high-desert scenery and have the opportunity to explore Cline Falls State Park next to the Deschutes River. You'll complete the loop by riding north on rural roads back to the town of Terrebonne, then end the route at Smith Rock State Park.

This ride begins in spectacular 641-acre Smith Rock State Park. This park features beautiful canyon scenery and is filled with magnificent 400-foot cliffs that shoot skyward from the canyon floor. From the main parking area on the canyon rim, you'll have a bird's-eye view of this spectacular canyon, and you may see rock climbers clinging to the multicolored cliffs. The park's rugged cliffs are remnants of ash deposits left from ancient volcanoes. The Gray Butte Complex, of which these volcanoes are a part, is made up of several different volcanic rock types that originate from the Miocene period, nearly 17 to 19 million years ago. Birds of prey, including golden eagles and peregrine falcons, nest in the high protected cliffs in the park. River otter, beaver, porcupine, deer, coyote, Canadian geese, blue heron, and a variety of ducks are among the wildlife you may see. Rest rooms, water, and picnic tables are available at the main parking area. There is also a bivouac area with walk-in tent sites.

From Smith Rock you'll pedal southwest on rural country roads, past large ranches and horse farms. At the 10-mile mark you'll pass Borden Beck Wildlife Preserve on your left. This day-use area is next to the Deschutes River, and its shady poplar trees and hiking trails give you a good break from the saddle. From here you'll continue your journey southwest on Lower Bridge Way as it winds past an old mining area and takes you through scenic high-desert country filled with fragrant sage and juniper.

After 29.4 miles you'll arrive in the small western-style town of Sisters. Sisters gets its name from the Three Sisters Cascade volcanoes

located southwest of the town. Logging was the main industry here in the early 1900s, as well as cattle ranching and farming. Today tourism is one of the mainstays of this small community, and it is worth stopping to explore the many funs shops and art galleries.

From Sisters you'll have a tough but scenic 2,100-foot-plus climb through a ponderosa pine forest to Dee Wright Observatory, located on a windswept lava flow. This stunning observatory is made from lava rock. A hiking path leads you to the inside of the observatory, which has viewing portals from which you can admire eleven gorgeous Cascade peaks, including Mount

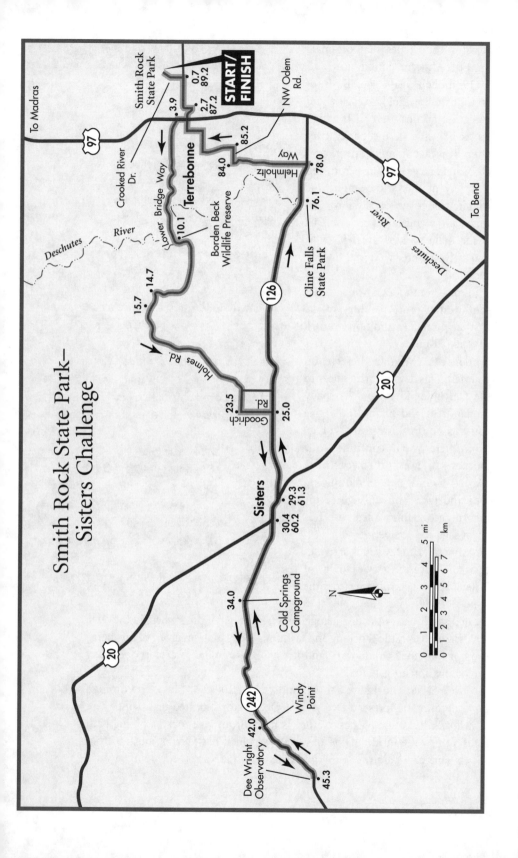

Smith Rock State Park–Sisters Challenge

To Madras

97

Smith Rock State Park

Crooked River Dr.

Deschutes River

Lower Bridge Way

Terrebonne

Borden Beck Wildlife Preserve

Helmholtz Way

NW Odem Rd.

START/FINISH

0.7
89.2

2.7
87.2

3.9

85.2

84.0

78.0

76.1

Cline Falls State Park

10.1

14.7

15.7

Holmes Rd.

126

Deschutes River

97

To Bend

20

23.5

25.0

Goodrich Rd.

29.3
61.3

30.4
60.2

Sisters

34.0

Cold Springs Campground

20

242

42.0

Windy Point

Dee Wright Observatory

45.3

N

0 1 2 3 4 5 mi

0 1 2 3 4 5 6 7 km

Start the ride from the Smith Rock State Park main parking area, and ride south on Crooked River Drive.

0.3 Pass the Smith Rock State Park bivouac area on your right. You can camp here for $4.00 per night. This camping area also has solar showers.

0.7 At the stop sign turn right onto Wilcox Avenue.

2.7 At the stop sign turn right onto Smith Rock Way. Go up the hill and through the small town of Terrebonne.

3.3 At the stop sign turn right (north) onto U.S. Highway 97. If you need to stock up on drinks, outdoor gear, or camping gear, you should stop at the Red Point Climber's Supply, which is on your right at this intersection.

3.9 Turn left onto Lower Bridge Way.

10.1 You'll pass Borden Beck Wildlife Preserve on your left. This day-use area is adjacent to the Deschutes River, and its shady poplar trees and hiking trails give you a good break from the saddle. Continue riding on Lower Bridge Way as it crosses over the Deschutes River and takes you past large ranches, alfalfa fields, and a juniper- and sage-filled landscape.

14.7 Turn left onto Holmes Road. (Lower Bridge Way turns to gravel here.)

15.7 Pass Long Hollow Ranch on your right. This ranch features a bed-and-breakfast and horseback riding.

22.3 Cross a cattle guard and then continue straight on Goodrich Loop. (Holmes Road goes left at this junction.)

23.5 Turn left onto Goodrich Road.

25.0 At the stop sign turn right (west) onto Highway 126.

29.4 Enter the small western-style town of Sisters.

29.7 Turn left onto West Hood Street. (After 0.2 mile of riding on West Hood Street, you have the option of riding to Sisters on the Green Park, which has a large grassy area with picnic tables, shade trees, a rest room, and water. To get to the park, turn left onto South Fir Street, ride 1 block, and turn right onto East Washington Street. The park is on your left after you turn onto East Washington Street.)

(continued)

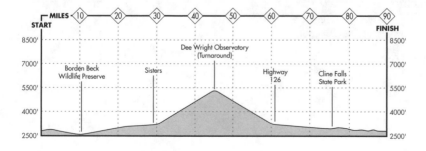

30.4 Turn left onto Highway 242 (the McKenzie Highway). Now you'll begin a long, difficult climb to the Dee Wright Observatory. Be sure you have plenty of water and food, and be sure to bring extras layers for the chilly descent.

34.0 Pass Cold Springs Campground on your right. This campground has vault toilets, water, and picnic tables.

42.0 Pass Windy Point viewpoint on your right. From here you have a grand view of Mount Washington and other prominent central Cascade volcanoes. As you continue west keep a sharp eye out for inattentive drivers who are looking at the view and not at the road.

45.3 Arrive at the Dee Wright Observatory on your right. Be sure to stop here to hike up the short path to the inside of the observatory and to read the interesting interpretive signs. You will be rewarded for all your hard work by a magnificent view of many central Oregon Cascade peaks. After you have had time to explore, turn around and head back to Sisters on Highway 242. Be sure to wear bright clothing on your descent. It is difficult for cars to see you on this shady highway.

60.2 Arrive back in Sisters, and turn right onto West Hood Avenue.

60.6 If you are in the mood for java, stop at Sisters Coffee Company on your right.

60.7 If you need to stock up on any biking or other outdoor supplies, stop at Eurosports on your left.

60.9 Turn right onto Highway 20.

61.3 Turn left onto Highway 126 East toward Redmond and Prineville. Use caution at this intersection!

76.1 Pass the turnoff to Cline Falls State Park on the right. This scenic state park has rest rooms, picnic tables, and hiking trails next to the Deschutes River.

78.0 Turn left onto NW Helmholtz Way.

81.7 At the stop sign turn right onto NW Coyner.

82.5 At the stop sign turn left onto Northwest Way.

84.0 Turn right onto NW Odem Road

85.2 Turn left onto NW 19th Street.

85.7 Turn right onto B Avenue.

86.5 At the stop sign cross U. S. Highway 97, and continue pedaling on B Avenue, which turns into Smith Rock Way.

87.2 Turn left onto Wilcox Avenue.

89.2 Turn left onto Crooked River Drive.

89.9 Arrive at the Smith Rock State Park main parking area.

Middle Sister and North Sister.

Bachelor, Broken Top, the Three Sisters, Mount Washington, and Mount Jefferson. Interpretive signs explain the amazing geology of the area. The lava flow surrounding the observatory was created when Belknap Crater erupted more than 2,900 years ago. Over the next thousand years, successive eruptions from Belknap Crater and Little Belknap Crater put the final touches on this moonlike landscape.

From the observatory you'll sail downhill back to Sisters. Wear bright clothing, and use caution on your descent. From Sisters you'll head east on Highway 126 toward Redmond for 6 miles to Cline Falls State Park. This nine-acre day-use park is located on the banks of the boulder-strewn Deschutes River and has picnic tables, rest rooms, and water. It is a good place to take a break. There are many great swimming holes along this stretch of the river.

A couple of miles past the park you'll turn north on Helmholtz Way. A curious attraction on this road is a reindeer farm. Over the next 8 miles, you'll pedal on backroads through rural countryside filled with farms, ranches, and rural residences back to the small town of Terrebonne. From Terrebonne, you'll head northeast back to your starting point at Smith Rock State Park.

ADDITIONAL RIDE INFORMATION

♦ State Parks and Recreation, 1115 Commercial Street NE, Suite 1, Salem, OR 97301-1002, (800) 551-6949, www.oregonstateparks.org.

Dee Wright Observatory.

LOCAL INFORMATION

♦ Redmond Chamber of Commerce, 446 SW Seventh Street, Redmond, OR 97756, (541) 923–5191, www.redmondcofc.com.
♦ Sisters Chamber of Commerce, 164 North Elm Street, Sisters, OR 97759, (541) 549–0251, www.sisterschamber.com.

LOCAL EVENTS/ATTRACTIONS

♦ Sisters Folk Festival, held the second weekend in September, PO Box 3500, PMB 304, Sisters, OR 97759, (503) 549–4979, www.sistersfolkfestival.com.
♦ Sisters Rodeo and Parade, held the second weekend in June, PO Box 1018, Sisters, OR 97759, (541) 549–0121, www.sistersrodeo.com.

RESTAURANTS

♦ El Rancho Grande, 150 East Cascade Avenue, Sisters, OR 97759, (541) 549–3594.
♦ Papandrea's Pizzeria, 442 East Hood Avenue, Sisters, OR 97759, (541) 549–6081.
♦ Sisters Bakery, 251 East Cascade Avenue, Sisters, OR 97759, (541) 549–0361.

◆ Sisters Coffee Company, 273 West Hood Street, Sisters, OR 97759, (800) 524–JAVA, www.sisterscoffee.com.

ACCOMMODATIONS

◆ Long Hollow Ranch, A Working Dude Ranch, 71105 Holmes Road, Sisters, OR 97759, (877) 923–1901, www.lhranch.com. Stay in a historic ranch house and eat a homemade breakfast for $95 per night.
◆ Blue Spruce B&B, 444 South Spruce Street, Sisters, OR 97759, (541) 549–6271, www.bluesprucebandb.com, $125 per night for two people, including a homemade breakfast.

BIKE SHOPS

◆ Eurosports, 182 East Hood Avenue, Sisters, OR 97759, (541) 549–2471.

REST ROOMS

◆ Mile 0.0: Smith Rock State Park.
◆ Mile 29.7: Sisters on the Green Park.
◆ Mile 30.4: Dee Wright Observatory.
◆ Mile 76.1: Cline Falls State Park.

MAPS

◆ USGS 7.5-minute quads Redmond, Cline Falls, Henkle Butte, Sisters, Black Crater, and Mount Washington; *DeLorme Oregon Atlas and Gazetteer,* maps 50 and 51.

Cove Palisades Cruise

T his loop tour takes you through the farming country surrounding Culver and Madras, where you'll have spectacular views of the Cascade Mountains to the west. It takes you across the historic Crooked River Bridge, which offers dramatic views of the Crooked River Gorge. You will also ride through the spectacular river canyon of Lake Billy Chinook and Cove Palisades State Park, where there are opportunities to camp and swim. From the park the route takes you back to the canyon rim, which offers more grand views of Lake Billy Chinook and the surrounding central Oregon high-desert country.

Crooked River Gorge.

This ride starts at the Peter Skene Ogden Scenic Wayside, perched on the rim of the striking Crooked River Canyon. Before you start the ride, be sure to walk across the expansive lawn to look down into the canyon. Once you begin riding you'll hook up with a pedestrian/ bike-only path that takes you across the historic Crooked River Gorge Bridge spanning the 300-foot-deep river canyon. Conde B. McCullough, a famous Oregon bridge engineer, designed this one. He is well known for bridges on the Oregon coast. Construction on the historic bridge began in 1925 at a cost of $180,000. At that time the bridge was the highest single-arch span bridge in the United States. This bridge was the final link for connecting the north and south borders along U.S. Highway 97 in central Oregon. Before it was built, travelers had to cross on a rickety wooden bridge about a mile upstream. Icy conditions made crossing the wooden bridge difficult during the winter, and traveling up the steep-walled gorge made the river crossing even more dangerous. When the historic bridge was dedicated on 15 July 1927, the *Oregonian* newspaper read: "The bridge stands as a symbol of all that the building of modern highways has meant to central Oregon. In it people see the fruition of their greatest hopes, the last link in the modern highway that stretches from north to south across the state, east of the Cascades, bringing tourists to their doors, bringing the farms closer to the cities, uniting the cities themselves in a spirit of neighborliness, where the lack of transportation in the old days meant isolation." Car traffic traveled on this historic bridge until October 2000, when the construction of a new bridge was completed at a cost of $18.3 million.

After you cross this historic bridge, you'll turn north onto busy U.S. Highway 97 and ride for about 7 miles, where you'll turn west onto the less traveled Culver Highway. The route takes you through a rural

THE BASICS

Start: Peter Skene Ogden Scenic Wayside in Terrebonne.
Length: 51.3-mile loop.
Season: Year-round (the roads can be icy during the winter months).
Approximate riding time: Four to five hours.
Recommended start time: 9:00 A.M.
Terrain: This route travels on rural roads and U.S. Highway 97. There are short sections of gravel road to three different viewpoints of Lake Billy Chinook.
Traffic and hazards: Use caution when riding on U.S. Highway 97, which has moderate to heavy traffic and a 3-foot shoulder. Use caution when descending on Jordan Road as you enter Cove Palisades State Park. This road is very narrow and windy and has no shoulder. Mountain View Road is very rough, and you'll have to negotiate uneven pavement and dodge multiple potholes. The short sections of road leading to the three viewpoints along Mountain View Road are gravel.
Getting there: From Redmond head 11.5 miles north on U.S. Highway 97 to the entrance road to the Peter Skene Ogden Scenic Wayside. Turn left onto the entrance road, and go 0.2 mile to a large parking area.

From Madras head approximately 14.5 miles south on U.S. Highway 97 to the entrance road to the Peter Skene Ogden Scenic Wayside. Turn right, and go 0.2 mile to a large parking area.

setting past farms and fields of mint and alfalfa and other commercial farm crops. To the west the central Cascade peaks dominate the horizon. Just shy of 10 miles, you'll pedal through the small community of Culver. From Culver the route continues west on rural roads through a sagebrush and juniper landscape.

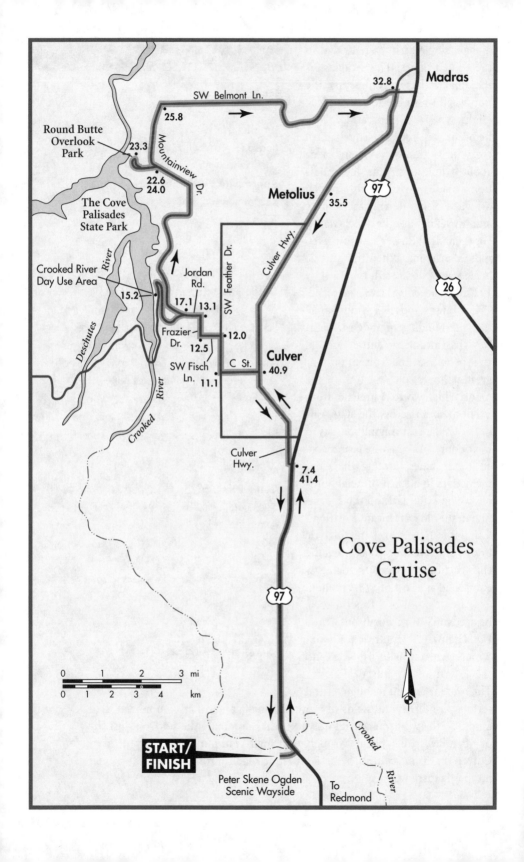

Cove Palisades Cruise

Madras

32.8

SW Belmont Ln.

25.8

Round Butte
Overlook
Park

23.3

Mountainview Dr.

22.6
24.0

Metolius

35.5

97

The Cove
Palisades
State Park

Deschutes River

Crooked River
Day Use Area

15.2

Jordan
Rd.

17.1   13.1

SW Feather Dr.

Culver Hwy.

Frazier
Dr.

12.0

12.5

Culver

C St.

40.9

SW Fisch
Ln.

11.1

Crooked River

26

Culver
Hwy.

7.4
41.4

97

START/
FINISH

Peter Skene Ogden
Scenic Wayside

To
Redmond

Crooked River

0   1   2   3 mi

0   1   2   3   4 km

N

Start by riding out the entrance road.

0.2 Turn left onto the pedestrian/bike-only paved road.

0.3 Cross the historic Crooked River Bridge. Be sure to stop and enjoy the awesome view of the 300-foot-deep Crooked River Gorge.

0.4 Turn left (north) onto U.S. Highway 97.

7.4 Turn left onto the Culver Highway, where a sign states COVE PALISADES STATE PARK and CULVER/ROUND BUTTE DAM.

9.7 Enter Culver.

10.1 Turn left onto C Street.

10.4 Cross railroad tracks.

11.1 At the T-intersection and stop sign, turn right onto SW Feather Drive, and follow the signs to Cove Palisades State Park.

12.0 Turn left onto SW Fisch Lane.

12.5 SW Fisch Lane curves sharply to the right and turns into Frazier Drive.

13.1 Turn left onto Jordan Road toward STATE PARKS.

13.3 Arrive at a road junction. Continue straight on unsigned Jordan Road, and begin a long, steep descent on a narrow, windy road with no shoulder. (Mountain View Drive heads right.)

13.4 Enter Cove Palisades State Park.

14.2 Pass a scenic overlook for Lake Billy Chinook on the left.

15.1 Arrive at a road junction. Take a sharp left toward DESCHUTES CAMP/DAY USE AREAS.

15.2 Turn into the Crooked River day-use area on the right. This recreation area is on the shores of the lake and has picnic tables, rest rooms, water, and a swimming area. This is your turnaround point. When you're finished exploring head back uphill on Jordan Road.

17.1 Turn left onto Mountain View Drive, where a sign states VIEWPOINTS 3/ROUND BUTTE OVERLOOK PARK 5/LAKE SIMTUSTUS 10. This section of the route is rough, and you'll have to dodge some potholes.

17.8 Pass a viewpoint of the lake on the left.

(continued)

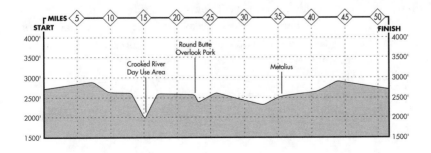

18.7 Pass a viewpoint of the lake on the left.

20.2 Pass a viewpoint of the lake on the left.

20.4 Cross a cattle guard.

21.0 Cross a cattle guard.

21.6 Arrive at a road junction. Turn left, and continue riding on Mountain View Drive (Round Butte Drive heads right). The road surface becomes smoother.

22.6 Arrive at the turnoff for the Round Butte Overlook Park. Turn left.

23.3 Arrive at the park and scenic overlook of Lake Billy Chinook. Rest rooms and water are available here. After enjoying the view head back out the entrance road to the park.

24.0 Turn left toward PELTON PARK/LAKE SIMUSTUS/PELTON WILDLIFE OVERLOOK.

25.8 At the stop sign and T-intersection, turn right onto SW Belmont Lane.

31.9 Cross railroad tracks.

32.8 At a stop sign and T-intersection, turn right onto Culver Highway.

35.5 Enter Metolius.

36.2 Pass the Desert Inn Restaurant on the right.

36.4 Pass Rico's Market on the right.

40.9 Enter Culver.

41.2 Pass Beetle Bailey Burgers on the right.

41.4 At the road junction stay to the left, and continue riding on the Culver Highway toward U.S. Highway 97.

43.9 Turn right (south) onto U.S. Highway 97.

50.9 Turn right onto the pedestrian/bike-only path.

51.1 Cross the historic Crooked River Bridge.

51.3 Arrive at the parking area at Peter Skene Ogden Scenic Wayside.

After 13 miles you'll begin a steep descent into the dramatic canyon that is home to Cove Palisades State Park and Lake Billy Chinook. Lake Billy Chinook is a huge reservoir that is fed by the Deschutes, Metolius, and Crooked Rivers. Dramatic canyon walls and spectacular high-desert scenery are this state park's draw. Two campgrounds are available if you want to stay overnight.

After 15 miles you'll arrive at the Crooked River day-use area, located on the shores of the lake, which has picnic tables, rest rooms, and a swimming area. If it's a hot summer's day, this is your chance to cool off!

After taking a break you'll crank more than 600 feet uphill to the canyon rim. From here the route travels north along the rim. Along the way you will have the chance to stop at three scenic viewpoints overlooking the lake.

You can see the lake from another perspective at Round Butte Dam Park at mile 23.3. This park is a shady oasis and has picnic tables, rest rooms, and an observation building perched above Round Butte Dam. Interpretive signs also explain the area's geology, history, and wildlife.

From here the route turns east toward Madras and takes you through more high-desert country. After 32.8 miles the route turns south onto the Culver Highway and takes you through the small town of Metolius. After 35 miles you'll complete the loop in Culver and retrace the route back to your starting point at the Peter Skene Ogden Scenic Wayside at mile 51.3.

ADDITIONAL RIDE INFORMATION

♦ Oregon State Parks and Recreation, 1115 Commercial Street NE, Suite 1, Salem, OR 97301-1002, (800) 551–6949, www.oregonstateparks.org/park_32.php.

LOCAL INFORMATION

♦ Madras-Jefferson County Chamber of Commerce, 274 SW 4th Street, Madras, OR 97741, (800) 967–3564, www.madras.net.
♦ Redmond Chamber of Commerce, 446 SW Seventh Street, Redmond, OR 97756, (541) 923–5191, www.redmondcofc.com.

LOCAL EVENTS/ATTRACTIONS

♦ Deschutes County Fair, held the first week in August, Deschutes County Fairgrounds, 3800 Airport Way, Redmond, OR 97756, (541) 548–2711, www.expo.deschutes.org.
♦ Eagle Watch, held the last weekend in February, Culver, OR. Contact Oregon State Parks, 1115 Commercial Street, Suite 1, Salem, OR 97301-1002, (541) 388–6211.

RESTAURANTS

♦ Black Bear Diner, 237 Southwest 4th Street, Madras, OR 97741, (541) 475–6632.
♦ Mexico City, 215 4th Street, Madras, OR 97741, (541) 475–6078.

ACCOMMODATIONS

♦ Best Western Rama Inn, 12 SW 4th Street, Madras, OR 97741, (888) 726–2466.
♦ Travelodge New Redmond Hotel, 521 SW 6th Street, Redmond, OR 97756, (800) 923–7378.

BIKE SHOPS

♦ Mountain Cycle, 411 Southwest Cascade Avenue, Redmond, OR 97756, (541) 923–2132.

REST ROOMS

♦ Mile 0.0: Peter Skene Ogden Scenic Wayside.
♦ Mile 15.2: Crooked River day-use area.
♦ Mile 23.3: Round Butte Overlook Dam.
♦ Mile 51.3: Peter Skene Ogden Scenic Wayside.

MAPS

♦ USGS 7.5-minute quads Opal City, Culver, and Round Butte Dam; *DeLorme Oregon Atlas and Gazetteer,* maps 51 and 57.

33

Drake Park–Shevlin Park– Tumalo State Park Ramble

This fun loop route begins in Drake Park in downtown Bend and takes you through a sage-scented landscape past Shevlin Park and Tumalo State Park.

The city of Bend is a good starting point for many excellent road tours. The city serves as a gateway to the Deschutes National Forest and the Cascade Lakes region and is surrounded by many gorgeous central Cascade peaks. There are many rural roads leading from Bend that wind through forests and through scenic farming and ranching country. The dry, sunny weather is an added bonus to this spectacular region of central Oregon.

This tour begins in Drake Park in downtown Bend and is a great introduction to some of the fantastic road riding Bend has to offer. Drake Park covers thirteen acres in

Central Oregon road riding at its best.

Start: Drake Park in downtown Bend.

Length: 15-mile loop.

Season: Year-round. Snow can be present during the winter months.

Approximate riding time: One to two hours.

Recommended start time: 11:00 A.M.

Terrain: This route travels on city streets and rural country roads in Bend.

Traffic and hazards: Riverside Boulevard, Galveston Avenue, NW 14th Street, Newport Avenue, Butler Market Road, Revere Avenue, Hill Street, and Franklin Avenue have light to moderate traffic. Shevlin Park Road, Johnson Road, and O. B. Riley Road have a bike lane and light to moderate traffic. Use caution when riding on U.S. Highway 97. There is a bike lane on the highway, but there is heavy traffic. It is recommended that you avoid this ride during peak morning and evening rush hour traffic.

Getting there: At the intersection of U.S Highway 97 and Franklin Avenue in downtown Bend, turn west onto Franklin Avenue Drive 0.8 mile on Franklin Avenue to a public parking area on the right side of the road in Drake Park.

a picturesque setting on the edge of Mirror Pond, which is fed by the Deschutes River. Towering ponderosa pine trees, paved paths, and picnic tables make this a great starting point for this short fun ride. From the public parking area adjacent to Drake Park, you'll pedal along the edge of the park on Riverside Boulevard. After 1.2 miles you'll turn west onto Newport Avenue, which takes you through the west side of Bend past several quiet residential areas. Newport Avenue soon turns into NW Shevlin Park Road, and after a few miles you'll enter the Deschutes National Forest. This amazing national forest is visited by more than 8 million people per year and is one of the most popular forests in the Northwest.

After 4.2 miles you'll pass Shevlin Park. This beautiful park covers 603 acres and was donated to the community of Bend in 1920. It is worth stopping at this park to explore the hiking trails that wind through towering ponderosa pines. Continue your journey by heading north on Shevlin Park Road as it takes you over rolling hills through a sage-scented, high-desert landscape.

After 9 miles you'll arrive at Tumalo State Park. Located on the Deschutes River, this quiet haven has trails that wind along the river underneath towering ponderosa pine, willow, and alder trees. Picnic tables, rest rooms, and water are available. This park also features a large campground that is open year-round.

From Tumalo State Park you'll turn south and head back into town on O. B. Riley Road, which intersects with busy U.S. Highway 97 after 13 miles. The Bend River Mall and several restaurants and hotels line this section of the highway. After 0.2 mile you'll turn off the highway and ride on quieter city streets back to your starting point at Drake Park. After your ride you can quench your thirst and hunger at the Deschutes Brewery in downtown Bend, which serves up great local microbrews and delicious food.

ADDITIONAL RIDE INFORMATION

♦ Bend Metro Park and Recreation District, 200 NW Pacific Park Lane, Bend, OR 97701, (541) 389–7275, www.bendparksandrec.org.

♦ Oregon State Parks and Recreation, 1115 Commercial Street NE, Suite 1, Salem, OR 97301-1002, (800) 551–6949, www.oregonstateparks.org.

LOCAL INFORMATION

♦ Bend Chamber Visitor and Convention Bureau, 63085 North Highway 97, Bend, OR 97701, (800) 905–2363, www.visitbend.com.

♦ Deschutes National Forest, 1645 Highway 20 East, Bend, OR 97701, (541) 383–5531, www.fs.fed.us/r6/centraloregon.

LOCAL ATTRACTION

♦ High Desert Museum, 59800 South U.S. Highway 97, Bend, OR 97702-7963, (541) 382–4754, www.highdesert.org. Learn about the history and flora and fauna of central Oregon at this outstanding museum. Hours 9:00 A.M. to 5:00 P.M. daily. Closed Thanksgiving, Christmas, and New Year's Day. Call for admission rates.

RESTAURANTS

♦ Baja Norte Mexican Grill, 801 NW Wall Street, Bend, OR 97701, (541) 593–9374.

♦ Deschutes Brewery, 1044 NW Bond Street, Bend, OR 97701, (541) 382–9242, www.deschutesbrewery.com.

♦ West Side Bakery & Café, 1005 NW Galveston Avenue, Bend, OR 97701, (541) 382–3426.

ACCOMMODATIONS

♦ Bend Hostel, 19 SW Century Drive, Bend, OR 97701, (541) 389–3813.

♦ Lara House B&B, 640 NW Congress, Bend, OR 97701, (541) 388–4064, www.larahouse.com. Stay in a magnificent 1910 craftsman historical B&B home overlooking Drake Park and Mirror Pond in downtown Bend. Call for current rates.

♦ The Inn of the Seventh Mountain, 18575 SW Century Drive, Bend, OR 97702, (800) 452–6810, www.innofthe7thmountain.com. This resort offers tennis, swimming, rafting, mountain biking, and other fun activities. Call for current rates.

♦ The Riverhouse, 3075 North Highway 97, Bend, OR 97701, (800) 547–3928, www.riverhouse.com. This hotel offers river-view rooms in downtown Bend. Call for current rates.

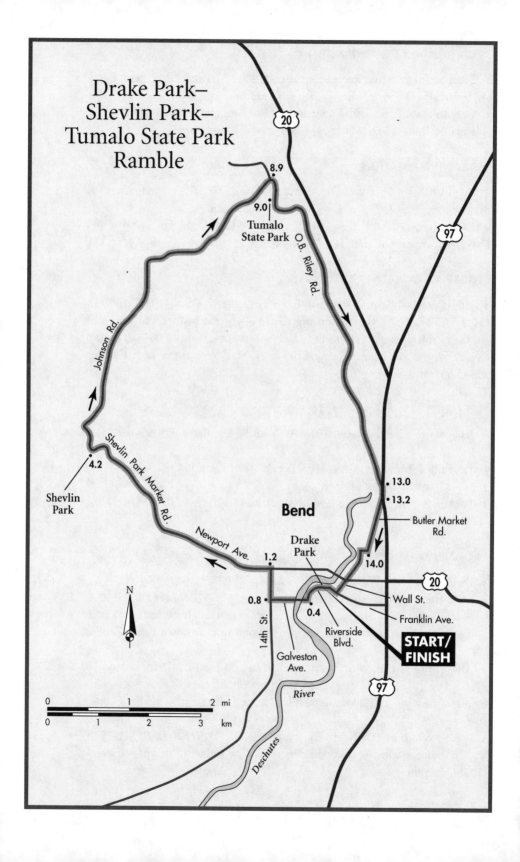

Drake Park–
Shevlin Park–
Tumalo State Park
Ramble

20

97

8.9

9.0
Tumalo
State Park

O.B. Riley Rd.

Johnson Rd.

4.2
Shevlin
Park

Shevlin Park Market Rd.

Newport Ave.

Bend

13.0
13.2

Butler Market
Rd.

1.2

Drake
Park

14.0

20

N

0.8

Wall St.

Franklin Ave.

14th St.

0.4

Galveston
Ave.

Riverside
Blvd.

START/
FINISH

River

97

Deschutes

0   1   2 mi
0   1   2   3 km

MILES AND DIRECTIONS

Start by turning right out of the public parking area at Drake Park onto Riverside Boulevard.

0.4 At the stop sign turn right onto Tumalo Street (which turns into Galveston Avenue).

0.8 At the stop sign turn right onto 14th Street.

1.2 At the stop sign turn left onto Newport Avenue (This road turns into NW Shevlin Park Road and then into Johnson Road.)

4.2 Pass Shevlin Park on your left. Rest rooms and water are available here.

8.9 At the stop sign turn right onto Tumalo Reservoir Road. At the next stop sign turn right onto O. B. Riley Road.

9.0 Pass the entrance to Tumalo State Park on your right. Rest rooms, water, and picnic tables are available at this park.

10.3 The bike lane begins again.

13.0 Turn right onto U.S. Highway 97.

13.2 Turn right onto Butler Market Road (this turns into Division Street).

14.0 At the stoplight turn right onto Revere Avenue.

14.1 At the stoplight turn left onto Hill Street (this turns into Wall Street).

14.9 At the stoplight turn right onto Franklin Avenue.

15.0 Arrive at the public parking area on your right.

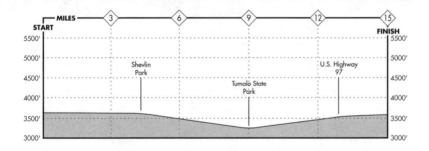

♦ Tumalo State Park Campground, Bend, OR. Contact Oregon State Parks, 1115 Commercial Street NE, Suite 1, Salem, OR 97301-1002, (800) 551–6949, www.oregonstateparks.org.

BIKE SHOPS

♦ Bend Cyclery, 853 NW Bond Street, Bend, OR 97701, (541) 385–5256.

♦ Century Cycles, 1135 NW Galveston, Bend, OR 97701, (541) 389–4224, www.centurycycles.org.

♦ Hutch's Bicycle Store, 725 NW Columbia Street, Bend, OR 97701, (541) 382–9253, www.hutchsbicycles.com.

- Pine Mountain Sports, 133 SW Century Drive, Bend, OR 97701, (541) 385–8080.
- Sunnyside Sports, 930 NW Newport Avenue, Bend, OR 97701, (541) 382–8018, www.kmx.com/sunnyside.

REST ROOMS

- Mile 0.0: Drake Park.
- Mile 4.2: Shevlin Park.
- Mile 9.0: Tumalo State Park.

MAPS

- USGS 7.5-minute quad Bend; *DeLorme Oregon Atlas and Gazetteer,* map 51.

Cascade Lakes Highway Challenge

T his spectacular route takes you into the high lakes region of central Oregon. The ride starts in Drake Park in downtown Bend and takes you on an uphill odyssey on the Cascade Lakes Highway. You'll pass many prominent central Oregon Cascade volcanoes, including Mount Bachelor, Broken Top, South Sister, and Middle Sister. The route then swings south and takes you past many beautiful alpine lakes, including Devil's Lake, Elk Lake, Lava Lake, and Little Lava Lake. The last section of the route takes you on paved forest service roads back to the Cascade Lakes Highway. An exhilarating descent back to Bend is the grand finale for this classic tour.

This tour takes you through the beautiful Cascade Lakes region west of Bend. The ride starts in picturesque Drake Park in downtown Bend. This park is nestled along the shores of Mirror Pond, which is home to graceful swans, Canada geese, and ducks. You'll pedal west on city streets through Bend's residential and tourist district for 2 miles, then turn onto Century Drive, which is the beginning of the Cascade Lakes Highway (Highway 46). Over the next 20 miles, you'll ascend 2,300 feet through the Deschutes National Forest, a sage- and pine-covered landscape with opportunities to view the lava flows and buttes that make up this spectacular volcano country.

Just past the 21-mile mark, you'll pass the world-class Mount Bachelor ski resort and 9,060-foot Mount Bachelor on the south side of the highway. This young volcano was formed about 14,000 years ago and is covered with thick stands of western and Engelmann spruce, ponderosa pine, Douglas fir, and sugar pine. During the summer months you can ride a chairlift to a scenic

Start: Drake Park in downtown Bend.
Length: 90-mile loop.
Season: Mid-June through October.
Approximate riding time: Seven to nine hours.
Recommended start time: 7:00 A.M.
Terrain: This route travels on city streets, a scenic highway, and paved forest service roads through the Deschutes National Forest.
Traffic and hazards: The Cascade Lakes Highway (Highway 46) has moderate traffic and a shoulder for part of its length. Forest Roads (FR) 40 and 45 do not have shoulders and have light traffic. Ride single file, and wear bright clothing on this route. This ride can also have a very chilly descent. Be sure to bring extra layers. If you are not used to riding at altitude, you may experience headaches or shortness of breath.

Getting there: From the intersection of U.S. Highway 97 and NW Franklin Avenue in downtown Bend, turn west onto NW Franklin Avenue. Drive 0.8 mile on NW Franklin Avenue (which turns into Riverside Boulevard) to a public parking area at Drake Park on the right side of the road.

viewpoint halfway up the mountain, where you'll enjoy a magnificent view of the surrounding Cascade peaks.

As you ride past Mount Bachelor, you'll sail down into an area called Dutchman Flat. This is a huge pumice field. As you ride along the edge of its broad expanse, look north to view the towering peaks of 9,175-foot Broken Top; 10,358-foot South Sister; and 10,047-foot Middle Sister. If you feel like stretching your legs and viewing some beautiful scenery in the Three Sisters Wilderness, stop at the Green Lakes Trailhead at the 26.4-mile mark. From the trailhead you can hike 4.4 miles north along the magical Fall Creek Trail to the pristine Green Lakes.

At 28.5 miles you'll pass Devil's Lake on the south side of the road. This forty-acre lake is stocked with rainbow trout and has a campground with walk-in tent sites. Not far past Devil's Lake, the highway swings to the south. At 32.8 miles you'll have the option of checking out Elk Lake and Elk Lake Resort. Elk Lake Resort offers cabin rentals, a café, and a restaurant. From the lakeshore Mount Bachelor rises majestically to the east, and the Three Sisters tower over the north end of the lake. This lake is a favorite for sailboaters and windsurfers. You can also stop at the day-use area located 1.5 miles south of the Elk Lake Resort turnoff to see the lake from a different perspective. Campgrounds are available at the lake if you want to stay overnight.

From Elk Lake continue south to the 38.3-mile mark, where you can turn off and explore Lava Lake and Little Lava Lake. There is a store at Lava Lake if you need to stock up on drinks and snacks. Lava Lake is spring fed and has good stocks of rainbow and brook trout. Little Lava Lake is located about a quarter mile south of Lava Lake and is the source for the Deschutes River. Campgrounds are present at both lakes.

Amazing mountain scenery on the Cascade Lakes Highway.

At 44.7 miles you'll turn off the Cascade Lakes Highway onto Forest Road (FR) 40. Over the next 15 miles, the road twists and turns through a pine-scented forest to the intersecton with FR 45. You'll turn left (north) onto FR 45 and over the next 11 miles you'll climb a few hundred feet back to the junction with the Cascade Lakes Highway. You'll finish the route by turning east onto the Cascade Lakes Highway and having an exhilarating descent back to Drake Park in downtown Bend.

ADDITIONAL RIDE INFORMATION

♦ Bend Metro Park and Recreation District, 200 NW Pacific Park Lane, Bend, OR 97701, (541) 389–7275, www.bendparksandrec.org.
♦ Deschutes National Forest, 1645 Highway 20 East, Bend, OR 97701, (541) 383–5300, www.fs.fed.us/r6/centraloregon.
♦ Oregon State Parks and Recreation, 1115 Commercial Street NE, Suite 1, Salem, OR 97301-1002, (800) 551–6949, www.oregonstateparks.org.

LOCAL INFORMATION

♦ Bend Chamber Visitor and Convention Bureau, 63085 North Highway 97, Bend, OR 97701, (800) 905–2363, www.visitbend.com.

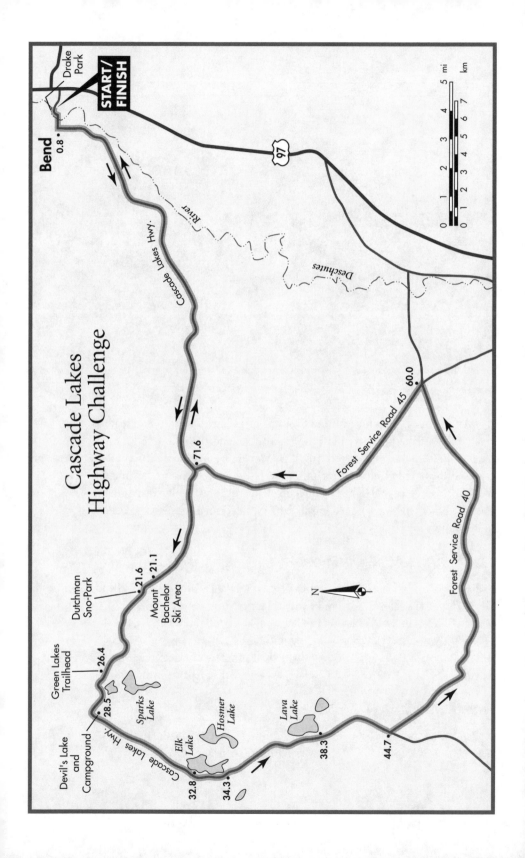

Cascade Lakes
Highway Challenge

Bend

Drake Park

START/
FINISH

0.8

97

Deschutes

River

Cascade Lakes Hwy.

71.6

Forest Service Road 45

60.0

Forest Service Road 40

N

Dutchman
Sno-Park

21.6

Mount
Bachelor
Ski Area

21.1

Green Lakes
Trailhead

26.4

28.5

Sparks
Lake

Devil's Lake
and
Campground

Cascade Lakes Hwy.

32.8

34.3

Elk
Lake

Hosmer
Lake

38.3

Lava
Lake

44.7

5 mi

km

0   1   2   3   4   5

0   1   2   3   4   5   6   7

Start by turning right out of the public parking area at Drake Park onto Riverside Boulevard.

0.3 At the stop sign turn right onto Tumalo Street (this turns into Galveston Avenue).

0.8 At the stop sign turn left onto NW 14th Street toward Mount Bachelor and the Cascade Lakes.

1.9 Arrive at a roundabout, and follow signs to Century Drive (this turns into the Cascade Lakes Highway/Highway 46). From this point you'll begin a long ascent as the highway winds through the Deschutes National Forest.

21.1 Pass the entrance to Sunrise Lodge and Mount Bachelor ski area on your left.

21.6 Pass the Dutchman Sno-Park on your right. There is a vault toilet here. From this point you'll have a spectacular view of Mount Bachelor, South Sister, Middle Sister, and Broken Top, and you'll begin an exhilarating descent down to Dutchman Flat.

26.4 Pass the Green Lakes Trailhead on your right. There are vault toilets here. You have the option here of hiking on the 4.4-mile Fall Creek Trail to Green Lakes.

28.5 Pass Devil's Lake on your left. Vault toilets are available here. There is also a free campground with walk-in tent sites.

32.8 Pass the turnoff to Elk Lake Resort on your left.

34.3 Pass Elk Lake day-use area on your left.

38.3 Pass the turnoff to Lava Lakes on your left.

44.7 Turn left onto FR 40 toward Cow Meadow.

60.0 Turn left onto FR 45 where a sign indicates MT. BACHELOR JUNCTION.

71.6 At the stop sign turn right onto the Cascade Lakes Highway, and begin a fast descent toward Bend.

88.2 Arrive at a roundabout, and follow signs to 14th Street.

89.3 At the stop sign turn right onto Galveston Avenue.

89.6 Pass the Westside Bakery and Café on your right.

89.7 Turn left onto Riverside Boulevard.

90.0 Arrive back at Drake Park.

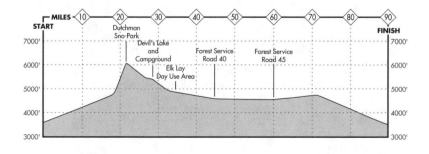

♦ High Desert Museum, 59800 South U.S. Highway 97, Bend, OR 97702-7963, (541) 382–4754, www.highdesert.org. Learn about the history and flora and fauna of central Oregon at this outstanding museum. Hours 9:00 A.M. to 5:00 P.M. daily. Closed Thanksgiving, Christmas, and New Year's Day. Call for admission rates.

♦ Mount Bachelor Chair Lift, located at the Mount Bachelor Ski Area, 20 miles west of Bend off the Cascade Lakes Highway, (541) 382–2442, www.mtbachelor. com. Open daily June 30 to September 3, 11:00 A.M. to 4:00 P.M. (Sunday–Thursday) and 11:00 A.M. to 8:00 P.M. (Friday–Saturday). Call for lift prices.

RESTAURANTS

♦ Baja Norte Mexican Grill, 801 NW Wall Street, Bend, OR 97701, (541) 593–9374.

♦ Deschutes Brewery, 1044 NW Bond Street, Bend, OR 97701, (541) 382–9242, www.deschutesbrewery.com.

♦ West Side Bakery & Café, 1005 NW Galveston Avenue, Bend, OR 97701, (541) 382–3426.

ACCOMMODATIONS

♦ Bend Hostel, 19 SW Century Drive, Bend, OR 97701, (541) 389–3813.

♦ Elk Lake Resort, PO Box 789, Bend, OR 97709, (541) 480–7228, www. elklakeresort.com.

♦ Lara House B&B, 640 NW Congress, Bend, OR 97701, (541) 388–4064, www.larahouse.com. Stay in a magnificent 1910 craftsman historical B&B home overlooking Drake Park and Mirror Pond in downtown Bend. Call for current rates.

♦ The Inn of the Seventh Mountain, 18575 SW Century Drive, Bend, OR 97702, (800) 452–6810, www.innofthe7thmountain.com. This resort offers tennis, swimming, rafting, mountain biking, and other fun activities. Call for current rates.

♦ The Riverhouse, 3075 North Highway 97, Bend, OR 97701, (800) 547–3928, www.riverhouse.com. This hotel offers river-view rooms in downtown Bend. Call for current rates.

BIKE SHOPS

♦ Bend Cyclery, 853 NW Bond Street, Bend, OR 97701, (541) 385–5256.

♦ Century Cycles, 1135 NW Galveston, Bend, OR 97701, (541) 389–4224, www.centurycycles.org.

- Hutch's Bicycle Store, 725 NW Columbia Street, Bend, OR 97701, (541) 382–9253, www.hutchsbicycles.com.
- Pine Mountain Sports, 133 SW Century Drive, Bend, OR 97701, (541) 385–8080.
- Sunnyside Sports, 930 NW Newport Avenue, Bend, OR 97701, (541) 382–8018, www.kmx.com/sunnyside.

REST ROOMS

- Mile 0.0: Drake Park.
- Mile 21.6: Dutchman Sno-Park.
- Mile 26.4: Green Lakes Trailhead.
- Mile 34.3: Elk Lake day-use area.

MAPS

- USGS 7.5-minute quads Elk Lake, South Sister, Broken Top, Bachelor Butte, Wanoga Butte, Benham Falls, Shevlin Park, and Bend; *DeLorme Oregon Atlas and Gazetteer,* maps 44, 45, 50, and 51.

35

Newberry National Volcanic Monument Cruise

*T*his strenuous route takes you on a tour of the geologic wonders in the Newberry Crater National Volcanic Monument. Dramatic lava flows, high volcanic peaks, alpine lakes, and cascading waterfalls are some of the attractions waiting to be explored in this magnificent monument. A $5.00 fee is charged to enter the monument. This ride is recommended for experienced and fit cyclists. You'll climb more than 2,200 feet in elevation.

East Lake.

This ride begins in La Pine State Park, which features miles of hiking and biking trails and a large campground. It also boasts Oregon's largest remaining ponderosa pine tree. This majestic tree is thought to be more than 500 years old. It is 191 feet high and 326 inches in circumfurence. From the state park you'll pedal on flat terrain for about 5 miles through a subalpine forest to U.S. Highway 97. You'll turn south onto busy U.S. Highway 97 for a short mile, then turn east onto Paulina Lake Road (FR 21). For the next 11 miles, you'll climb more than 2,200 feet through a scenic forest into the Newberry National Volcanic Monument. Created in November 1990 this national monument boasts more than 50,000 acres of high alpine lakes, lava flows, and scenic mountain peaks. The crown jewel is the 500-square-mile Newberry Crater caldera, which houses Paulina and East Lakes.

Once you enter the monument, there are several opportunities to stop and take a break to enjoy the superb scenery. Your first chance is at Paulina Creek Falls at 18.7 miles. This spectacular waterfall can be seen from a fenced-off viewpoint about 100 yards from the parking area. Paulina Creek spills over a bouldery cliff, creating a magnificent 60-foot cascade. At 19 miles you have the option of turning off at Paulina Lake Resort, which has a general store with drinks and snacks. This resort also rents cabins during the summer if you want to stay overnight. Once you are at this point, you'll enjoy a grand view of Paulina Lake and impressive 7,984-foot Paulina Peak. As you continue the route swings around the south side of Paulina Lake. If you want to hike around the lakeshore, you can

turn into the Paulina Lake Trailhead at 19.2 miles. A 7.5-mile trail travels past sandy beaches and through lava flows and pine-scented forest.

If you'd like to see Oregon's youngest lava flow, be sure to stop at the Big Obsidian Flow Trailhead at 21.4 miles. This flow covers 1.1 square miles and has an average depth of 150 feet. It is about 1,300 years old and features glasslike obsidian. A 0.7-mile trail loops through the lava flow past piles of shiny black obsidian. Native Americans used this rock to make arrowheads,

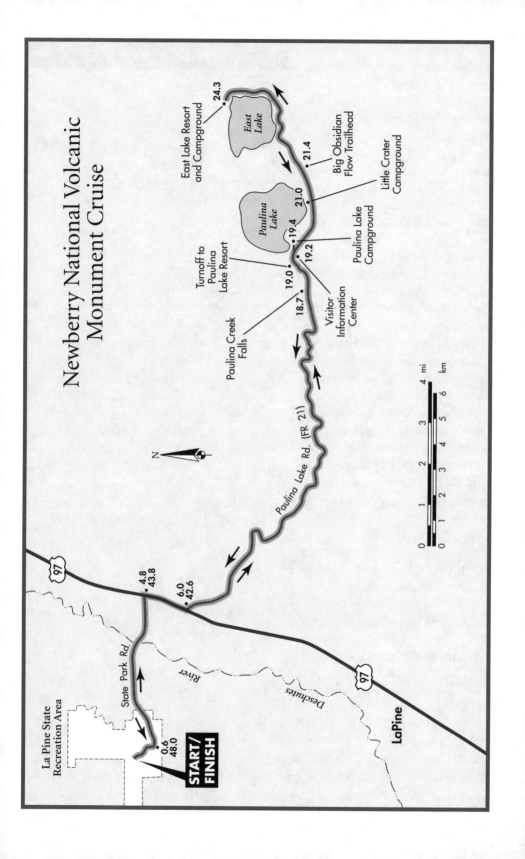

Start from the picnic and day-use area in La Pine State Park. Ride south on the paved road.

0.4 At the stop sign and T-intersection, turn right onto the unsigned paved road.

0.6 At the road junction turn left onto State Park Road at the U.S. 97 sign.

4.4 Cross the railroad tracks.

4.8 At the stop sign and T-intersection, turn right (south) onto U.S. Highway 97.

6.0 Turn left onto Paulina Lake Road (FR 21).

6.1 Pass an information station and pullout on the left describing the attractions in the Newberry National Volcanic Monument.

16.6 Pass a scenic overlook on the right.

17.6 Pass the entrance station to the national monument on your left.

18.7 Pass the turnoff to Paulina Creek Falls on your left. Rest rooms are available.

19.0 Pass the turnoff to Paulina Lake Resort on your left. Snacks and drinks are available at the general store.

19.2 Pass the Paulina Lake Trailhead on your left. You have the option here of hiking 7.5 miles around Paulina Lake. There are rest rooms at this trailhead. The Paulina Lake Visitors Center is located on the right side of the road at this junction.

19.4 Pass the entrance to Paulina Lake Campground on your left. Rest rooms and water are available here.

21.0 Pass the entrance to Little Crater Campground on your left. Rest rooms and water are available here.

21.4 Pass the Big Obsidian Flow Trailhead on your right. A hike on the 0.7-mile Big Obsidian Flow Trail takes you on a tour of Oregon's youngest lava flow.

23.2 Pass the entrance to East Lake Campground on your left.

23.9 Pass the Hot Springs Boat Ramp on your left. Rest rooms and water are available here.

24.3 Arrive at East Lake Resort and Campground on your left. This is your turnaround point. Rest rooms are present here.

(continued)

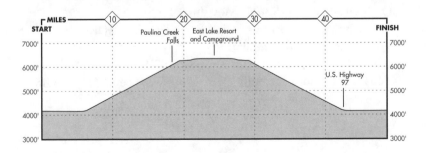

42.6 Turn right (north) onto U.S. Highway 97.

43.8 Turn left onto State Park Road toward La Pine State Park.

44.2 Cross the railroad tracks.

48.0 The road forks. Turn right where a sign indicates CAMPING/DAY USE.

48.2 Turn left at the signed DAY USE/PICNIC AREA.

48.6 Arrive at the day-use picnic area.

jewelry, knives, and tools. Artifacts have been found here that are more than 10,000 years old.

After 24.3 miles you'll arrive at East Lake Resort and your turnaround point. This resort is located on the shores of quiet 1,050-acre East Lake and has cabins, rooms, and three campgrounds. Like Paulina Lake, East Lake is popular for fishing, and record-size brown trout are caught here frequently. Until 1912 Paulina and East Lake did not have any fish stocks. Rainbow fingerlings were hauled from Bend on a long, tough journey and since that time have been the predominate catch at both lakes.

From here head back down Paulina Lake Road on a fun, fast downhill to U.S. Highway 97. Watch your speed on this often chilly descent. From U.S. Highway 97 retrace your route back to La Pine State Park.

ADDITIONAL RIDE INFORMATION

♦ Oregon State Parks and Recreation, 1115 Commercial Street NE, Suite 1, Salem OR 97301-1002, (800) 551–6949, www.oregonstateparks.org/park_41.php.

♦ Newberry National Volcanic Monument, Deschutes National Forest, 1645 Highway 20 East, Bend, OR 97701, (541) 383–5300, www.fs.fed.us/r6/centraloregon/index-monument.html.

LOCAL INFORMATION

♦ Bend Chamber Visitor and Convention Bureau, 63085 North Highway 97, Bend, OR 97701, (800) 905–2363, www.visitbend.com.

♦ Deschutes National Forest, 1645 Highway 20 East, Bend, OR 97701, (541) 383–5531, www.fs.fed.us/r6/centraloregon.

♦ Central Oregon Wheelers, PO Box 8269, Bend 97708, 541-385-0948.

♦ Klah Klahnee Cycling Club, 930 NW Newport Ave., Bend, 541-382-8018.

LOCAL ATTRACTIONS

♦ High Desert Museum, 59800 South U.S. Highway 97, Bend, OR 97702-7963, (541) 382–4754, www.highdesert.org. Learn about the history and flora and fauna of central Oregon at this outstanding museum. Hours 9:00 A.M. to 5:00 P.M. daily. Closed Thanksgiving, Christmas, and New Year's Day. Call for admission rates.

RESTAURANTS

♦ Baja Norte Mexican Grill, 801 NW Wall Street, Bend, OR 97701, (541) 593–9374.
♦ Bend Brewing, 1019 NW Brooks Street, Bend, OR 97701, (541) 383–1599, www.sharplink.com/bbc.
♦ Deschutes Brewery, 1044 NW Bond Street, Bend, OR 97701, (541) 382–9242, www.deschutesbrewery.com.
♦ West Side Bakery & Café, 1005 NW Galveston Avenue, Bend, OR 97701, (541) 382–3426.

ACCOMMODATIONS

♦ East Lake Resort, Newberry National Volcanic Monument, PO Box 95, 22430 Paulina Lake Road, La Pine, OR 97739, (541) 536–2230, www.eastlakeresort.com. This resort rents cabins and camping rooms. Three large campgrounds are also located here.
♦ La Pine State Park Campground, La Pine, OR. Contact Oregon State Parks, 1115 Commercial Street NE, Suite 1, Salem, OR 97301-1002, (800) 551–6949, www.oregonstateparks.org/park_41.php.
♦ Lara House B&B, 640 NW Congress, Bend, OR 97701, (541) 388–4064, www.larahouse.com. Stay in a magnificent 1910 craftsman historical B&B home overlooking Drake Park and Mirror Pond in downtown Bend. Call for current rates.
♦ Paulina Lake Campground, Paulina Lake, Deschutes National Forest, 1645 Highway 20 East, Bend, OR 97701, www.fs.fed.us/r6/centraloregon. Open May through October.
♦ Paulina Lake Resort, PO Box 95, La Pine, OR 97739, (541) 536–2240. Open mid-December through mid-March and from May through October.

BIKE SHOPS

♦ Bend Cyclery, 853 NW Bond Street, Bend, OR 97701, (541) 385–5256.
♦ Century Cycles, 1135 NW Galveston, Bend, OR 97701, (541) 389–4224, www.centurycycles.org.

♦ Hutch's Bicycle Store, 725 NW Columbia Street, Bend, OR 97701, (541) 382–9253, www.hutchsbicycles.com.
♦ Pine Mountain Sports, 133 SW Century Drive, Bend, OR 97701, (541) 385–8080.
♦ Sunnyside Sports, 930 NW Newport Avenue, Bend, OR 97701, (541) 382–8018, www.kmx.com/sunnyside.

REST ROOMS

♦ Mile 0.0: La Pine State Park day-use area.
♦ Mile 18.7: Paulina Lake Falls.
♦ Mile 19.2: Paulina Lake Trailhead.
♦ Mile 19.4: Paulina Lake Campground.
♦ Mile 21.0: Little Crater Campground.
♦ Mile 23.2: East Lake Campground.
♦ Mile 23.9: Hot Springs Boat Ramp.
♦ Mile 24.3: East Lake Resort and Campground.

MAPS

♦ USGS 7.5-minute quads Anns Butte, Finley Butte, Paulina Lake, and East Lake; *DeLorme Oregon Atlas and Gazetteer,* maps 44 and 45.

Prineville–Painted Hills Classic

T his tough route takes you into the heart of Oregon's outback. You'll begin in downtown Prineville and head east on Highway 26, which takes you on a challenging 1,800-foot climb through the Ochoco Mountains and Ochoco National Forest. After a fast descent you'll pedal into the fascinating Painted Hills country of the John Day Fossil Beds National Monument, where you can view beautiful multi-colored hills and explore fascinating fossil beds. After your tour of the national monument, you have the option of spending the night in Mitchell or camping at Ochoco Divide Summit Campground on your return trip to Prineville.

This ride starts in downtown Prineville at Pioneer Park. Established in 1868, Prineville was the first city in central Oregon. The town is located at the junction of Highway 26 and Highway 126 in Crooked River Valley at the foot of the Ochoco Mountains. Prineville has strong ranching roots and is known as "The Cowboy Capitol of Oregon."

From Pioneer Park you'll head east through downtown Prineville on Third Street, which soon turns into Highway 26. Be sure to stock up on water at the park before you leave. Your next water stop is at the picnic area at the Painted Hills Unit of the John Day Fossil Beds at mile 51.5. At 7.5 miles you'll pass Ochoco Lake State Park on your right. This shady spot is located on the shores of the lake and has a campground, rest rooms, and boat ramp. The route continues east on Highway 26, and over the next 24 miles you'll climb more than 1,800 feet through the Ochoco National Forest to Ochoco Summit at 32.1 miles. Just before the summit you'll pass Ochoco Divide Campground. If you

Start: From Pioneer Park in Prineville.
Length: 109.4-mile loop.
Season: June through October.
Approximate riding time: One to two days.
Recommended start time: 7:00 A.M.
Terrain: This route travels on Highway 26 and paved and gravel rural roads.
Traffic and hazards: Highway 26 has a shoulder for only the first 12 miles of the route. This route has 6.9 miles of well-graded dirt/gravel road riding. Touring bikes have no trouble with this surface, but skinny-tired road bikes may have a rough ride. Be sure to have a good water cache before heading out—water holes are few and far between. This is a very strenuous tour and should only be attempted by experienced and fit cyclists.
Getting there: Prineville is located 35 miles northeast of Bend and 19 miles east of Redmond off Highway 126, and 29 miles southeast of Madras off Highway 26. Highway 126 and Highway 26 merge in downtown Prineville and turn into Third Street. This ride begins at Pioneer Park, located at the intersection of Third Street and Elm Street in downtown Prineville. Pioneer Park is in the center of town on the south side of Third Street. Parking is available on Third and Elm Streets. Rest rooms and water are available at the park.

plan on camping overnight, this is a good spot to stay on your return trip to Prineville. From the summit continue east on a fast, fun downhill.

At 45.2 miles you'll turn off Highway 26 and ride on Burnt Ranch Road over some sections of rough pavement for about 6 miles to the turnoff for the information center and picnic area for the Painted Hills Unit of the John Day Fossil Beds National Monument. At this point the road turns to gravel— the road is well graded, and you shouldn't have a problem riding. The route continues winding through the spectacular painted hills of the John Day Fossil Beds.

Your first stop is the Painted Hills Overlook at 52.7 miles. The round, multicolored hills surrounding you are made up of different layers of ash that were deposited here more than 30 million years ago. Millions of years of erosion have exposed the different layers of the hills. The different colors are a result of combinations of the various minerals, such as calcium, titanium, sodium, iron, silicon, aluminum, manganese, magnesium, and others. When it rains the colors of the hills change because the clay absorbs water, causing more light reflection. When the clay begins to dry out, it contracts. This causes surface cracking, which diffuses the light. Plants don't grow on these hills because the clay is nutritionally poor and the dense soil cannot absorb much moisture. From the Painted Hills Overlook Viewpoint you can hike on a 1 mile out-and-back trail that gives you a chance to see the hills from a different perspective.

Your next stop is the Painted Cove Trail at 54 miles. Here you have the option of hiking on a 0.25-mile boardwalk trail that gives you a close-up look at a bright red soil of a small painted hill. Next you can explore plant fossils on

0.25-mile Leaf Fossil Trail at mile 55.5. The fossilized remains of thirty-five different plant species have been discovered in this area, including alder, beech, maple, hornbeam (now extinct), oak, grape, fern, redwood, and pine. This is your turnaround point for the route. From here you'll ride back to Highway 26. Once you reach the highway, you have the option of traveling about 5 miles east on Highway 26 to the small community of Mitchell and spending the night at the Historic Oregon Hotel B&B (call ahead for availability), or heading west toward Prineville and camping at the Ochoco Divide Campground. If you choose the latter, you'll need to stock up on water at the monument's picnic area because there is no water available at the campground.

ADDITIONAL RIDE INFORMATION

♦ John Day Fossil Beds National Monument, HCR 82, Box 126, Kimberly, OR 97848-9701, (541) 987–2333, www.nps.gov/joda.

LOCAL INFORMATION

♦ Crook County Chamber of Commerce, 390 North Fairview, Prineville, OR 97754, (541) 447–6304, www.prineville.org.

LOCAL EVENTS/ATTRACTIONS

♦ A. R. Bowman Museum, 246 North Main Street, Prineville, OR 97754, (541) 447–3715, www.bowmanmuseum.org.

Admiring the Painted Hills in the John Day Fossil Beds National Monument.

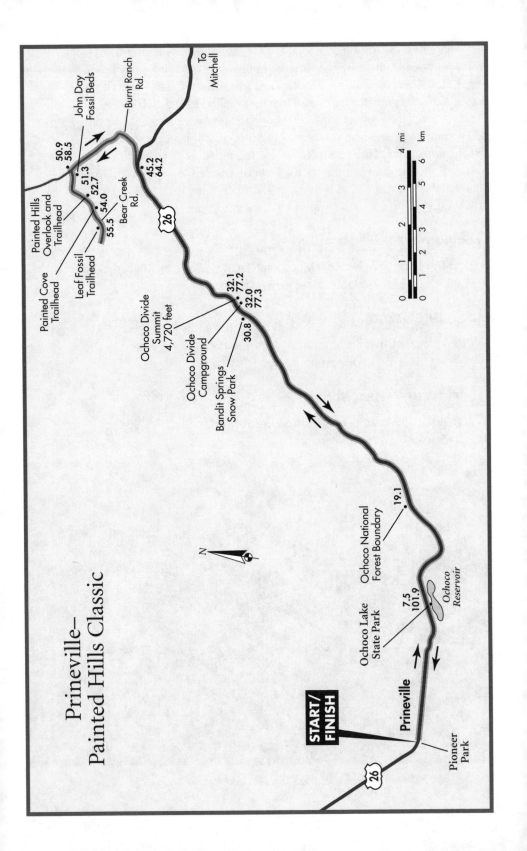

Prineville–Painted Hills Classic

John Day Fossil Beds

Burnt Ranch Rd.

To Mitchell

50.9
58.5

Painted Hills Overlook and Trailhead

51.3
52.7

Bear Creek Rd.

54.0

Painted Cove Trailhead

55.5

Leaf Fossil Trailhead

45.2
64.2

26

32.1
77.2

Ochoco Divide Summit 4,720 feet

32.0
77.3

Ochoco Divide Campground

30.8

Bandit Springs Snow Park

N

Ochoco National Forest Boundary

19.1

Ochoco Lake State Park

7.5
101.9

Ochoco Reservoir

START/FINISH

Prineville

Pioneer Park

26

0 1 2 3 4 mi
0 1 2 3 4 5 6 km

Start by turning right (east) onto Third Street (Highway 26).

1.8 Pass the Ochoco Ranger Station on the right.

7.5 Pass Ochoco Lake State Park on your right. Rest rooms are available here (no water).

19.1 Enter Ochoco National Forest Park. Begin a steep ascent.

30.8 Pass Bandit Springs Snow Park parking area on your left. Rest rooms are available (no water).

32.0 Pass Ochoco Divide Campground on the right. Rest rooms are available (no water).

32.1 Arrive at the 4,720-foot Ochoco Summit. Begin a steep descent.

45.2 Turn left onto Burnt Ranch Road at the JOHN DAY FOSSIL BEDS/PAINTED HILLS sign.

45.3 Cross a cattle guard. Watch out for RVs on this narrow road.

46.0 Cross a cattle guard. The road becomes rough here.

50.9 Turn left onto Bear Creek Road. Cross a cattle guard. Continue on the rough road.

51.3 Turn left at the INFORMATION/RESTROOMS/PICNIC AREA sign. From this point on the route is gravel.

51.5 Arrive at the picnic area and information booth. Water and rest rooms are available here. From here head back out to the main road.

51.7 Turn left onto Bear Creek Road where a sign states PAINTED HILLS OVERLOOK 1/ TRAILS 2.

52.6 Turn left where a sign states CARROLL RIM TRAIL.

52.7 Arrive at the Painted Hills Overlook Trail and a spectacular viewpoint for the Painted Hills. You have the option here of hiking on a 1-mile out-and-back trail to another viewpoint of the Painted Hills. After enjoying the views, head back down the dirt road to Bear Creek Road. Turn left onto Bear Creek Road toward the Painted Cove and Leaf Hill Trailheads. *Note:* Across the road from this turnoff is the Carroll Rim Trailhead, which takes you on a 1.5-mile out-and-back trip to the top of Carroll Rim.

(continued)

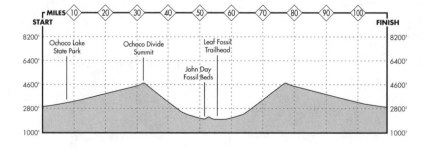

53.6 The road forks. Turn right onto a dirt road toward PAINTED COVE.

54.0 Arrive at the Painted Cove Trailhead on your left. You have the option of hiking the 0.25-mile Painted Cove Trail. When you are finished exploring, turn right out of the parking area onto an unsigned dirt road.

54.4 Arrive at a T-junction. Turn right onto a dirt road toward the Leaf Hill Trailhead.

55.5 Arrive at the Leaf Fossil Trailhead on your right and your turnaround point. You have the option of hiking the 0.25-mile trail, where you can view ancient plant fossils. When you're finished exploring, turn left onto a dirt road.

56.6 At the road junction continue straight (right).

58.2 The road turns to pavement.

58.5 Cross a cattle guard and turn right onto Burnt Ranch Road.

64.1 Cross a cattle guard.

64.2 At the stop sign, turn right (west) onto Highway 26, and begin a long 13-mile climb to the Ochoco Summit. You also have the option of turning left (east), riding about 5 miles to Mitchell, and spending the night at the Historic Oregon Hotel B&B (call ahead for availability).

77.2 Arrive at 4,720-foot Ochoco Summit. Begin a steep descent.

77.3 Pass Ochoco Divide Campground (no water) on left.

78.5 Pass Bandit Springs Snow Park parking area on your right. Rest rooms are available (no water).

101.9 Pass the picnic area and entrance to Ochoco Lake Campground on your right. Rest rooms are available here.

109.4 Arrive back at Pioneer Park in downtown Prineville.

♦ Crook County Fair, Crook County Fairgrounds, 590 SE Lynn Boulevard, Prineville, OR 97754, (541) 447–6575. This fun county fair is held Wednesday through Sunday during the third week in July.

♦ Crooked River Roundup, Crook County Fairgrounds, 590 SE Lynn Boulevard, Prineville, OR 97754, (541) 447–4479. This annual rodeo is held the last weekend in June and features bronco riding, calf roping, bull riding, and other exciting rodeo events.

RESTAURANTS

♦ Ranchero Mexican Restaurant, 969 Northwest 3rd Street, Prineville, OR 97754, (541) 416–0103.

ACCOMMODATIONS

♦ Best Western Prineville Inn, 1475 East Third Street, Prineville, OR 97754, (541) 447–8080 or (800) 528–1234.

♦ Historic Oregon Hotel B&B, 104 Main Street, Mitchell, OR 97750, (541) 462–3027.

♦ The Elliot House B&B, 305 West First Street, Prineville, OR 97754, (541) 416–0423, www.empnet.com/elliotthouse/.

♦ Ochoco Inn, 123 NE 3rd Street, Prineville, OR 97754, (541) 447–6231 or (888) 800–9948, www.ochocoinn.com.

♦ Ochoco Lake State Park, located 7.5 miles east of Prineville, off Highway 26, Prineville, OR 97754, (541) 447–1209. This park has a campground with eighteen campsites and is open April through October. No water is available at the park.

BIKE SHOPS

Bend

♦ Bend Cyclery, 853 NW Bond Street, Bend, OR 97701, (541) 385–5256.

♦ Century Cycles, 1135 NW Galveston, Bend, OR 97701, (541) 389–4224, www.centurycycles.org.

♦ Hutch's Bicycle Store, 725 NW Columbia Street, Bend, OR 97701, (541) 382–9253, www.hutchsbicycles.com.

♦ Pine Mountain Sports, 133 SW Century Drive, Bend, OR 97701, (541) 385–8080.

♦ Sunnyside Sports, 930 NW Newport Avenue, Bend, OR 97701, (541) 382–8018, www.kmx.com/sunnyside.

Redmond

♦ Mountain Cycle, 411 Southwest Cascade Avenue, Redmond, OR 97756, (541) 923–2132.

REST ROOMS

♦ Mile 0.0: Pioneer Park in Prineville.

♦ Mile 7.5: Ochoco Lake State Park picnic area (no water).

♦ Mile 30.8: Bandit Springs Snow Park (no water).

♦ Mile 32.0: Ochoco Divide Campground (no water).

♦ Mile 51.5: Picnic area at the Painted Hills Unit of the John Day Fossil Beds National Monument.

MAPS

♦ USGS 7.5-minute quads Prineville, Ochoco Reservoir, Whistler Point, Lawson Mountain, Mitchell, Sutton Mountain, and Painted Hills; *DeLorme Oregon Atlas and Gazetteer,* map 80.

Jacksonville—Applegate Lake Cruise

This tour begins in the historic community of Jacksonville and climbs more than 400 feet to Applegate Lake in Rogue National Forest. This lake is nestled in the foothills of the Siskiyou Mountains and offers camping, hiking, and swimming opportunities during summer months. Additional highlights of this tour include an opportunity to sample fine wines at the Valley View Winery and to stop and view the McKee covered bridge. This route is also close to Ashland, which is host to the famous Oregon Shakespeare Festival.

Jacksonville is one of the oldest settlements in southern Oregon and has preserved many of its historic buildings. It was established in the mid-1850s to help support the bustling gold boom in the Rogue River Valley. Many merchants quickly prospered from the booming economy and built lavish homes. When the railroad reached Medford in the 1920s, the center of trade moved to Medford, and Jacksonville's population began to decline. The 1960s brought a renewed interest in reviving the town's historic heritage, and the community was registered as a National Historic Landmark District. To learn more about Jacksonville's history, visit the Jacksonville Museum of Southern Oregon History at 206 North 5th Street. This museum is housed in the former 1883 county courthouse.

From Jacksonville the route heads southwest on Highway 238—use caution when riding on this highway because it does not have a shoulder and can have moderate traffic. You'll begin climbing a fairly steep grade (with about 500 feet

Start: Jacksonville.

Length: 52 miles out and back.

Season: Year-round. The roads can be icy during the winter months.

Approximate riding time: Four to six hours.

Recommended start time: 10:00 A.M.

Terrain: Major highway and rural roads.

Traffic and hazards: Moderate traffic is present on Highway 238. Applegate Road does not have a shoulder—use caution when riding on this road.

Getting there: From I–5 South in Medford, take exit 27 for medford/barnett road. At the end of the off-ramp, turn right onto Barnett Road, and get into the right lane. Go 0.2 mile, and turn right onto Riverside Avenue/Highway 99 North toward CITY CENTER/ JACKSONVILLE. Continue 0.9 mile on Main Street through downtown Medford. Turn left onto Highway 238 toward Jacksonville. Continue west on Highway 238 for about 5.6 miles to a downtown public parking area on the right side of the road.

of elevation gain) to the 2,167-foot summit of Jacksonville Hill at just less than 3 miles. After the summit you'll cruise downhill and turn west off the highway onto Applegate Road in the small town of Ruch. If you want to fuel up for your next climb, stop at the Ruch Natural Foods and Deli at mile 7.7. At 8.5 miles you'll have the opportunity to stop at Valley View Winery. This winery was established in 1850 by famous photographer Peter Britt and specializes in producing cabernet sauvignon, merlot, chardonnay, syrah, and cabernet franc.

At 15.9 miles you'll turn off Applegate Road to view the McKee covered bridge. This historic bridge was built

Downtown Jacksonville.

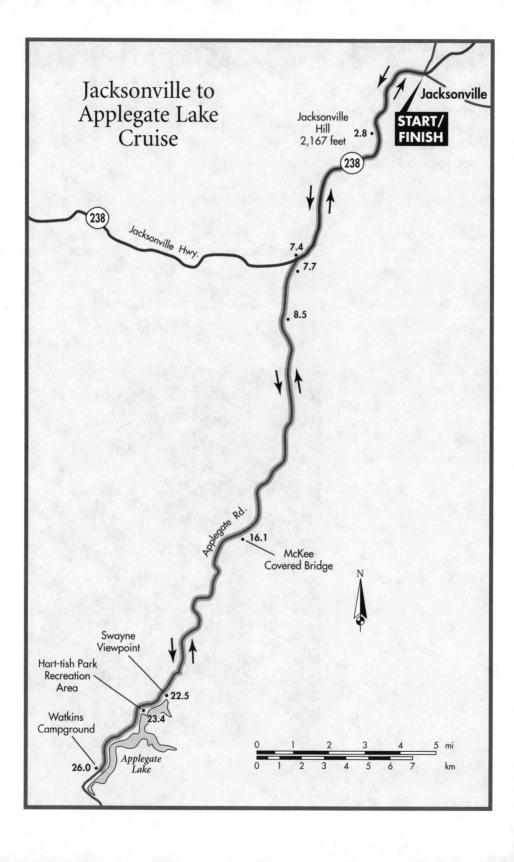

Jacksonville to Applegate Lake Cruise

Jacksonville

START/FINISH

Jacksonville
Hill
2,167 feet

2.8

238

238

Jacksonville Hwy.

7.4

7.7

8.5

Applegate Rd.

16.1

McKee
Covered Bridge

N

Swayne
Viewpoint

Hart-tish Park
Recreation
Area

22.5

23.4

Watkins
Campground

26.0

Applegate
Lake

0   1   2   3   4   5 mi

0 1 2 3 4 5 6 7 km

Start by exiting the public parking area and turning right onto Oregon Street.

0.1 Turn right onto Highway 238, and begin climbing.

2.8 Reach the summit of 2,167-foot Jacksonville Hill.

7.0 Arrive in the town of Ruch.

7.4 Turn left onto Applegate Road, and begin climbing.

7.7 Pass Ruch Natural Foods and Deli on the left.

8.5 Pass Valley View Winery on the right.

13.9 Pass the Star Ranger Station on the left.

15.9 Turn left to view the McKee covered bridge.

16.1 Arrive at the McKee covered bridge and a large picnic area with rest rooms and water. After viewing the bridge, turn around and head back out to Applegate Road.

16.3 Turn left onto Applegate Road.

22.5 Pass Swayne Viewpoint on your left. Rest rooms are available at this location.

23.4 Pass the Hart-tish Park Recreation Area on the left. Rest rooms and water are available at this location.

26.0 Arrive at Watkins Campground. Rest rooms and water are available here. This is your turnaround point. Retrace the route back to your starting point in Jacksonville.

52.0 Arrive in the public parking area in Jacksonville.

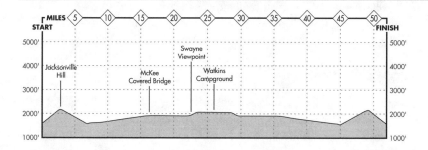

in 1917 and is 122 feet long. It spans the Applegate River and is open to pedestrian traffic. Adjacent to the bridge is a shady picnic area that has rest rooms. From here the route continues northwest on Applegate Road. After about 10 more miles of pedaling past farms and forest, you'll arrive at Swayne Viewpoint, which offers a good view of Applegate Lake and the Applegate Dam (completed in 1980). This scenic lake is located at the foot of the Siskiyou Mountains in the Rogue River National Forest. The lake covers 988 acres and is more than 4.5 miles long. It is a popular recreation spot and has many campgrounds and day-use areas along its scenic shores. A hiking trail circles the lake, and many other hiking trailheads can be accessed off Applegate Lake Road. At 26 miles you'll reach your turnaround point at Watkins Campground. From here, retrace the route back to your starting point in Jacksonville.

LOCAL INFORMATION

♦ Rogue River National Forest, Applegate Ranger District, 6941 Upper Applegate Road, Jacksonville, OR 97530-9314, (541) 899–3800, www.fs.fed.us/r6/rogue/.
♦ Jacksonville Chamber of Commerce, 185 North Oregon Street, Jacksonville, OR 97523, (541) 899–8118, www.jacksonvilleoregon.org.

LOCAL EVENTS/ATTRACTIONS

♦ Britt Music Festival, events held in Jacksonville throughout the summer, 517 West 10th Street, Medford, OR 97501, (800) 882–7488.
♦ Jacksonville Museum of Southern Oregon History, 206 North 5th Street, Jacksonville, OR 97530, (541) 773–6536.
♦ Oregon Shakespeare Festival, 15 South Pioneer Street, Ashland, OR 97520, (541) 482–4331, www.orshakes.org.
♦ Valley View Winery, 1000 Upper Applegate Road, Jacksonville, OR 97530, (800) 781-WINE, www.valleyviewwinery.com.

RESTAURANTS

♦ McCully House Inn Restaurant, 240 East California Street, Jacksonville, OR 97530, (800) 367–1942, www.mccullyhouseinn.com.
♦ Pony Espresso Café, 545 North 5th Street, Jacksonville, OR 97530, (541) 899–3757.

ACCOMMODATIONS

♦ McCully House Inn, 240 East California Street, Jacksonville, OR 97530, (800) 367–1942, www.mccullyhouseinn.com/index.htm.
♦ Watkins Campground, Applegate Lake, OR. Contact Applegate Ranger District, 6941 Upper Applegate Road, Jacksonville, OR 97530-9314, (541) 899–3800, www.fs.fed.us/r6/rogue.

BIKE SHOPS

♦ Cycle Analysis, 535 North 5th Street, Jacksonville, OR 97530, (541) 899–9190.

REST ROOMS

- Mile 0.0: Public parking area in Jacksonville.
- Mile 16.1: Picnic area at McKee covered bridge.
- Mile 22.5: Swayne Viewpoint.
- Mile 23.4: Hart-tish Park Recreation Area.
- Mile 26.0: Watkins Campground.

MAPS

- USGS 7.5-minute quads Medford West, Carberry Creek, Ruch, and Squaw Lakes; *DeLorme Oregon Atlas and Gazetteer,* maps 19 and 20.

Frenchglen–Peter French Round Barn Challenge

Τhis out-and-back tour takes you through the wild open spaces of southeast Oregon. You'll begin the tour in the small town of Frenchglen, which is the gateway to the Steens Mountain Recreation Area. From Frenchglen you'll ride north through prime cattle country and pedal past the western edge of the magnificent 186,500-acre Malheur Wildlife Refuge. Additional attractions on this route include the unique geologic formation in the Diamond Craters Outstanding Natural Area and the historic 1880 Peter French Round Barn.

This relatively flat tour begins in the small historic town of Frenchglen, which can be found on the southern boundary of the 186,500-acre Malheur Wildlife Refuge and at the western edge of the Steens Mountain Recreation Lands. You'll begin by riding north on Highway 205 through an open sunny landscape filled with fragrant sagebrush, rimrock plateaus, and cattle ranches. There is no water along the route, so be sure to stock up before you head out. To the east you'll have a magnificent view of 9,773-foot Steens Mountain, which rises prominently above the Blitzen Valley.

As you pedal north on Highway 205, you'll pass by the western boundary of the Malheur Wildlife Refuge, which supports a variety of bird life. The expansive refuge is busiest during the spring months, when more than 130 species of birds are nesting. Northern pintails, tundra swans, snow geese, white-fronted geese, and sandhill cranes arrive on the scene in February. Waterfowl species arrive in April, shorebirds in May, and songbirds in June.

Young pronghorn and mule deer fawns can also be seen during May and June. In the fall great flocks of sandhill cranes gather in the southern end of the Blitzen Valley for their migration south to the Central Valley in California. Canada geese and large flocks of ducks can also be seen migrating south. While you are in this area, it is worth taking the time to visit the refuge visitors center and museum, which is located approximately 38 miles southeast of Burns off Highway 205.

After 28.4 miles you'll pass by a trailhead to a double-track road that leads you through many diverse geologic formations in the 17,000-acre Diamond Craters Outstanding Natural Area. This geologic area was formed about 25,000 years ago, when lava oozed from wide fissures, creating a 6-mile-long pool of molten lava. After the original lava cooled and hardened, more lava oozed under the original layers, forming low-lying lava domes. You can ride or walk up a double-track road for more than 4 miles to view different geologic formations, such as cinder cones, pit craters, and maar craters (shallow depressions in the ground, edged with rock fragments that were hurled from the center of the crater during a large volcanic explosion).

After 35.2 miles you'll arrive at the turnoff for the Peter French Round Barn State Heritage Site. Note that you'll have to ride on a dirt road for a mile to view the round barn. This road is well graded and is easily traveled if you ride slowly. When you reach the round barn, your turnaround point for this tour, take the time to walk inside and read the interpretive signs explaining its history. This fascinating barn was built by Peter French in 1880 and is the only remaining round barn left out of three that were built during the same period. This local cattle baron ran the P Ranch in the Blitzen Valley. Over a twenty-eight-year period, the P Ranch became the largest single cattle ranch in the United States, covering 200,000 acres. The uniquely shaped round barn was used during the winter months to break the 300 head of horses and mules that were foaled on

THE BASICS

Start: From the Frenchglen Hotel State Wayside in Frenchglen.

Length: 72.4 miles out and back.

Season: April to October.

Approximate riding time: Seven to nine hours.

Recommended start time: 8:00 A.M.

Terrain: This route follows Highway 205 and county roads in Harney County in southeast Oregon.

Traffic and hazards: Highway 205 has a 1-foot shoulder and light traffic. The remaining paved county roads on this tour have very light traffic and no shoulder. There are 2 miles of dirt road riding on a well-graded dirt road. Use caution when crossing this route's metal cattle guards.

Getting there: This tour begins at the Frenchglen Hotel State Wayside in the small town of Frenchglen. Frenchglen is located approximately 60 miles south of Burns on Highway 205.

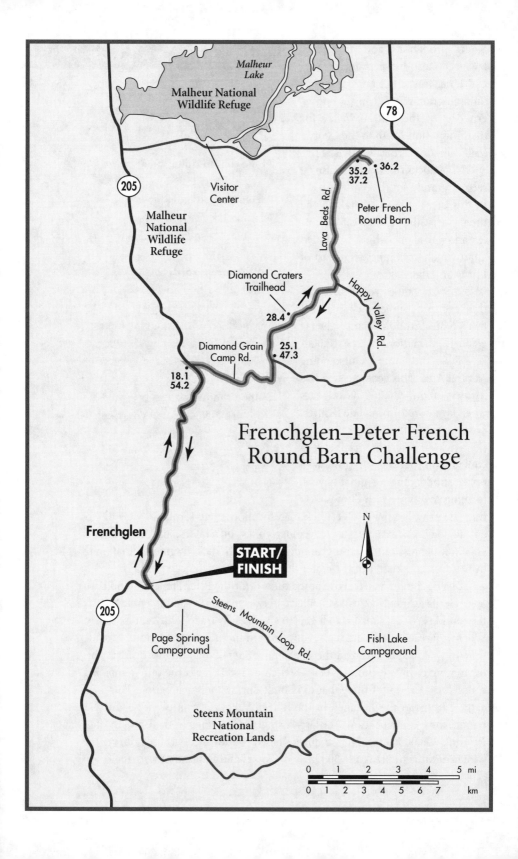

Start by turning left (north) onto Highway 205 from the Frenchglen Hotel State Wayside (water and pit toilet are available here).

18.1 Turn right onto Diamond Grain Camp Road, where a sign indicates DIAMOND CRATERS/FRENCH ROUND BARN 17/DIAMOND 13.

25.1 Turn left onto Lava Beds Road, where a sign indicates DIAMOND CRATERS 2.

27.0 Enter the Diamond Craters Outstanding Natural Area.

28.4 Diamond Craters Trailhead is on your left. You have the option of riding (if you have a burly bike) or hiking on this road to view a variety of geologic formations, including cinder cones, pit craters, and maar craters. The road passes through different geologic formations for more than 4 miles.

35.2 Turn right onto a dirt road where a sign indicates WELCOME TO PETER FRENCH ROUND BARN STATE HERITAGE SITE. You'll have to ride on a well-graded dirt road for 1 mile to view the barn.

35.3 Cross a cattle guard.

36.2 Arrive at the Peter French Round Barn, your turnaround point for this tour. Take time to read the interpretive signs and to explore this fascinating historic structure. After you're finished exploring, head back out to the paved Lava Beds Road.

37.1 Cross a cattle guard.

37.2 Turn left onto the Lava Beds Road where a sign indicates FRENCHGLEN 35 MILES.

47.3 At the stop sign and T-intersection, turn right onto Diamond Grain Camp Road, where a sign indicates FRENCHGLEN 24 MILES.

54.2 At the stop sign and T-intersection, turn left onto Highway 205, where a sign indicates FRENCHGLEN 18 MILES.

72.4 End the tour at the Frenchglen Hotel State Wayside on the right side of the road.

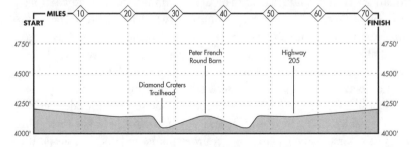

the ranch each year. The barn houses a 60-foot-wide circular stone corral supported by sturdy juniper posts. This 9-foot-high corral is made up of more than 250 tons of lava rock that was hauled to this site from more than 8 miles away. An outer 20-foot-wide circular paddock completes the dimensions of the

The Peter French Round Barn was built in 1880 and was used to break horses for the P Ranch.

barn. The unique round shape of the barn provided a way to more easily break horses because its round contours do not have corners that could force a horse to stop its natural gait. After you're finished exploring the barn, head back on the same route to the Frenchglen Hotel State Wayside.

If you want to stay and explore the area, you can stay at this hotel (open March 15 through November 15), Steens Mountain Resort (3 miles east of Frenchglen off Steens Mountain Loop Road), or Page Springs Campground (4 miles east of Frenchglen off Steens Mountain Loop Road). Additional camping opportunities are available off Steens Mountain Loop Road at Fish Lake, Jackman Park, and South Steens. The Steens Mountain Loop Road is also known as the Steens Mountain Back Country Byway. This dirt road travels for 66 miles over the top of 9,773-foot Steens Mountain and through several eco-zones that support a wide variety of animal and plant life. Western juniper, mountain mohogany, and sagebrush steppe grace the lower slopes of the mountain between 4,000 and 6,000 feet. Higher up, groves of quaking aspen stand sentinel over high mountain lakes and provide shelter for mule deer and pronghorn antelope. As the road reaches its highest point, a fragile rocky tundra covers the landscape. There are several viewpoints and hiking trails off this road with opportunities to see magnificent glacial-carved gorges and dramatic cliffs and canyons. Note that Steens Mountain Loop Road is usually open from July 1 through October 31 depending on snow conditions.

LOCAL INFORMATION

♦ Bureau of Land Management, Burns District Office, HC 74-12533 Hwy 20 West, Hines, OR 97738, (541) 573–4400, www.or.blm.gov/Steens.

♦ Harney County Chamber of Commerce, 18 West D Street, Burns, OR 97720, (541) 573–2636.

♦ Oregon State Parks and Recreation, 1115 Commercial Street NE, Suite 1, Salem, OR 97301-1002, (800) 551–6949, www.oregonstateparks.org.

LOCAL EVENTS/ATTRACTIONS

♦ Malheur National Wildlife Refuge, HC 72 Box 245, Princeton, OR 97721, (541) 493–2612. Visitors center hours are 7:00 A.M. to 4:30 P.M. Monday through Thursday and 7:00 A.M. to 3:30 P.M. Friday.

♦ P Ranch, Frenchglen, OR. Contact the Bureau of Land Management, Burns District Office, HC 74–12533 Highway 20 West, Burns, OR 97738, (541) 573–4400. Visit the historic ranch operated by Peter French. To get to this historic site from Frenchglen, drive south on Highway 205, and take an immediate left onto a dirt road where a sign indicates STEENS MOUNTAIN LOOP/FISH LAKE 18. Drive 1.6 miles, and turn left where a sign indicates P RANCH. Drive 0.4 mile to a gravel parking area and the ranch site. No fees are charged.

♦ Steens Mountain National Back Country Byway, Frenchglen, OR. Contact the Bureau of Land Management, Burns District Office, HC 74–12533 Highway 20 West, Burns, OR 97738, (541) 573–4400. This 66-mile dirt road loops over the top of Steens Mountain past dozens of hiking trails and natural lakes. You can hike, mountain bike, camp, and enjoy breathtaking views from this backcountry byway. The road is open from July 1 through October 31 (depending on the snow conditions). This dirt road is accessed just south of the Frenchglen Hotel off Highway 205 in Frenchglen.

RESTAURANTS

♦ Frenchglen Hotel, Frenchglen, OR. Contact Oregon State Parks, 1115 Commercial Street NE, Suite 1, Salem, OR 97301-1002, (541) 493–2825, www.oregonstateparks.org/park_3.php. A homemade breakfast is $3.00 to $7.00 (served 7:30 A.M. to 9:30 A.M.), lunch is $4.00 to $7.00 (served 11:30 A.M. to 2:30 P.M.), and dinner is $13.50 to $16.00 (served at 6:30 P.M.) The hotel restaurant is open from March 15 to November 15.

ACCOMMODATIONS

♦ Frenchglen Hotel, Frenchglen, OR 97736, 541-493-2825, www.oregon-stateparks.org/park_3.php. Relax in the historic luxury of this quiet 1916 hotel. Rates are $60–$63 per night. The hotel is open from March 15 to November 15.

◆ Page Springs Campground, Frenchglen, OR. Contact the Bureau of Land Management, Burns District Office, HC 74–12533 Highway 20 West, Burns, OR 97738, (541) 573–4400. To get to the campground from Frenchglen, drive south on Highway 205, and turn left onto Steens Mountain Loop Road. Drive 3.2 miles to a T-intersection. Turn right, and arrive at the campground in 0.2 mile.

BIKE SHOPS

◆ There are no bike shops in this area.

REST ROOMS

◆ Mile 0.0: Frenchglen Hotel State Wayside.

MAPS

◆ USGS 7.5-minute quads Frenchglen, Irish Lake, Krumbo Reservoir, Diamond Swamp, Diamond, Barton Lake, and Adobe Flat; *DeLorme Oregon Atlas and Gazetteer,* maps 74 and 78.

39

John Day Fossil Beds Classic

*T*his challenging two-day tour climbs more than 3,000 feet and takes you through the center of two magnificent river canyons in northeast Oregon: the John Day and the North Fork of the John Day. Dramatic canyon scenery, smooth-flowing rivers, and small friendly towns make this tour one of a kind. As an added bonus you'll pedal through John Day Fossil Beds National Monument, a fantastic geologic wonder that has encapsulated the fossilized remains of plants and animals from millions of years ago.

This strenuous yet beautiful route climbs more than 3,000 feet and travels through the heart of John Day River country through the Sheep Rock Unit of the John Day Fossil Beds National Monument. If you plan on camping, you can stay at Asher's RV Park at mile 42.4, or you can camp at Lone Pine Park (mile 53.4) or Big Bend Park (mile 54.7). These latter two parks are located on the banks of the North Fork of the John Day River. Although they do not have running water, you can get water by filtering it from the river. If you are looking for more posh accommodations, stay at the Land's Inn Bed and Breakfast in Kimberly (be sure to call ahead for availability).

You'll begin the route at Clyde Holliday State Park just east of the small hamlet of Mount Vernon. From here you'll pedal west on U.S. Highway 26 through Mount Vernon and the small community of Dayville. Dayville started growing in the late 1880s, and it was originally called Cottonwood. It was officially incorporated in 1914. Its main industries are agriculture, timber, and tourism. If you want to take a break from the saddle, check out the Dayville Mercantile and the Dayville Café.

Start: From Clyde Holliday State Park in Mount Vernon.

Length: 118.4-mile loop.

Season: June to October.

Approximate riding time: Two days.

Recommended start time: 7:00 A.M.

Terrain: This route follows Highway 26, Highway 19, Kimberly-Long Creek Highway, and U.S. Highway 395.

Traffic and hazards: Highway 26 has a wide shoulder and can have moderate traffic. Use extreme caution on Highway 19 when you are traveling through Picture Gorge—the highway does not have a shoulder through the gorge and is very narrow. Highway 19 usually has light traffic. The Kimberly-Long Creek Highway has very light traffic. U.S. Highway 395 has light to moderate traffic and a wide shoulder. This tour is designed as a two-day tour. Summertime temperatures can get into the 90s. Bring plenty of sunscreen and shoes for hiking (if you plan on exploring any of the trails in the John Day Fossil Beds National Monument).

Getting there: This tour begins at Clyde Holliday State Park, 1 mile east of Mount Vernon on Highway 26. This state park is approximately 8 miles west of John Day and 23 miles east of Dayville on Highway 26.

From Dayville the route continues on a flat route west on Highway 26. At mile 30.7 you'll enter Picture Gorge, which is part of the Sheep Rock Unit of the John Day Fossil Beds National Monument. This magnificent river gorge is carved by the John Day River and has high sheer rock walls. The highway narrows severely in this gorge, and there is no shoulder. Use extreme caution when riding on the short 1.5-mile section through the gorge.

Established in 1975, the John Day Fossil Beds National Monument covers 14,000 acres and is made up of three units: Sheep Rock, Clarno (18 miles west of Fossil off Highway 218), and Painted Hills (9 miles northwest of Mitchell off Highway 26). Millions of years ago the landscape here was very different. Clarno was formed 54 to 37 million years ago, when plant-browsing animals lived in wet tropical forests and rainfall averaged 100 inches per year. The Cascade Mountain range had not yet formed, and warm, moist air extended inland from the Pacific Ocean. Volcanic activity was also frequent during this time, and ash covered the region. Heavy rain turned the ash to mud. This mud covered dead and dying plants, and over millions of years these plants and animals were preserved as fossils. The John Day formation was formed 39 to 20 million years ago, when the landscape changed to a deciduous forest that supported animals such as horses, rhinoceroses, rodents, camels, dogs, cats, and oreodonts. As the Cascade Mountain range formed, the climate became drier because the moist Pacific air was cut off by the growing mountain range. As a result grassy plains dominated the scene at the time of the Mascall Formation (15 to 20 million years ago) and the Rattlesnake

Riding through the open expanse of the John Day Fossil Beds National Monument.

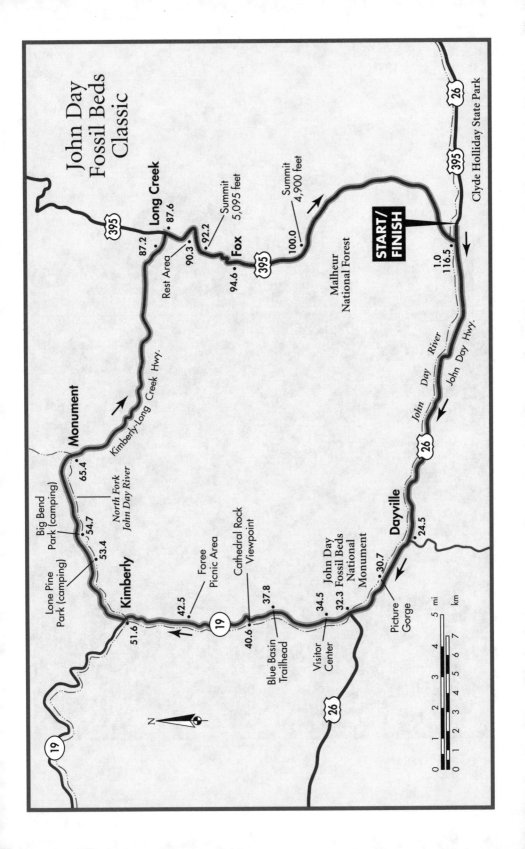

John Day Fossil Beds Classic

Long Creek
87.6

87.2

Rest Area
90.3

Summit
5,095 feet
92.2

Fox
94.6

Summit
4,900 feet
100.0

START/FINISH

Malheur National Forest

1.0
116.5

John Day River

John Day Hwy.

Clyde Holliday State Park

Kimberly-Long Creek Hwy.

Monument
65.4

North Fork
John Day River

Big Bend
Park (camping)
54.7

53.4

Lone Pine
Park (camping)

Kimberly
51.6

42.5

Foree
Picnic Area
40.6

Cathedral Rock
Viewpoint
37.8

Blue Basin
Trailhead

Visitor
Center
34.5

John Day
Fossil Beds
National
Monument
32.3

30.7

Dayville
24.5

Picture
Gorge

N

5 mi

km

0 1 2 3 4 5

0 1 2 3 4 5 6 7

Start by turning left (west) on U.S. Highway 26 from Clyde Holliday State Park.

1.0 Mount Vernon.

24.5 Dayville.

25.1 Dayville Mercantile on your right. Food and drinks are available here. If you want to try some local cuisine, check out the Dayville Café right across the street from the Dayville Mercantile.

30.7 Enter Picture Gorge in the John Day Beds National Monument. Use extreme caution on this section of the road. There is no shoulder, and the road is very narrow.

32.3 Turn right onto Highway 19, where a sign indicates VISITORS CENTER 2/ ARLINGTON 121.

34.2 Pass Sheep Rock Overlook on the right.

34.5 Pass Thomas Condon Visitors Center (water and rest rooms are available here) on the right. You can stop here and look at a collection of fossils, view short films about the geology and history of the area, visit the gift shop (which has a good collection of books about the geology and history of the John Day Valley), and explore the historic buildings on the grounds.

37.8 Pass Blue Basin Trailhead on the right (rest rooms are present but no water). You have the option here of hiking on the 1.4-mile Island in Time Trail or the 3-mile Blue Basin Overlook Trail.

40.6 Pass Cathedral Rock Viewpoint on your left.

42.4 Pass Asher's RV Park on the right.

42.5 Pass Foree Picnic Area on the right. You have the option here of hiking the 0.25-mile Flood of Fire Trail or the 0.25-mile Story in Time Trail.

51.6 Kimberly. Turn right on the Kimberly-Long Creek Highway where a sign indicates MONUMENT 14/LONG CREEK 35. Food and drinks are available at the Kimberly Center Store, on your right before this turn.

53.4 Pass Lone Pine Park on the North Fork of the John Day River. You have the option of camping here overnight. There are rest rooms at this campground but

(continued)

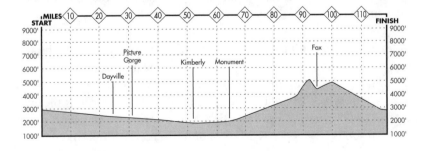

no water. Retrieve water from the North Fork of the John Day River and use your water filter.

54.7 Pass Big Bend Park. You have the option of camping here overnight. There are rest rooms at this campground but no water. Retrieve water from the North Fork of the John Day River and use your water filter.

65.4 Monument. You have the option of stocking up on groceries and drinks at the local market.

87.2 Long Creek.

87.5 Pass a park with water (no rest rooms) on the right.

87.6 At the stop sign and four-way intersection turn right onto U.S. Highway 395. You can stock up on drinks and food at the Northside Café and Store, located on the other side of U.S. Highway 395 at this intersection.

90.3 Pass a rest area on the right. Water and rest rooms are available here.

92.2 Reach the summit at 5,095 feet. Begin a steep descent.

94.6 Fox.

100.0 Reach another summit at 4,900 feet. Begin a steep descent.

116.5 At the four-way stop in Mount Vernon, turn left (east) onto Highway 26 toward John Day and Burns.

118.4 End your ride at Clyde Holliday State Park on right. Camping is available here.

Formation (8 to 6 million years ago), and grazing animals thrived in a much drier cooler environment.

After 32.3 miles you'll turn north onto Highway 19 toward Kimberly. In 2 short miles, you'll arrive at the Thomas Condon Visitors Center at the Sheep Rock Unit of the John Day Fossil Beds National Monument. Be sure to stop here and explore the fascinating fossil exhibits, browse the large collections of books about the geology and history of the area, and walk around the grounds, which display historic buildings and antique farming equipment. If you want to see more fossils, be sure to stop at the Blue Basin Trailhead (37.8 miles) or the Foree Picnic Area (42.5 miles). Both of these trailheads lead to trails that give you unique glimpses at some of the plant and animal fossil remains in the monument.

After 51.6 miles you'll turn east onto the Kimberly-Long Creek Highway, and your long climbing journey of 3,000-plus feet will begin. Be sure to stock up on drinks and food at the Kimberly Store at this junction. As you travel through Kimberly, you'll be amazed to see green orchards dominating the dry landscape. The Kimberly-Long Creek Highway travels through another beautiful river canyon carved by the North Fork of the John Day River. On this section of the route, you'll enjoy peace and solitude as you pedal past farms and ranches. At 65.4 miles you'll arrive in the small town of Monument, which also has a grocery store where you can stock up on supplies. Early settlers named this town after Monument Mountain in 1869. Your next chance for supplies is in the town of Long Creek, which you'll reach just after mile 87. Lodging is also available here if you decide to complete most of the route the first day.

At this point you'll turn south onto U.S. Highway 395 and begin climbing steeply through a wild sage and juniper landscape dominated by dramatic cliffs. You'll reach your first summit of 5,095 feet at just past 92 miles, then you'll cruise downhill into the small town of Fox. From Fox (at 4,390 feet), you'll complete another 5.4-mile climb to an approximate 4,900-foot summit. From there you'll enjoy a fast downhill cruise back to Mount Vernon and Clyde Holliday State Park at 118.4 miles.

LOCAL INFORMATION

♦ Grant County Chamber of Commerce, 281 West Main Street, John Day, OR 97845, (800) 769–5664, www.grantcounty.cc.
♦ John Day Fossil Beds National Monument HCR 82, Box 126, Kimberly, OR 97848-9701, (541) 987–2333, www.nps.gov/joda.
♦ Oregon State Parks and Recreation, 1115 Commercial Street NE, Suite 1, Salem, OR 97301-1002, (800) 551–6949, www.oregonstateparks.org.

LOCAL EVENTS/ATTRACTIONS

♦ Grant County Fair, held the first week in August, 281 West Main Street, John Day, OR 97845, (800) 769–5664.

RESTAURANTS

♦ Dayville Café, 212 West Franklin Avenue, Dayville, OR 97825, (541) 987–2132.
♦ Peggy's Place, 110 East Main Street, Long Creek, OR 97856, (541) 421–3099.

ACCOMMODATIONS

♦ Asher's RV Park, HC 82, Box 113, Kimberly, OR 97848, (541) 934–2712.
♦ Big Bend Campground, Bureau of Land Management, Prineville District Office, 3050 NE Third Street, Prineville, OR 97754, (541) 416–6700, www.or.blm.gov/Prineville/recreation/. Located on the North Fork of the John Day River, 3.1 miles northeast of Kimberly toward Monument on the Kimberly-Long Creek Highway. Rest rooms. No water.
♦ Clyde Holliday State Park, Mount Vernon, OR. Contact Oregon State Parks, 1115 Commercial Street NE, Suite 1, Salem, OR 97301-1002, (800) 551–6949, www.oregonstateparks.org/park_11.php.

♦ Fish House Inn, B&B and RV Park, 110 Franklin, Dayville, OR 97825, (888) 286–FISH.

♦ Land's Inn Bed and Breakfast, HC 1 Box 117, Kimberly, OR 97848, (541) 934–2333.

♦ Lone Pine Campground, Bureau of Land Management, Prineville District Office, 3050 NE Third Street, Prineville, OR 97754, (541) 416–6700, www.or.blm.gov/Prineville/recreation/. Located on the North Fork of the John Day River, 1.8 miles northeast of Kimberly toward Monument on the Kimberly-Long Creek Highway. Rest rooms. No water.

BIKE SHOPS

♦ There are no bike shops in this area.

REST ROOMS

♦ Mile 0.0: Clyde Holliday State Park.
♦ Mile 34.5: Thomas Condon Visitors Center.
♦ Mile 37.8: Blue Basin Trailhead.
♦ Mile 42.5: Foree Picnic Area.
♦ Mile 53.4: Lone Pine Park.
♦ Mile 54.7: Big Bend Park.
♦ Mile 90.3: U.S. Highway 395 rest area.

MAPS

♦ USGS 7.5-minute quads Mount Vernon, Wolfinger Butte, Shop Gulch, Aldrich Mount North, Dayville, Picture Gorge East, Picture Gorge West, Misery, Kimberly, Bologna Basin, Monument, Steet Mountain, Hamilton, Fox, Belshaw Meadows, Johnson Saddle, and Long Creek; *DeLorme Oregon Atlas and Gazetteer,* map 81.

Elkhorn Scenic Byway Classic

This strenuous two-day loop tour follows the Elkhorn Scenic Byway, takes you through the majestic forested Elkhorn Mountains of northeast Oregon, and drops into the desert valley surrounding Baker City. The route then travels along the banks of the scenic Powder River past Phillips Reservoir back to your starting point at Sumpter Dredge State Park. On this tour you'll be able to explore the Sumpter Dredge at Sumpter Dredge State Park, stay overnight at scenic Anthony Lake, explore the historical buildings in Haines and Baker City, enjoy the dramatic river canyon carved by the Powder River, and go swimming at Phillips Reservoir.

This tour begins in Sumpter Dredge State Park in the small town of Sumpter, once a thriving gold-mining town. The main attraction at this small state park is the Sumpter gold dredge. The Powder River Gold Dredging Company assembled the first dredge in the Sumpter area in late 1912. This monster contraption was 100 feet long, 45 feet wide, and had sixty-five buckets. Each bucket held 9 cubic feet of earth, and the contraption could dig at a rate of 7 yards of earth per minute. The entire dredge was made of wood and was powered by an electric motor. The buckets dumped the gold-rich dirt into a hopper, and the dirt was sifted through ¾-inch holes and deposited into sluice boxes. The gold-filled sand and water settled to the bottom, and the coarser rocks and dirt were deposited via conveyor belt behind the dredge into ugly mountains of dirt and rock called tailings. The dredge located at the state park was a "new and improved version" of its previous cousin and was built and put into operation in 1934, when the price of gold went from $20 to $35 per ounce. Over a nineteen-year period, this dredge produced $4.5 million

Start: From Sumpter Valley Dredge State Park in Sumpter.

Length: 108.7-mile loop.

Season: June through October .

Approximate riding time: Two days.

Recommended start time: 7:00 P.M.

Terrain: This route follows forest service roads, rural roads, and major highways on the Elkhorn Scenic Byway.

Traffic and hazards: Elkhorn Drive (Forest Road [FR] 73) is narrow and windy, has no shoulder, and has light traffic. Highway 30 and Highway 7 have light to moderate traffic. This is a strenuous tour and should only be attempted by experienced cyclists. If you are not used to riding at altitude, you may experience headaches or shortness of breath.

Getting there: From Prairie City drive approximately 18 miles east on Highway 26. Turn left (north) onto Highway 7 toward Sumpter and Baker City. Proceed 26.1 miles, and turn left onto Sumpter Highway at the SUMPTER DREDGE STATE PARK sign. Drive 2.9 miles and turn left into Sumpter Dredge State Park.

worth of gold (based on the 1934 price of $35 per ounce) from the Powder River Valley.

From Sumpter you'll travel uphill through a thick forest of lodgepole pine, ponderosa, and pine and Douglas fir for 7.6 miles to Blue Springs Summit at 5,864 feet. After 17.2 miles you'll arrive in the small town of Granite. If you want to stock up on food and drinks, stop at the Granite Store. Over the next 26 miles you'll climb more than 2,100 feet as the route winds along steep ridges and provides spectacular views of the towering granite peaks of the Elkhorn Mountains. At 41.4 miles you'll reach the Elkhorn Summit at 7,392 feet. Anthony Lake is your next stop at 43 miles. This beautiful alpine lake has a campground, and it is recommended that you stay here overnight. The lake is surrounded by towering peaks and is ringed with Douglas fir, white fir, lodgepole pine, and tamarack trees. Anthony Lake Campground is located on the edge of the lake. Be sure to hike the 1-mile trail around the lake.

From Anthony Lake the route travels a steep downhill grade on a rough, narrow road for more than 8 miles. Watch your speed on this descent! The route soon leaves the mountains and forest behind and enters the flat Baker Valley, which is filled with open grassy pastures dominated by farms and ranches. Haines is your next major stop at 67 miles. This small community was established in 1884 and grew into a major farm supply and railroad shipping center. Many historic buildings are still here, including the 1893 Haines Methodist Church (at the corner of 4th Street and Roberts Street) and the 1908 Haines City Hall (on Cole Street between 3rd and 4th Streets). You can also view the Chandler Cabin in Haines 1880s Park, located on the left side of the road before you turn onto Highway 30. This cabin was built in 1861 and is thought to be the first pioneer cabin built in Baker County. It was moved here in 1993 from its original site 5 miles south of Haines.

From Haines the route heads south on Highway 30 for 10 miles to down-

Anthony Lake.

town Baker City. Baker City includes many historic stone buildings and is the location of the National Historic Trail Interpretive Center, located 5 miles east of town off Highway 86. As you leave Baker City, the route travels south on Highway 7 through dry grasslands, then enters a deep river canyon with sharp lava outcroppings covered with juniper and sage. The road swings northwest and begins climbing as it follows the course of the Powder River and then enters the Wallowa-Whitman National Forest. Keep your eye out for osprey fishing along the banks of the river.

After 98.5 miles you'll pass the Union Creek Recreation Area and Phillips Reservoir. This recreation area boasts a scenic campground set amongst ponderosa pine along the shores of the reservoir. There are great swimming opportunities here. A 16.4-mile hiking and mountain biking trail also surrounds the reservoir. About 3 miles past the reservoir, you'll pass the turnoff to the Sumpter Valley Historic Railroad. On weekends from Memorial Day through Labor Day, you can ride on a historic steam train from McEwen Station 5 miles to the Sumpter Depot. The tour ends back at Sumpter Dredge State Park at 108.7 miles.

LOCAL INFORMATION

♦ Eastern Oregon Visitors Association, PO Box 1087, Baker City, OR 97814, (800) 332–1843.
♦ Grant County Chamber of Commerce, 281 West Main Street, John Day, OR 97845, (800) 769–5664, www.grantcounty.cc.

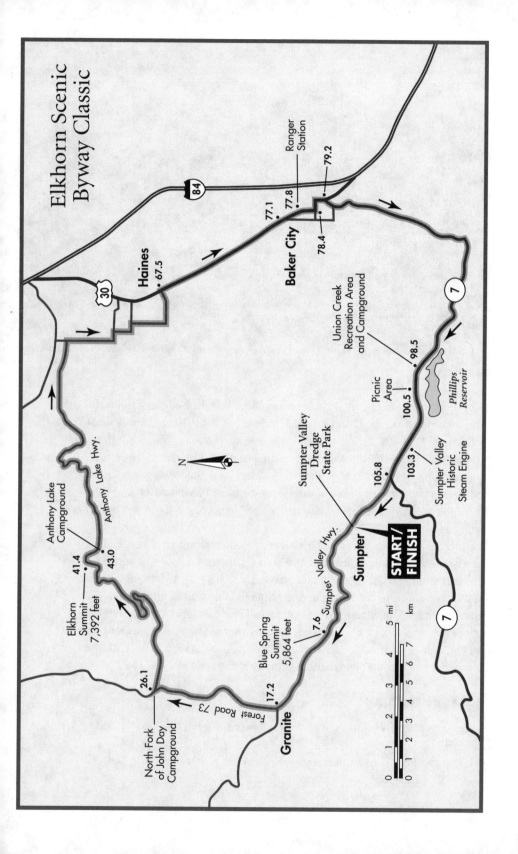

Start by turning left onto the Sumpter Highway. You'll pedal through the small town of Sumpter.

7.6 Reach Blue Springs Summit at 5,864 feet. Start descending steeply. Watch your speed. The road is narrow, windy, and rough in spots.

10.0 Pass an interpretive sign and pullout on the left. This interpretive sign explains the growth of a lodgepole pine forest.

17.2 Arrive at a four-way intersection in Granite. Continue straight on FR 73 (Elkhorn Drive) toward ANTHONY LAKE 26/UKIAH 50. Begin climbing on a rough road. If you want to stock up on food and drinks, turn right at this intersection and ride a short distance to the Granite Store.

26.1 Turn right at the road junction, and continue pedaling on Elkhorn Drive (FR 73) where a sign indicates ANTHONY LAKE 17 MILES. After this intersection you'll continue your steep climb. *Note:* If you continue straight at this intersection, you'll reach the North Fork of John Day Campground in 0.1 mile on your left. No water is available.

41.4 Reach Elkhorn Summit at 7,392 feet.

43.0 Anthony Lakes Campground. It is recommended that you camp here overnight. Turn right, and follow signs to the campground. Water and rest rooms are available here.

59.0 Turn right onto the Anthony Lakes Highway toward Haines and Baker City. Enjoy the wonderful view of the Elkhorn Range.

63.2 At the road junction stay left, and continue riding on the Anthony Lakes Highway (Muddy Creek Lane goes right at this junction).

65.7 At the road junction stay left toward Haines and Highway 30. (Pocahontas Road goes right at this junction.)

67.5 Haines. Cross the railroad tracks. At the stop sign and T-intersection, turn right onto Highway 30. You have the option here of exploring the Chandler Cabin (on your left at this intersection).

77.1 Baker City.

(continued)

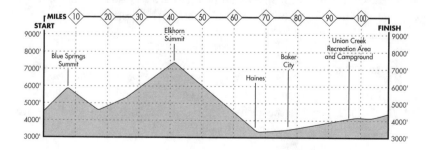

77.8 Pass a ranger station on the right (water and rest rooms).

78.4 At the flashing yellow light, turn left, and continue following Highway 30 east.

79.0 At the stoplight turn right onto Main Street, and ride through downtown Baker City.

79.2 At the stoplight continue straight on Highway 7 toward Sumpter and John Day.

98.5 Pass the Union Creek Recreation Area and Phillips Reservoir on your left. Rest rooms and water are available here. There is also a campground if you want to stay overnight.

100.5 Pass a picnic area with rest rooms at Phillips Reservoir on your left.

103.3 Pass a turnoff on the left to the McEwen Station for the Sumpter Valley Historic Steam Engine.

105.8 Turn right onto the Sumpter Highway (unsigned) toward Sumpter.

108.7 Arrive at Sumpter Dredge State Park on the left.

♦ Oregon State Parks and Recreation, 1115 Commercial Street NE, Suite 1, Salem, OR 97301-1002, (800)551–6949 or (541) 894–2486, www.oregonstateparks.org/park_239.php.

♦ Wallowa-Whitman National Forest, 1550 Dewey Avenue, Baker OR 97814, (541) 523–6391, www.fs.fed.us/r6/w-w.

LOCAL EVENTS/ATTRACTIONS

♦ National Historic Oregon Trail Interpretive Center at Flagstaff Hill, Highway 86, PO Box 987, Baker City, OR 97814-0987, (541) 523–1843, www.or.blm.gov/NHOTIC/.

♦ Sumpter Valley Railway, PO Box 389, Baker City, OR 97814-0389, (541) 894–2268, www.svry.com. The railway is open weekends from Memorial Day through Labor Day. Three train rides are run each day. Call for current rates.

RESTAURANTS

♦ Barley Browns Brewpub, 2190 Main Street, Baker City, OR 97814, (541) 523–4266.

♦ Borellos, 175 South Mill Street, Sumpter, OR 97877, (541) 894–2480.

♦ Scoop-N-Steamer Station, 363 South Mill Street, Sumpter, OR 97877, (541) 894–2236.

ACCOMMODATIONS

♦ Until Tomorrow Bed and Breakfast, 1790 4th Street, Baker City, OR 97814, (541) 523–2509. Stay in a beautiful Victorian home in Baker City. Rates are $60–$75, which includes a gourmet breakfast.

◆ Scoop-N-Steamer Station & Log Cabins, 363 South Mill Street, Sumpter, OR 97877, (888) 894–2236.

BIKE SHOPS

◆ Flagstaff Sports, 2101 Main Street, Baker City, OR 97814, (541) 523–3477.

REST ROOMS

◆ Mile 0.0: Sumpter Dredge State Park.
◆ Mile 26.1: North Fork of John Day Campground.
◆ Mile 43: Anthony Lake.
◆ Mile 77.8: Ranger station in Baker City.
◆ Mile 100.5: Picnic area at Phillips Reservoir.

MAPS

◆ USGS 7.5-minute quads Sumpter, Bourne, Mount Ireland, Granite, Trout Meadows, Crawfish Lake, Anthony Lakes, Rock Creek, Haines, Wingville, Baker City, Bowen Valley, Blue Canyon, and Phillips Lake; *DeLorme Oregon Atlas and Gazetteer,* maps 82 and 83.

Gold dredge at Sumpter State Park.

Resources

Beaverton Bicycle Club
13939 NW Cornell Road
Portland, OR 97229
(503) 649–4632

The Bike Gallery Bicycle Club
5329 NE Sandy Boulevard
Portland, OR 97213
(503) 281–9800

Blueberry Rides
8508 NE Schuyler
Portland, OR 97220
(503) 252–6680
www.blueberryrides.com

Central Oregon Wheelers
PO Box 8269
Bend, OR 97708
(541) 385–0948

Emerald Velo
15050 SW Carolwood
Beaverton, OR 97007
(503) 293–6505

Greater Eugene Area RiderS
   (GEARS)
PO Box 10244
Eugene, OR 97440
(541) 345–3181
www.geocities.com/Colosseum/
   Hoop/4419/gears.html

Klah Klahnee Cycling Club
930 NW Newport Avenue
Bend, OR 97708
(541) 382–8018

Klamath Freewheelers
PO Box 7485
Klamath Falls, OR 97602
(541) 882–3921

Lake Oswego Velo Club
15290 SW 100th
Tigard, OR 97224
(503) 620–5007

Mid-Valley Bicycle Club
PO Box 1283
Corvallis, OR 97339-1283
(541) 752–4639
www.mvbc.com

Portland Wheelman Touring Club
PO Box 2972
Portland, OR 97208-2972
(503) 257–7982
www.pwtc.com

Raindance Velo
PO Box 10475
Portland, OR 97210
(503) 221–1176

Rose City Wheelmen
9205 NW Skyline
Portland, OR 97231
(503) 286–6298

Salem Bicycle Club
PO Box 2224
Salem, OR 97308
(503) 363–7725
www.salembicycleclub.org

Santiam Slow Spokes
PO Box 739
525 North Santiam Avenue
Lebanon, OR 97355
(541) 259–3923
www.geocities.com/
santiamslowspokes

Siskiyou Velo Club
PO Box 974
Ashland, OR 97520
(541) 535–4116
www.mind.net/siskiyouvelo

Umpqua Velo Club
PO Box 84
Roseburg, OR 97470
(541) 440–3070

University of Oregon Cycling Club
Erb Memorial Union, Room 5
University of Oregon
Eugene, OR 97403
(541) 346–3733

Vancouver Bicycle Club
PO Box 1456
Vancouver, WA 98668
(360) 693–0195
www.vancouverbicycleclub.com

Vernonia Velo Club
57109 Timber Road.
Vernonia, OR 97064
(503) 429–9581

GEAR

Bike Nashbar
6103 State Route 446
Canfield, OH 44406
(800) 627–4227
www.nashbar.com

Burley Design Cooperative
4020 Stewart Road
Eugene, OR 97402
(800) 311–5294
www.burley.com

Performance Bike
Performance, Inc.
One Performance Way
Chapel Hill, NC 27514
(919) 933–9113
www.performancebike.com

R.E.I., Inc.
1700 45th Street East
Sumner, WA 98390
(800) 426–4840
www.rei.com

Albany/Linn County
Albany/Linn County Bicycle Map
Albany Public Works Department
333 Broadalbin Street SW
Albany, OR 97321
(541) 917–7777
Cost: $4.00

Clackamas County
Clackamas County Bike Map
Clackamas County Department of
  Transportation
902 Abernathy Road
Oregon City, OR 97045
(503) 655–8521
Cost: $3.50 plus $1.50 shipping and
  handling

Columbia River Gorge
Columbia River Gorge Bike Map
Oregon Department of
  Transportation
355 Capitol Street NE
Salem, OR 97301-3871
(503) 731–8234
Cost: Free

Corvallis/Benton County
Corvallis Area Bikeways
Public Works Department
PO Box 1083
Corvallis, OR 97339
(541) 682–5471
Cost: Free

Deschutes County
Deschutes County Bicycling Guide
Deschutes County Road Department
61150 SE 27th Street
Bend, OR 97702
(541) 388–6581
Cost: Free

Douglas County Bicycling Guide
Roseburg Visitors and Convention
  Bureau
410 Spruce Street
Roseburg, OR 97470
(541) 672–9731
Cost: Free

Eugene and Springfield
Eugene/Springfield Bikeways Map
City of Eugene Public Works
858 Pearl Street
Eugene, OR 97401
(541) 682–5471
Cost: Free

Jackson County
Jackson County Bicycling Guide
Jackson County Roads and Parks
200 Antelope Road
White City, OR 97503
(541) 774–8184
Cost: $2.00

Lane County
Lane County Bicycle Map
Lane County Public Works
3040 North Delta Highway
Eugene, OR 97408-1696
(541) 682–6900
Cost: $3.00

Multnomah County
Multnomah County Bicycling Guide
Department of Environmental
  Services
1620 SE 190th Avenue
Portland, OR 97232
(503) 248–5050
Cost: Free

Oregon
Oregon Bicycling Guide
Oregon Coast Bike Route Map
355 Capitol Street NE, Room 210
Salem, OR 97301-1354
(503) 986–3556
Cost: Free

Portland Area
Bike There
Metropolitan Service District
Transportation Department
600 NE Grand Avenue
Portland, OR 97232
(503) 797–1742
Cost: $3.95 plus $1.00 shipping and
handling

Washington County
Getting There by Bike
Washington County Visitors
   Association
5075 SW Griffith Drive, Suite 120
Beaverton, OR 97005
(800) 537–3149
Cost: Free

ORGANIZATIONS

Bicycle Program Manager
Oregon Department of Transportation
Room 210, Transportation Building
Salem, OR 97310
(503) 986–3555
www.odot.state.or.us/techserve/
   bikewalk

Bicycle Transportation Alliance
PO Box 9072
Portland, OR 97207-9072
(503) 226–0676
www.bta4bikes.org

PUBLICATIONS

Adventure Cyclist
150 East Pine Street
PO Box 8308
Missoula, MT 59807
(800) 755–2453
www.adv-cycling.org

Bicycling Magazine
Rodale, Inc.
135 North Sixth Street
Emmaus, PA 18098
(800) 666–2806
www.bicycling.com

Oregon Bicyclist Manual
Transportation Safety Division
235 Union Street NE
Salem, OR 97301
(503) 986–4190
www.odot.state.or.us/techserv/
   bikewalk/manual

Oregon Cycling
455 West 1st Avenue
Eugene, OR 97401
(541) 686–9885
www.efn.org/~ocycling

Adventure Cycling Association
PO Box 8308
Missoula, MT 59807-8308
(406) 721–1776
www.adv-cycling.org

Bicycle Adventures
P.O. Box 11219
Olympia, WA 98508
(800) 443–6060
www.bicycleadventures.com/who/
  contact.html

Cycle Oregon Inc.
8700 SW Nimbus Avenue, #8
Beaverton, OR 97005-7119
(800) 292–5367
www.cycleoregon.com

Hell's Canyon Bicycle Tours
102 West McCully
Joseph, OR 97846
(541) 432–2453

Scenic Cycling Adventures
1324 NW Vicksburg
Bend, OR 97701
(541) 385–5257
www.oregonbicycleride.org/#